MW01228244

The solution provided in the book makes intuitive sense and is exciting in that it ties together a broader range of Biblical history and revelation.
-Sanjay Merchant, PhD, Professor of Theology, Moody Bible Institute

It has been one of the most powerful extra-biblical books I perhaps have ever read.
-M. Coolidge

I found I couldn't put it down when I started. The data is very persuasive and convincing – in fact – overwhelming. You can't come to other conclusions after all the evidence was given and verified.
-L. Coffman

It is a worthwhile read. I gained a lot from how the evidence was laid out and from many of the arguments presented. The author claims (page 4) to have produced a work that is truly different and new, and after reading the book, I would agree. This is a manuscript that definitely deserves to be published and many of its insights should be seriously considered
-Jonathan K. Paulien, PhD, Professor, Religion-Theological Studies, Loma Linda University

I couldn't put it down. I love that everything is backed by scripture. No other book outside the Bible have I enjoyed reading more.
-A. Breivogel

THREE PROOFS
OF GOD

THREE PROOFS OF GOD

James Brown

Released on Palm Sunday

2024

Shilohhouse.com

Three Proofs of God
Published by Shiloh House, LLC
Gilbert, Arizona, U.S.A.

Scripture quotations taken from the (NASB®) New American Standard Bible®, Copyright © 1960, 1971, 1977, 1995, 2020 by The Lockman Foundation. Used by permission. All rights reserved. lockman.org.

Directly quoted text is presented as it appears in its referenced source without alteration to style, spelling, etc. In quoted secular text, interpolations appear in brackets (e.g., "A simple reading of [Daniel 9] verse 25") and redactions appear as bracketed ellipses; any added emphasis is noted. Quoted scriptural verses appear in a dedicated font and are not altered. In case of any discrepancy between the print, eBook, and/or audio versions, the most recent print edition in the English language shall be considered the definitive version.

BROWN, JAMES, Author
THREE PROOFS OF GOD
Library of Congress Control Number: 2023924062
Internal Control Number: MS040312

ISBN: 979-8-9892652-1-3, 979-8-9892652-3-7 (paperback)
ISBN: 979-8-9892652-4-4 (hardcover)
ISBN: 979-8-9892652-2-0 (digital)

RELIGION / Christian Theology / Apologetics
RELIGION / Biblical Commentary / Old Testament / Prophets
RELIGION / Biblical Commentary / New Testament / Jesus, the Gospels & Acts

QUANTITY PURCHASES: Churches, schools, companies, professional groups, clubs, and other organizations may qualify for special terms when ordering large quantities of this title. For information, email sales@shilohhouse.com.

CONTACT: Send non-sales-related inquiries to editor@shilohhouse.com

AT A GLANCE

This book IS
- \+   new, objective evidence of God
- \+   interpreting Scripture at face-value
- \+   written in plain language

This book is NOT
- −   about the end times
- −   using codes or numerology
- −   a rehash of previous work

This book will give YOU
- objectively verifiable evidence of God's existence
- a deep understanding of large parts of the Bible
- many examples of history, archaeology, and science harmonizing with the biblical account.

VIDEO PREFACE

Scan the QR code below to see a short
introduction of this book.

CONTENTS

1. The Big Question 1
2. Daniel 7
3. Seventy Weeks 13
4. Nehemiah 21
5. Palm Sunday 27
6. "Everything" 31
7. The Seal 37
8. Cyrus 45
9. Origin 49
10. Israel 57
11. Darius the Great 65
12. Temple 69
13. Temple Mount 73
14. Ezra 79
15. Baptism 83
16. Jerusalem 87
17. The Progression 95
18. High Sabbaths 105
19. Triple-Check 109
20. The Final Word 113
Appendix A—Details 121
Appendix B—The Calendar 155
Appendix C—Key Dates 161
Appendix D—An Absolute Chronology 171
Appendix E—Attestations 183
Endnotes 185
Works Cited 215
Select Subject Index 221
Scripture Index 227
Acknowledgments 231
About the Author 232

If one man alone had made a book of predictions about Jesus Christ, as to the time and the manner, and Jesus Christ had come in conformity to these prophecies, this fact would have infinite weight.

—Blaise Pascal

1

Read this to me

THE BIG QUESTION

Does God Exist?

IT'S OUR GREATEST QUESTION. Over the centuries, people have found many ways to approach it. This book will take a logical path—one that starts with hard evidence and ends with a case you could present in court. So, what might direct evidence of God look like?

Consider this: if there were no God, meaning no supernatural entity at all, then the universe would reflect only the unguided laws of nature. Those natural laws would never be truly broken. Fundamentals like gravity, energy, and time would always operate according to their natures. Everything we observe would have a strictly scientific explanation—even if we humans didn't fully understand it. That type of universe would show no real evidence of anything supernatural.

If on the other hand God does exist, then we might observe those basic natural laws undeniably broken.[1]

Let's now focus on the nature of *time*.

Natural law forbids us from observing the future. Although we can make forecasts and have lucky guesses, our focus here is different: truly predicting the future—accurately foretelling human events in precise detail, centuries in advance. That is simply forbidden by the laws of nature.

> Observing human events and accurately describing them centuries before they occur alters the direction of time's flow. That would disrupt the order of cause and effect, a basis of reason itself. That type of *true prediction* could violate natural law and is certainly beyond human capability.[2]

So, what would a *true prediction* look like? A true prediction must pass some key tests. It must be precise and not ambiguous. It can't be self-fulfilling. It must be recorded long enough before its foretold event that it couldn't have been calculated or anticipated by pattern. The foretold event must be improbable enough that it's unlikely to have happened on its own—ideally unique in all history, something that had never happened before.

Truly predicting not only *what*, but also *when* a unique event will occur, if proven, could show that the laws of nature have been broken.[3]

Something proven to break natural law is by definition *supernatural*. A true prediction is evidence of the supernatural, and maybe—depending on details—even of God. The key word of course is *proven*.

The Special Case of Daniel (c. 620–535 BC)

The Bible's book of Daniel predicts many historical events, such as Persia's fall (330 BC) and Alexander the Great's death (323 BC). Even the hardest skeptics concede that Daniel accurately describes those.[4]

But those same skeptics also claim that Daniel was written after those events occurred. In contrast, Daniel itself claims to have been written before them. Although debate continues over the time of Daniel's composition, *all* sides of that debate agree that Daniel was written in the BC era, before Jesus was born.[5]

> The oldest recovered copy of Daniel, found among the Dead Sea Scrolls, dates to c. 125 BC.[6] As with all books of the Bible, we have not recovered the original document.

This means that if Daniel accurately describes events in Jesus' life, then it might be a *true prediction*, one that might break natural law. But is Jesus foretold in the book of Daniel? Many people insist he is.

Daniel wrote that "Messiah" will be "cut off" before "the city and the sanctuary" are destroyed.[7] Many see this as predicting Jesus' crucifixion four decades before Rome destroyed Jerusalem and the temple in the year AD 70. But is Jesus Daniel's foretold Messiah? How can we know for sure?

Fortunately, Daniel provides the exact timing of Messiah's arrival—cryptically for sure, but precisely—using exact numbers:

> So you are to know and understand that from the issuing of a decree to restore and rebuild Jerusalem, until Messiah the Prince, there will be seven weeks and sixty-two weeks; it will be built again, with streets and moat, even in times of distress. (Daniel 9:25)

Daniel's promised Messiah would arrive "seven weeks and sixty-two weeks" after "the issuing of a decree to restore and rebuild Jerusalem." This is the only text in the entire Bible that gives us, in hard numbers, Messiah's exact timing. Here, Daniel makes a *testable prediction*. It's either true or it's not, and we can check—the Bible even urges us to check.

Because here, Daniel wrote that we should *know and understand* this prediction. He directly urged us to figure it out.

This is a key part of a Bible passage called the "Seventy Weeks of Daniel." This book will present a new and verifiable solution to it.

> Why *seventy* weeks? Another week is presented in Daniel 9:27. All seventy weeks are referenced in Daniel 9:24–27. The accounting is: 7 + 62 + 1 = 70.

What Is Daniel's Seventy Weeks?

The Seventy Weeks of Daniel foretells many events, including the timing of the promised Messiah.[8] It's one of the Bible's most important passages. Jesus referred to it, and to Daniel by name.[9] For centuries, people have considered it crucial. *Just how crucial?*

The Seventy Weeks of Daniel has been called "the most important revelation in all Scripture," the "backbone" and "crown jewels of the Old Testament," that "provides a time framework to which most other prophecies can be attached," and "the key that unlocks all Scriptures."[10]

Isaac Newton

Sir Isaac Newton, who wrote as much on the Bible as on physics,[11] agreed:

> In those things which relate to the last times, he [Daniel] must be made the key to the rest.[12] (Newton)

Newton, one of the greatest minds in history, viewed the Seventy Weeks of Daniel as a *foundation* of the Christian faith.[13]

But despite its importance, the Seventy Weeks' precise solution has eluded us for centuries. Hundreds of proposals have been offered, yet none of them holds consensus support. If there's any consensus at all, it's that we haven't quite figured it out yet—at least not in full detail—and certainly not to everyone's satisfaction.[14]

Note that the exact years of Jesus' birth and resurrection are still subject to debate, with no dominant consensus. If we did have consensus on Daniel 9:25, then we would also expect to see consensus on those milestone years of Jesus. But until now we don't.

Daniel 9 is less-frequently taught today, as it can provoke heated dispute. If you are Bible-literate yet unfamiliar with Daniel's Seventy Weeks, this may be one reason why.

You may ask, *how could something so important remain unsolved for centuries?* Maybe we shouldn't be too surprised, because Daniel told us directly that his words would be "secret and sealed."

> And he said, "Go your way, Daniel, for these words will be kept secret and sealed up until the end time. (Daniel 12:9)

Daniel's prophecies, including the Seventy Weeks, would remain unsolved, far into his future.[15] And so they have. Despite our best efforts, this seal has remained intact for centuries, as Daniel said it would.

Yet that same verse makes it equally clear that Daniel's prophecies, including the Seventy Weeks, will be fully understood one day.

What Will We Discover?

This book will present a new, literal solution to Daniel 9:25 and verify it with exacting precision. It will then set another major biblical prophecy into the framework of Daniel's *true prediction* and verify that it too is fulfilled precisely to the day. It won't just claim Daniel to be the master key to prophecy—it will show it to be, using objective evidence. This solution will identify Jesus as the promised Messiah and provide new, direct evidence of God.

The discoveries in this book are truly new, not just a revision of other work.

Is This Book for You?

If you seek direct, objective evidence of God, then this book is for you. You won't need deep knowledge of history or the Bible—that will be presented to you in plain language. But first, here is a word of advice: no matter how tempting, *don't skip text.* If you skip or skim as you read, you will miss *everything.* This book presents a structured thesis that introduces key concepts along the way as it builds upon itself. It's written to be read carefully and conventionally—from the beginning, each page in order.

So, What "Proofs" Are We Working Toward?

Here's a preview of the first proof of the three (we'll see it again). It is *deductive*, meaning if its two premises are true, then its conclusion is true:

> Premise 1: If a *true prediction* (as defined previously) exists, then a supernatural entity must exist. Premise 2: Daniel provides a *true prediction*. Conclusion: A supernatural entity exists.

A *true prediction*, as previously described, requires a supernatural entity. The second premise—that Daniel provides this type of *true prediction*—will be established in the following chapters. Proofs two and three will establish that this supernatural entity is indeed the God of the Bible.

> This book interprets Scripture at face value and makes a strictly rational case *in plain English*. It does *not* use codes or numerology[16] but it does use arithmetic. After all, Daniel did give us numbers to work with. This book's mathematical statements have been audited and confirmed correct (see appendix E.1).
>
> This book is not a devotional. It won't ask you to accept or reject anything on faith. It doesn't focus on end times. It presents prophecy that has been fulfilled to an extent not yet recognized. This book does not introduce doctrine to divide over, nor does it impact salvation, nor does it set dates for Jesus' return. It does, however, present objective evidence for God's existence, Jesus' messiahship, and Scripture's reliability.

Chapter 1 Key Points

- Daniel 9:25 is a *testable prediction*. It foretells the precise timing of the promised Messiah's key advents (arrivals).

- This book will show Daniel's prediction to be *verifiably true*.

- Once verified, it will provide direct evidence that God exists, that Jesus is Messiah, and that Scripture is reliable.

These are extraordinary claims. It's right to approach them with extreme skepticism. After all, we've seen such claims before. But do approach—as a matter not only of faith but also of fact.

Do this, and you will find a clear answer to our greatest question.

> If you hold a reason-based approach to Scripture to be improper, know the Bible tells us directly to take precisely this approach to this exact passage (see appendix A.1.1).

It's been said that "extraordinary claims require extraordinary evidence."[17]

What follows is that evidence.

Figure 1. The Neo-Babylonian Empire during Daniel's lifetime.

2

DANIEL

> This chapter summarizes the historical context of Daniel's lifetime. It also presents the date of Babylon's fall—a key anchor point of ancient chronology.

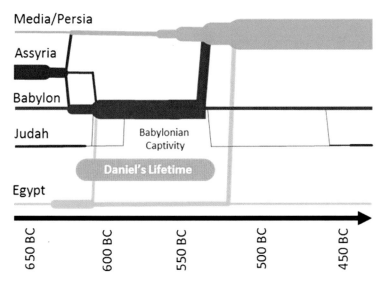

Figure 2. Approximate strength of nations from 650 to 450 BC depicted as thickness of the bars. Note: BC year numbers decrease over time.

ANIEL WAS BORN ABOUT 620 BC in Judah, a little kingdom wedged between the old superpowers of Egypt, Assyria, and a resurgent Babylon.

When Daniel was a young teenager, a Babylonian army besieged Jerusalem. They took spoils and captives, selecting healthy, intelligent youths to serve the government in Babylon. Daniel was among those taken.[18] That day marks the beginning of a key period in Jewish history, often called the "Babylonian captivity."[19]

In 605 BC, Babylon crushed Egypt and Assyria at the pivotal battle of Carchemish.[20] Over the next two decades, Babylon deported Judah's population in waves, and then destroyed Jerusalem and the temple. Babylon stood as the dominant power of the known world for seven decades.

In Babylon, young Daniel was stripped of his family, his home, and even his name. He was now a captive stranger in a strange land who lost everything except his faith. But his life changed yet again when Babylon's King Nebuchadnezzar had a terrifying dream.[21]

Upon awakening from his nightmare, the rattled king commanded Babylon's wise men and magicians to interpret his dream without first describing it to them. When they couldn't, the king angrily accused them of being frauds and ordered every one of them, including their teenage apprentice Daniel, to be executed.[22]

Suddenly, young Daniel found himself condemned to die for something he had no part of. But Daniel boldly declared that God could reveal the king's dream and its meaning. The king gave him one chance.

The next day, Daniel described the king's dream in detail and interpreted its exact meaning. The king was so impressed and thankful that he appointed Daniel over the wise men of Babylon.[23]

Over the next four decades, Daniel served as a royal advisor. When King Nebuchadnezzar died in 562 BC,[24] Daniel began many years of comfortable semi-retirement. But his eventful life was far from over.

By Daniel's eightieth birthday, Jews had flourished in Babylon for almost seven decades. Then late one autumn night, something happened that changed the course of world history forever.

October 12, 539 BC—Babylon

That night,[25] the people of Babylon were out raucously celebrating a festival, despite their army's fresh defeat at the hands of Persia's King Cyrus. All of Babylon knew Cyrus was now coming for them. But everyone felt completely secure behind their enormous city walls.

At worst, people expected a long siege. Babylonians had stockpiled provisions to last for years,[26] and thanks to the Euphrates River, they would never run out of water both inside and around their massive, moated walls. The proud city considered itself unconquerable. But just like the unsinkable *Titanic*, Babylon would go down fast.

Recreated Ishtar Gate from the wall of Babylon.

That night, Babylonian King Belshazzar threw a lavish festival banquet. The vast hall was packed with Babylon's nobility. The king was in high spirits until the strangest thing happened. He and some of his guests saw a floating human hand write strange words on the wall. The king was so shocked that his face bleached white and his legs buckled.[27]

Not everyone saw the hand, but everyone did see the words. No one could understand them. Given the military threat, the king certainly felt some urgency about their meaning. He offered money and high honors to anyone who could make sense of those words. But no one there had a clue.

The king summoned Babylon's wise men and magicians to read the strange writing. They couldn't. Finally, someone remembered how Daniel had interpreted King Nebuchadnezzar's dreams long ago, when the experts failed. Maybe Daniel could *read the writing on the wall?*

Out of retirement, Daniel was again summoned to advise the king of Babylon. Daniel told the king:

> "Now this is the inscription that was written:
> 'MENĒ, MENĒ, TEKĒL, UPHARSIN.'
> This is the interpretation of the message:
> 'MENĒ'—God has numbered your kingdom and put an end to it.
> TEKĒL'—you have been weighed on the scales and found deficient.
> PERĒS'—your kingdom has been divided and given to the Medes and Persians." (Daniel 5:25-28)

This occurred hours, if not minutes, before the event it foretold—a major watershed of world history—the fall of Babylon. That night, October 12 in 539 BC, an army of Medes and Persians captured the city of Babylon without

Belshazzar's Feast by Rembrandt. Daniel's account of this event gave us the common phrase "to read the writing on the wall."

a fight. Scholars are certain of the date. Babylon's fall is also recorded in the terse but reliable Babylonian Chronicle:[28]

> Ugbaru, governor of Gutium, and the troops of Cyrus entered Babylon without a battle.[29] (Babylonian Chronicle)

Never before was such a great city conquered bloodlessly. Despite Babylon's colossal city walls, Persian troops simply walked in and took over. They slipped in silently through the water gates where the Euphrates River flowed under the city walls (figure 3). Persian engineers had diverted the river upstream, reducing its level "about to the middle of a man's thigh,"[30] which created "a high-road into Babylon."[31] Persian soldiers breached the mighty walls of Babylon, suffering nothing more than wet feet.

Remarkably, history records only minimal violence. A band of elite soldiers who knew Babylon's streets raced straight to the palace and arrested the king.[32] Babylonians put up no resistance. Many didn't even notice a foreign power had taken over until days later. Some may have even viewed the Medes and Persians as liberators.[33]

The fall of Babylon had a profound impact. For decades, Babylon stood as the cultural, financial, and political center of the world around it. Arguably never has a single city been so dominant in its day, certainly not outside of Rome. Babylon was enormously important. So was its fall.

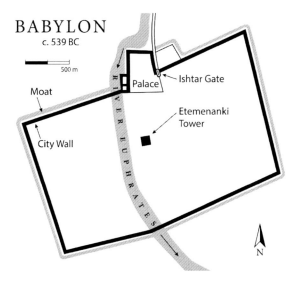

Figure 3. The city of Babylon. The area inside the city walls is roughly twice the size of New York City's Central Park, and slightly larger than the walled section of Rome at the time of Caesar Augustus (Servian Wall). Note the Euphrates River crosses the city walls at two points. Note also the Etemenanki Tower, from which Babylonian astronomers recorded eclipse observations, whose exact dates are verified by modern astronomy.

Persia's King Cyrus was not in Babylon that night. The commander who took Babylon was a Mede named Ugbaru. He remained the military authority[34] until October 29, when Cyrus entered Babylon, ended martial law, and promoted Ugbaru to rule in Babylon as a vassal (subordinate) king.

> Peace was declared. Cyrus to all Babylon sent greetings. Ugbaru his governor appointed governors in Babylon.[35] (Babylonian Chronicle)

The chronicle confirms Ugbaru acted as Emperor Cyrus' agent in Babylon and appointed regional governors. Those are kingly duties. Daniel refers to this same person using the throne name "Darius the Mede."[36]

> So Darius the Mede received the kingdom at about the age of sixty-two. It pleased Darius to appoint 120 satraps over the kingdom, to be in charge of the whole kingdom (Daniel 5:31–6:1)

Darius appointed Daniel to oversee some of those satraps (governors).[37] Daniel once again found himself in high government administration.

Chapter 2 Key Points

- Babylon fell to the Medes and Persians on October 12 in 539 BC.

- That October 29, Persian emperor Cyrus the Great appointed the Median general Ugbaru to rule as a vassal (subordinate) king in Babylon.

- Daniel referred to Ugbaru as "Darius the Mede."

For deeper discussion on Daniel's Darius the Mede, see appendix A.2.1.

How can we know the exact BC years of these ancient events? See appendix D.1.

This chapter recounts only *parts* of Daniel's eventful life. The first six chapters of Daniel present many other episodes in a very readable form. Those stories are an excellent introduction to the Bible for anyone of any age.

Ishtar Gate inscription (c. 575 BC) introduces King Nebuchadnezzar and explains why he constructed the gate. This inscription was installed when Daniel was in his mid-forties, so he was certainly familiar with it. These are the original bricks. You are now seeing something with your own eyes that Daniel also saw directly with his. (Photo credit mtr/shutterstock.com)

Then, about a year later, at age eighty-two, Daniel received one of the most profound messages recorded anywhere in the Bible.

3

Read this to me

SEVENTY WEEKS

> This chapter introduces the Seventy Weeks Prophecy, the structure of Daniel 9:25, and prior attempts to interpret it. It then presents a new approach—a path not yet taken.

538 BC—Persian Babylon

SOON AFTER BABYLON'S FALL, Daniel advised a new king in a new empire and was certainly the most influential Jew of his day. But despite his power and prestige, something deeply troubled him. Daniel's heart yearned for his people's promised return to Jerusalem.

Daniel read Jeremiah's prophecy that Jerusalem would be desolate for seventy years.[38] Daniel knew it had been about seventy years since his own captivity began, and Babylon's rule had recently ended. But Jews were not returning to God, and Daniel feared God would extend those seventy years due to his people's unrepentance.[39] This greatly distressed him.

One evening, Daniel fell into one of the most passionate prayers recorded in the Bible.[40] In response, God sent an angel with a reply[41] that far exceeded Daniel's expectations—nothing less than a summary of God's plan for Israel:

> [24] Seventy weeks have been decreed for your people and your holy city, to finish the wrongdoing, to make an end of sin, to make atonement for guilt, to bring in everlasting righteousness, to seal up vision and prophecy, and to anoint the Most Holy Place.
> [25] So you are to know and understand that from the issuing of a decree to restore and rebuild Jerusalem, until Messiah the Prince, there will be seven weeks and sixty-two weeks; it will be built again, with streets and moat, even in times of distress.
> [26] Then after the sixty-two weeks, the Messiah will be cut off and have nothing, and the people of the prince who is to come will destroy the city and the sanctuary. And its end will come with a flood; even to the end there will be war; desolations are determined.

²⁷ And he will confirm a covenant with the many for one week, but in the middle of the week he will put a stop to sacrifice and grain offering; and on the wing of abominations will come the one who makes desolate, until a complete destruction, one that is decreed, gushes forth on the one who makes desolate. (Daniel 9:24–27)

This text covers a long span of history. It's one of the most information-dense summaries found anywhere in the Bible. It packs centuries of events into extremely few words. One of those events—the timing of the promised Messiah's arrival in verse 25—is our focus.

Daniel 9:25 is the only verse in the Bible that foretells Messiah's exact timing. It urges us to "know and understand," suggesting we may find a literal meaning.[42] Intriguingly, the Gospels also urge us to "understand" this passage.[43] This is the only text that both Old and New Testaments directly call the reader to understand (appendix A.3.1)—not just *believe*, but *understand*.

Daniel's Hebrew word for "Messiah" appears without a leading *the*. This book uses "Messiah" instead of "the Messiah" to match Daniel's exact wording. For detail on Daniel's "Messiah the Prince," see appendix A.3.2.

Daniel divides the seventy weeks into three parts: seven, sixty-two, and one.[44] Later chapters will show these divisions are significant.

Figure 4. The book of Daniel presents these seventy weeks in three segments: the first two in verse 25 and the last in verse 27. Our focus is verse 25's "seven weeks and sixty-two weeks."

Verse 25 presents the first two segments. It's an exact mathematical statement: *from point A to point B will take exactly X amount of time.* In other words, from the issuing of a decree until Messiah will take seven weeks and sixty-two weeks. This is a *testable prediction*. It has these major elements:

1. **Start point:** "from the issuing of a decree to restore and rebuild Jerusalem"
2. **End point:** "until Messiah the Prince"
3. **Time span:** "seven weeks and sixty-two weeks"

Start point: The Bible contains four decrees to restore and rebuild Jerusalem.[45] Scholars typically ask, *which one of these decrees does Daniel* *indicate?* only to select one and dismiss the other three. We will later pose this same question, but in a slightly different form, to find a clear and direct answer in Scripture, one that unlocks the precise solution to Daniel 9:25.

End point: Messiah the Prince (Hebrew: *mashiach nagid*) is the arrival (advent) of Messiah, specifically of someone of extremely high importance, anointed by God to rule (appendix A.3.2).

Time span: Daniel's Hebrew for "weeks," *shabuim* (singular *shabua*), is a plural from the root word for "seven." But seven of what, exactly? Daniel didn't tell us what he counted. A Hebrew week (*shabua*) might refer to seven days or seven years.[46] We know Daniel does not refer to seven days here. First, seventy weeks of days are 490 days, or about sixteen months. That isn't enough time to rebuild a ruined Jerusalem, much less achieve the promises of Daniel 9:24.[47]

> To Hebrews, a week of seven years is a *sabbatical cycle*. Hebrews also group seven sabbatical cycles into *jubilee cycles* of forty-nine years.[48] Elsewhere, Daniel writes "weeks [of] days" (*shabuim yamim*)[49] in contrast to the "weeks" (*shabuim*) of Daniel 9:24–27. Both Christians and Jews view the weeks in Daniel 9:25 as groups of seven "years"[50] (quotation marks intentional).

Second, Daniel foretells events lasting 2,300 days, during the final seventieth week of this same prophecy.[51] These cannot fit a week of days but do easily fit a week of years. By near-universal consensus among both Christians and Jews, the weeks of Daniel 9:25 are groups of seven "years."[52]

At first glance, the phrase "seven weeks and sixty-two weeks" indicates sixty-nine sets of seven "years," totaling 483:

$$69 \times 7 = 483$$

But what type of *year*? Hebrews in Daniel's day didn't observe solar years as we do today. Hebrew years were lunar, normally 354 days long, which is eleven days short of a solar year. To keep holidays from drifting out of season, Hebrews added an extra month every two or three years to create a 384-day, (13 lunar month) leap year (appendix B). Those leap years came in unpredictable sequence. This unpredictability made it impossible for Daniel to specify any date centuries in advance using Hebrew lunar years.

But Daniel did have one viable option.

The Bible itself defines a unit of time equal to 360 days.[53] We know Daniel intended this unit of time because Scripture confirms it directly.

In short, Daniel and Revelation describe the same duration of certain events as 1,260 days, 42 months, and 3½ "times."[54] Here, "time" equates to exactly 360 days. How do we know Daniel's weeks are seven of these 360-day "times"? Because those same events are set to occur during Daniel's seventieth week, the final week of this same prophecy, thus in the same units[55] (appendix A.3.3). Note that any period for Daniel 9:25 other than 360 days would create a scriptural contradiction. Daniel's weeks are seven 360-day periods, often called *prophetic years*.

> Whenever the Bible references a numbered span of years or months *and* the equivalent number of days, it always equates to a 360-day "year." There are several examples and *no exceptions*. The Bible never defines a "year" of any different length. The prophetic year is scriptural. It is *not* lunar. (A 360-day period cannot derive from 29.53-day lunar cycles.) The prophetic year is for prophecy, not for our calendar. For more detail on the 360-day prophetic year, see appendix A.3.3.

Daniel's "seven weeks and sixty-two weeks" (sixty-nine weeks of seven prophetic years) from decree to Messiah equal 173,880 days:

$$69 \times 7 \times 360 = 173,880 \text{ days}$$

This gives us a decree at the start, Messiah at the end, and 173,880 days in between.[56] This might seem straightforward, but people have struggled for centuries to agree on a single solution.

Prior Attempts

The most quoted solution is from **Sir Robert Anderson's** 1881 book, *The Coming Prince*. It starts with Persian King Artaxerxes' decree to his Jewish servant Nehemiah and ends with Jesus' triumphal entry into Jerusalem, allegedly in AD 32. Anderson claimed the two events were precisely 173,880 days apart.[57] Anderson's solution has errors, making its specific dates impossible. Yet even now, most precise-to-the-day presentations of Daniel 9:25 are still of the Anderson solution.

> Anderson was not the first to apply the prophetic year to Daniel's Seventy Weeks. Bishop William Lloyd, an editor of the 1701 King James Bible, asserted a 360-day "Chaldee year"[58] but didn't publish any solution calculated to the precise day.

Dr. Harold Hoehner's 1977 refinement of Anderson's solution starts with the same decree to Nehemiah and ends at Jesus' triumphal entry, allegedly in AD 33. Hoehner asserted the events were precisely 173,880 days apart.[59] He corrected most of Anderson's errors but made another, rendering those dates impossible.

> Anderson and Hoehner each applied sound interpretation but overlooked technical details (appendix A.3.4). Still, their works remain significant advancements.

Isaac Newton's solution starts with a different decree by the same King Artaxerxes to the Jewish scribe Ezra, allegedly in 457 BC. Newton adds the full seventy weeks to reach Jesus' crucifixion, allegedly in AD 34.[60] (When adding BC and AD years, one must be subtracted as there is no "year zero" between 1 BC and AD 1.) Newton claimed precision to the year but not to the day.

Another solution, loosely related to Newton's, starts with the same decree to Ezra, adds sixty-nine weeks of solar years, and ends with Jesus' baptism, allegedly in AD 27. This solution is commonly taught today. It also claims precision to the year but not to the day.

> Some see **symbolic** or **spiritualized** meaning in Daniel's numbers. Note three points. First, although the biblical number seven is richly symbolic, the number sixty-two is plainly unsymbolic. Second, a symbolic or spiritualized interpretation, even if valid, does not exclude a literal one, nor vice-versa. One doesn't negate the other. Third, this book will find a literal, mathematical interpretation and then objectively verify it.

Hundreds of other solutions exist that haven't gained as much traction.[61]

A New Approach

Remember, the Seventy Weeks of Daniel is the only Old Testament prophecy that the Gospels directly ask us to understand[62] (appendix A.3.1). When we turn there, we see that Daniel further focuses our attention on verse 25, urging us to "know and understand" the timing of "Messiah the Prince." These words introduce a message of key importance.

Intriguingly, Daniel twice confirmed that his prophecies are "secret and sealed up" until "the end time" (Daniel 12:4, 9). In other words, they won't be fully understood until long after he wrote them. This gives us a valuable and long-overlooked clue.

Consider this for a moment. How could Daniel 9:25 be so highly important, yet its full meaning remain elusive for centuries, just as Daniel foretold it would? How could Daniel, or anyone for that matter, accomplish such a thing? Because this is exactly what happened—it stayed sealed.

Daniel's Seventy Weeks would not unravel easily. Its solution wasn't meant to be simple or intuitive—quite the opposite in fact. If it were easy, it would have been solved centuries ago. It was instead *meant* to remain hidden, not yielding to traditional interpretive methods. It was essentially timelocked, designed to elude us until the appointed time arrived.

This timelock is its *recursive* structure.[63] Unlocking it requires bits of evidence that would appear much later. Put simply, it takes parts of the answer to properly frame the question. Only then can it be understood after remaining shrouded for centuries, as Daniel rightly foretold it would.

> This prophecy might have stumped the generations, but Daniel understood it fully. In Daniel 9:22-23, Gabriel instructed Daniel to *understand* the vision. This would remain "secret and sealed" until "the end time" (Daniel 12:4, 9) and intriguingly, that *Daniel* should seal it. Note that Scripture wasn't divided into chapters until the Middle Ages, so *the seal* may apply to the entire book of Daniel, and with certainty to its prophetic text (Daniel 2 and 7-12) including Daniel 9:25.

The Gospels ask us to *understand* this prophecy. Daniel urges us to *know and understand* the seven and sixty-two weeks, not to just believe them in an abstract sense. Those numbers serve a purpose. They are in Scripture for a reason—Daniel made a direct mathematical statement, in hard numbers. This suggests we may find a direct mathematical solution to Daniel's prophetic statement.[64] This is where we start.

> Many studies interpret Scripture broadly, even allegorically, to avoid missing intended meanings. We will take the opposite approach—that Scripture may indeed point accurately to its inspired messages, even if key details are omitted, and even if some Bible writers (e.g., Ezekiel, Luke) did not grasp the full meaning of the words penned by their hands. Therefore, we can test whether Scripture, taken at face-value, points to a literal solution of Daniel 9:25. A valid solution could establish, by demonstration, that Scripture is reliable and that our steps to interpret it are valid.[65]
>
> This approach is not circular reasoning (i.e., assuming reliability to prove reliability) because along the way, it must produce a valid solution to one of mankind's most enduring mysteries.[66]
>
> A face-value approach to Scripture is practical, not dogmatic, for a couple of reasons. First, taking the Bible at face value ensures we are evaluating the Bible and not something *other* than the Bible. Second, our aim here is to *find* the message, not to *avoid missing* it. We'll know we've found it when it fits the entire body of scriptural, historical, and physical evidence.

Chapter 3 Key Points

- Daniel divides the seventy weeks into seven, sixty-two, and one.

- Daniel's weeks are groups of seven "years," not seven days.

- Daniel's "years" are periods of 360 days each. Some refer to these 360-day periods as "prophetic years."

- "Seven weeks and sixty-two weeks" are 173,880 days.

A Timeline of Daniel 9:25

Anderson and Hoehner agreed on three major elements of Daniel 9:25:

1. **Start point**: Persian King Artaxerxes' decree to Nehemiah "in the month Nisan, in the twentieth year of King Artaxerxes"[67]

2. **End point**: Jesus' triumphal entry into Jerusalem on Palm Sunday of the crucifixion year[68]

3. **Time span**: 173,880 days (sixty-nine weeks of seven prophetic years each)

> The next two chapters are the most technically challenging of the book. Once you understand them, you will be well equipped to understand the rest.

Sir Robert Anderson and Dr. Harold Hoehner were both on the right path. The next two chapters will pick up where they left off, repair a couple of technical points, while following their valid approach to discover a viable solution. This will then point us toward a much larger, more robust, and verifiable solution than any presented before.

Hebrew Months

1.	**Nisan**	**(Mar/Apr)**	**7.**	**Tishri**	**(Sep/Oct)**
2.	Iyyar	(Apr/May)	8.	Heshvan	(Oct/Nov)
3.	Sivan	(May/Jun)	9.	Kislev	(Nov/Dec)
4.	Tammuz	(Jun/Jul)	10.	Tevet	(Dec/Jan)
5.	Av	(Jul/Aug)	11.	Shevat	(Jan/Feb)
6.	Elul	(Aug/Sep)	12.	Adar	(Feb/Mar)
	There are many spelling variants		*13.*	*Adar II*	*(Feb/Mar)*

Figure 5. Biblical Hebrew months. Adar II is a leap month added once every two or three years to keep the 354-day lunar year from drifting out of solar season. For more detail, see appendix B.

Cuneiform tablet **LBAT 1419** (BM 32234) dates King Xerxes' murder to August 465 BC in agreement with the Greek histories *(Fasti Hellenici)* referenced by Anderson. This tablet's first scholarly translation was published in 2001.
Photo © The Trustees of the British Museum. All rights reserved.

All mathematical statements of this book (including the appendices and endnotes) have been audited and confirmed correct (see appendix E.1).

4

Read this to me

NEHEMIAH

> This chapter finds the year of King Artaxerxes' decree to Nehemiah, presented in the Old Testament book of Nehemiah's second chapter.

OTH ANDERSON AND HOEHNER'S starting date for Daniel's "seven weeks and sixty-two weeks" is Persian King Artaxerxes' decree allowing his Jewish cupbearer Nehemiah to rebuild Jerusalem's walls. (For detail on Daniel's word for *decree*, see appendix A.4.1.)

Nehemiah dates this to "Nisan, in the twentieth year of King Artaxerxes."[69] *Nisan* is a Hebrew springtime month. The king in question is undoubtedly Persian King Artaxerxes I (Longimanus), a king well known to history. But which BC year was his twentieth? Over the years, scholars have asserted 446, 445, or 444 BC. First, we must know when Artaxerxes became king. The exact date wasn't certain until fairly recently.[70]

> The following steps (A, B, and C) for finding Judean dates are presented here in detail. This three-step method will be applied consistently going forward.

A. (*Accession Date*) **Artaxerxes Became King in August 465 BC.**

King Artaxerxes was a teenager when he took the Persian throne. His father, King Xerxes, was murdered by his trusted officer Artabanus, commander of the royal bodyguard.[71]

Immediately, Artabanus falsely accused Artaxerxes' older brother, the Crown Prince, of murdering his father, and then coerced a terrified young Artaxerxes to order his brother's immediate execution.[72] Artaxerxes then became king, but in name only. Artabanus was the power behind the throne.

Over the next seven months, Artabanus plotted to dispose of Artaxerxes and establish his own dynasty. He unwisely sought help from a nobleman who was also unhappily married to Artaxerxes' older sister. Despite the marital problems, the young king's brother-in-law secretly warned him of Artabanus' plot. The boy king was forced to come of age quickly. He made a few key palace alliances and, with his own hands, killed Artabanus in March of 464 BC.[73]

> The date of King Xerxes' murder appears on cuneiform tablet **LBAT 1419** recovered in Babylon. This tablet also records eclipses, verified by modern astronomy, which authenticate the date of Xerxes' murder, in agreement with the Greek histories (*Fasti Hellenici*). Scholarly translation of LBAT 1419 was first formally published in 2001.[74]

We can't find Artaxerxes' twentieth year by just subtracting 20 from 465 BC. Methods of counting kings' years varied across eras and cultures.[75] The "twentieth year of King Artaxerxes" is *Nehemiah's* date. The entire passage is written in first person.[76] We must know how *Nehemiah* counted Artaxerxes' years and apply that same method. This requires two more steps.

B. (*Begin Counting*) Nehemiah Began Counting at "Year One."

Next, we must know if Nehemiah counted Artaxerxes' first day as king to "year zero" or "year one." Both methods were used at the time. Babylonians and Persians counted a king's first day on the throne to a "year zero" called an "accession year." Scholars name this the accession-year method (AY).[77] In contrast, Greeks and Egyptians counted a king's first day to a first year, or "year one." Scholars name this the nonaccession-year method (NAY).[78] The question is simply whether to start counting at *zero* or *one*.

> Nonaccession-year counting gives a year number one higher (+1) than accession year counting.[79] Even if all other aspects are correct, but this one is not, then the wrong year will be indicated in every case. It's absolutely vital to get it right.

At times, Hebrews used the accession year (year zero) and at other times the nonaccession year (year one).[80] Which did Nehemiah use? Put simply, did Nehemiah start counting at zero or one?

A careful study, shown in appendix A.4.2, indicates that Nehemiah counted Artaxerxes' first day as king (in August of 465 BC) to his **first year.**

C. (*Count Up*) Nehemiah Counted up Each Month of *Tishri*.

The third step is to know when to count up—in other words, on what day did Artaxerxes' first year end and his second year begin? Babylonians and Persians advanced kings' years on the first day of the springtime month *Nisan* (c. April). Jews advanced kings' years on either *Nisan* 1 or on the first day of the autumn month *Tishri* (c. October).[81]

Nehemiah advanced Artaxerxes' years at **Tishri**. We know this because Nehemiah 1:1 dates a prior event, before Nisan, also to the king's twentieth year, making a Nisan advance impossible.[82]

To Nehemiah, Artaxerxes' first year began when he became king in August of 465 BC, and his second year began on Tishri 1 (c. October) in 465 BC, only two months later. Nehemiah's "Nisan, in the twentieth year of King Artaxerxes" falls in March/April of 446 BC, as the chart shows.

Artaxerxes' Years per Nehemiah

From	BC	Year	BC	To	
Aug	465	1	465	Oct	
Oct	465	2	464	Oct	
Oct	464	3	463	Oct	
Oct	463	4	462	Oct	
Oct	462	5	461	Oct	
Oct	461	6	460	Oct	
Oct	460	7	459	Oct	
Oct	459	8	458	Oct	
Oct	458	9	457	Oct	
Oct	457	10	456	Oct	
Oct	456	11	455	Oct	
Oct	455	12	454	Oct	
Oct	454	13	453	Oct	
Oct	453	14	452	Oct	
Oct	452	15	451	Oct	
Oct	451	16	450	Oct	
Oct	450	17	449	Oct	
Oct	449	18	448	Oct	
Oct	448	19	447	Oct	
Oct	447	20	446	Oct	Nisan - 446 BC

Figure 6. Nehemiah's count of Artaxerxes' years. October is proxy for Tishri. Nisan falls in March/April. Nisan in Artaxerxes' twentieth year fell in 446 BC.

The Date

King Artaxerxes' decree to Nehemiah issued in *Nisan* (c. April), 446 BC.[83] The Bible doesn't state the exact day in Nisan. *Can we find it?*

Daniel 9:25 starts at "the issuing" of a decree. The Hebrew is *min motsa dabar*, also translated as "From the time the word goes out" (NIV)—in other words, not necessarily the day the word originated, but rather the day it physically traveled forth. Nehemiah carried that decree.[84] The key question here is: on what day did Nehemiah set out for Jerusalem? Scripture does not tell us directly.[85] It only mentions the Hebrew springtime month *Nisan*.

Fortunately, we know exactly when *Nisan* of 446 BC started and ended. The scholarly standard reference *Parker & Dubberstein's Babylonian Chronology* (PDBC), authoritative for Persia, places it between March 26 and April 25.[86] This frames a window of possible dates for this decree:

Start:	March 26, 446 BC
End:	April 25, 446 BC

The next chapter finds the exact date. A later chapter verifies it.

Richard Parker and Waldo Dubberstein's book *Babylonian Chronology 626 BC–AD 75* (*PDBC*) is a gold-standard scholarly reference for ancient chronology. It reconstructs the lunar calendar used in Babylon and Persia by matching modern astronomical calculations to ancient, dated cuneiform tablets. *PDBC* identifies actual intercalations (leap months) during this era and lists the Julian calendar date on which each lunar month began. *PDBC* has withstood many scholarly challenges over the decades and remains authoritative for dates referenced from Persia and Babylon in the biblical era.

Note: Internet calendar converters are not reliable for biblical Hebrew dates. Internet converters use the algorithmic modern (Hillel II) Hebrew calendar, adopted in c. AD 359, long after the biblical era. Using the internet to convert biblical dates is now probably the *single most common mistake* in biblical chronology.

The modern (Hillel II) Hebrew calendar uses a fixed cycle of leap years and fixed month lengths.[87] In contrast, biblical era Jews declared months and leap years by eyewitness observation of the moon and natural springtime, not by a fixed cycle. Declaring months and years was discretionary, not fixed, in the entire biblical era (appendix B). Thus, converting biblical Hebrew dates to Julian dates requires either the lunar phases (appendix C) or *PDBC*. The modern (Hillel II) Hebrew calendar, adopted c. AD 359, is the basis for internet date converters which do not apply to the biblical era.

Why does this book use the Julian calendar? By convention, scholars date events, including eclipses, prior to 1582 AD on the Julian calendar, and events thereafter on the Gregorian (modern) calendar. In this book, Julian AD years carry a leading AD, (e.g., AD 31) while Gregorian years carry a lagging AD (e.g., 1948 AD) or no AD at all.

Chapter 4 Key Points

- Nehemiah dated Artaxerxes' regnal years with:

  A.   his reign starting in August of 465 BC,

  B.   a nonaccession year "year one" (appendix A.4.2), and

  C.   a Tishri advance.

- Nisan of Artaxerxes' twentieth year fell in 446 BC (figure 6).

- In 446 BC, Nisan spanned March 26 to April 25.

- The exact date that Artaxerxes' decree to Nehemiah issued will be identified in the next chapter and then confirmed in a later chapter.

Why is Artaxerxes' year 1 only two months long? Note that the ancients numbered their king's years to name their civil years. They didn't have a seamlessly continuous count of years as we do today. The ancients named each year after the current king and the numbered year of his reign. When a king died and a new king ascended, a new count started. That could happen on any day of the year, even the last day of the year, so in theory, a king's year could be as short as one day long.

This is because ancient cultures advanced a king's year count on their New Years Day. On that day, the old year ended and a new one began, so the king's year counted up by one. For Jews, New Years Day was Tishri 1 (*Rosh Hashanah*). Jews advanced Judean kings (and *conspicuously* also Artaxerxes) at Tishri 1, but advanced other foreign kings at Nisan 1. Persia and Babylon also advanced kings on Nisan 1 (their New Years Day).

We moderns can refer to 2024, 1945, or 1066 and expect everyone to understand the correct year. This is because the world now observes a standard year count, where years are numbered from AD 1 and advance each New Years Day. Some may count modern kings' years, but only for the sake of their kings, not their calendars. Those counts don't influence our civil calendar as they did in the ancient era.

To recap, a new king could arise at any point of the year. For ancients, kings' year counts advanced on each New Years Day. So, a king's first year could be as short as even only one day. Each New Years Day started a new calendar year and required a new year number. This was vital to civil society; every contract, lease, tax bill, etc., bore a date which had to be universally understood.

If our calculations are correct that Nisan in Artaxerxes' twentieth year falls in the spring of 446 BC, and that the required time span is indeed 173,880 days, then Daniel 9:25 predicts an advent of Messiah to fall somewhere in the year AD 31. This is plausibly during Jesus' earthly ministry.

But when exactly?

Rejoice greatly, daughter of Zion!
Shout in triumph, daughter of Jerusalem!
Behold, your king is coming to you;
He is righteous and endowed with salvation,
Humble, and mounted on a donkey,
Even on a colt, the foal of a donkey.
(Zechariah 9:9)

You Are
Here

Decree   Messiah

5

Read this to me

PALM SUNDAY

> This chapter places Jesus' triumphal entry into Jerusalem on Sunday, April 22 in AD 31. This is 173,880 days after Nehemiah's decree issued, by calculation, on April 1 in 446 BC. These dates will be verified in a later chapter.

AD 31—Jerusalem

ANDERSON AND HOEHNER EACH placed the end point of Daniel's "seven weeks and sixty-two weeks" at Jesus' triumphal entry into Jerusalem on Nisan 10 of the crucifixion year. On that day, Jesus entered Jerusalem on a donkey and was received with loud adoration, as foretold five centuries earlier by the prophet Zechariah (facing page). Traditionally, we call this event "Palm Sunday."

> Per Mosaic law, on every Nisan 10, Jews accepted a lamb for sacrifice on Passover. This parallels Jesus' presentation on Nisan 10 and crucifixion at Passover.[88] On that Palm Sunday, Jesus also lamented that nobody recognized the time of his coming.[89] It's plausible that Daniel 9:25 refers to Jesus' triumphal entry on Nisan 10.

To review, chapter 4 identified a start date between March 26 and April 25, 446 BC and a span of 173,880 days. This reaches into AD 31. In that year, Nisan 10 fell on Sunday, April 22 (appendix C.5). Is this Palm Sunday? If so, then these dates must fit. There are two ways to check, and we'll use both.

> The triumphal entry didn't happen on a Sabbath. Riding a donkey on a Sabbath explicitly breaks Mosaic law which Jesus fulfilled perfectly. We know because the Pharisees, who always tried to entrap Jesus, rebuked Jesus for his noisy followers but did not accuse him of breaking Sabbath for his riding a donkey.[90] It wasn't a Sabbath.

Method 1. Julian Day Number (JDN)

The first method is by Julian Day Number (JDN), a tool astronomers use to calculate long time spans quickly and easily. The JDN is simply a continuous count of days. Each date in history has its own JDN.[91] To know the number of days between any two dates in history, simply subtract their JDNs. (Appendix A.5.1 introduces the JDN's function and gives a table of key JDNs.) JDNs are easily verified using astronomy websites such as NASA's.[92]

The end date, April 22, AD 31, is JDN 1,732,492.[93] If Artaxerxes' decree truly issued 173,880 days earlier, then it should have issued in 446 BC between March 26 and April 25 (chapter 4).

End	JDN 1,732,492	Apr 22, AD 31
Minus:	**-173,880**	days
Start	JDN 1,558,612	**Apr 1, 446 BC**

This does indeed fall in the target window of Nisan, 446 BC. But is it *correct*? How can we verify the exact number of days from April 1, 446 BC, to April 22, AD 31? Let's double-check the JDN result using longhand math.

Method 2. Longhand Math

The second method is by familiar arithmetic. There are exactly 476 Julian calendar years between April 1, 446 BC, and *April 1*, AD 31 (exact years). In those 476 years, there are 173,859 days (476 x 365.25 days per Julian calendar year—this also accounts for Julian leap years).

> 446 + 31 – 1 = 476 years from 446 BC to AD 31
>
> We must subtract one year because there is no "year zero" between 1 BC and AD 1. For example, there is only one year from 1 BC to AD 1. Thus, 1 + 1 – 1 = 1 is correct. There are two years from 1 BC to AD 2, so, 1 + 2 – 1 = 2 is correct, and so forth.

To this, we add 21 days from *April 1* to April 22 in AD 31. So:

$$173,859 + 21 = 173,880 \text{ days}$$

Longhand math confirms the JDN result. It seems Daniel's prediction could in fact be true. The next question is: *does AD 31 fit known evidence?*

The Crucifixion Year

Historically, scholars have placed the crucifixion year loosely between AD 26 and AD 36, with most assertions spanning AD 30 to AD 33.[94]

Almost all scholars agree that Jesus was crucified in the Hebrew month of *Nisan*, on or around Passover, just days after his triumphal entry into Jerusalem. Scripture tells us his empty tomb was discovered on the following Sunday morning. That much is nearly universally accepted.

An AD 31 crucifixion is a minority, yet historically attested view.[95] Some scholars exclude AD 31, erroneously assuming it would place the crucifixion on a Monday or Tuesday, violating the Gospel chronology of that week.

> Scholars have asserted the crucifixion on either a Wednesday, Thursday, or Friday, but virtually everyone, including this book, excludes the crucifixion on a Saturday, Sunday, Monday, or Tuesday.

But those who exclude AD 31 almost uniformly make the same mistake—namely, applying the modern (Hillel II) Hebrew calendar to this era, long before it was adopted. [96] The modern Hebrew calendar was not observed in the biblical era (appendix B). Applying it to AD 31 would start Nisan in March. But in AD 31, Nisan began in April, which places the crucifixion in a scripturally viable window of Wednesday, Thursday, or Friday. How can we know Nisan of AD 31 started in April and not March? Appendix A.5.2 presents detailed reasoning.

Of course, this alone doesn't prove AD 31—it only shows we cannot exclude it from consideration, as too many have done too quickly.

> The crucifixion day of the week question is vigorously debated. Wednesday, Thursday, and Friday are each staunchly advocated. This book will not seek to resolve this day of the week question, as the Nisan moon of AD 31 can, in theory, allow any of the three.

Yet there is also positive evidence for AD 31. This book will verify each of the four fulfillments, including this one. Verification that Jesus' triumphal entry occurred in AD 31 is presented in a later chapter because it works in tandem with another fulfillment.

It seems Daniel may have indeed predicted, five centuries in advance, the precise date that Messiah would enter Jerusalem triumphantly, as Zechariah foretold. And yet, we've barely begun to scratch the surface of Daniel 9:25.

Figure 7. Daniel 9:25—corrected Anderson/Hoehner solution timeline

Chapter 5 Key Points

- Jesus triumphantly entered Jerusalem on Sunday, April 22, AD 31. This is 173,880 days after Artaxerxes' decree to Nehemiah issued on April 1 in 446 BC (to be verified).

- The modern Hebrew calendar—the basis for internet calendar converters—is not valid for Hebrew dates in the biblical era.

- Time spans may be calculated using the JDN (appendix A.5.1) and by longhand arithmetic. This book uses both.

- This is one of four fulfillments of Daniel 9:25. This fulfillment will be verified in a later chapter.

> Jesus' triumphal entry is one of four advents foretold by Daniel 9:25. Intriguingly, it's only one small part of a larger, more precise, and robust fulfillment. In all seriousness, don't stop here. To this point, we have followed the Anderson/Hoehner approach with a couple of technical fixes and found a solution that fits both Scripture and math. Credit for this solution is due to them. The new discoveries start in the following chapters. Remember, this book is written to be read conventionally, each page in order. Skipping text will result in confusion.
>
> Note again that internet date converters are not reliable for the biblical era because they use the modern, algorithmic Hebrew calendar which wasn't adopted until AD 359.
>
> *Congratulations!* You have now survived this book's most challenging part, specifically the two concepts of (1) Judean dating method (ABC) in chapter 4, and (2) Julian Day Number (JDN) in chapter 5. These will be used consistently going forward.

It's far too soon to declare the prophecy valid and stop right here. First, we shouldn't assume this is all Daniel intended. As it turns out, he foretells much more. The next chapter indicates there is more to Daniel 9:25 than that Palm Sunday alone. In fact, Scripture indicates several starting points and several advents (arrivals). Jesus' triumphal entry is the fourth of these advents.

Read this to me

6

"EVERYTHING"

This chapter shows that Daniel 9:25 indicates more than Jesus' triumphal entry alone.

SHORTLY BEFORE ASCENDING TO heaven, Jesus spoke to his disciples:

> Now He said to them, "These are My words which I spoke to you while I was still with you, that all the things that are written about Me in the Law of Moses and the Prophets and the Psalms must be fulfilled." (Luke 24:44)

The phrase "all the things" (Greek, *panta*) also translated as "everything" (NIV) means *all* messianic Scripture,[97] without exception, indicates Jesus. We know we have found Truth when *everything* fits. That's a high standard of evidence—maybe even the highest possible standard. But we have it in Jesus' own words: ***everything***.

By this standard, Daniel 9:25 foretells more than just Palm Sunday. In fact, Scripture suggests that people should have known of Messiah's arrival also *before* Palm Sunday. Consider these passages:

> You hypocrites! You know how to analyze the appearance of the earth and the sky, but how is it that you do not know how to analyze this present time? (Luke 12:56)

Here, Jesus lamented long before Palm Sunday that no one understood the significance of that time. People should have known the importance of "this present time" as it was spoken.[98] Palm Sunday had not yet occurred. Daniel 9:25 is the only verse foretelling the exact timing of Messiah. This implies Daniel might have also foretold an advent of Messiah *before* Palm Sunday. Another example:

"Behold, I am sending My messenger, and he will clear a way before Me. And the Lord, whom you are seeking, will suddenly come to His temple; and the messenger of the covenant, in whom you delight, behold, He is coming," says the LORD of armies. (Malachi 3:1)

This is one of the last prophecies in the Old Testament, and it foretells an advent of Messiah. The timing clue is "will suddenly come to His temple" in the *future*. Malachi wrote this in c. 400 BC when the Second Temple was standing. Jesus entered that temple at age twelve,[99] long before Palm Sunday. It is possible that Daniel 9:25 could also indicate this prophetic event.[100] Yet another example:

The scepter will not depart from Judah,
Nor the ruler's staff from between his feet,
Until Shiloh comes,
And to him shall be the obedience of the peoples.
(Genesis 49:10)

Here, in c. 1800 BC, Jacob foretold an advent of Messiah. Both Christians and Jews understand "Shiloh" as Messiah.[101]

Messiah: What is his name? The school of R' Sheila say:
Shiloh is his name, as it is stated: "Until Shiloh comes"[102]
(Talmud)

This book doesn't ascribe scriptural authority to the Talmud but cites it as a reliable historical source, just as it cites Josephus, Tacitus, or other ancient sources.

Traditionally, "scepter" and "ruler's staff" refer to royal authority and the right to administer law.[103] Jacob's blessing foretells that Judah's descendants should both reign *and* enforce the law until Messiah comes.[104] The theology isn't our focus; the chronology is.

Jacob spoke these words four centuries before Israel received the Mosaic law (Torah) and nearly a millennium before its first king. Despite Israel's division (c. 930 BC), dispersion of the Northern Kingdom (c. 720 BC), and Babylonian captivity, Judah retained a prince.[105] So when did Judah lose *both* regency *and* legal authority? The short answer is the year AD 6.

In AD 6, Rome reduced Judea's status from client state to province, and replaced Judean king Archelaus with a Roman procurator named Coponius, who had "the power of death put into his hands by Caesar."[106] Rome now held supreme authority in Judea.[107]

Losing both regency and legal authority *at the same time* indicates this prophecy was fulfilled in AD 6. Jews at that time could have already known Messiah had arrived. Therefore, Daniel 9:25 might have also indicated an advent of Messiah before AD 6.[108]

A Closer Look

A careful reading of Daniel 9:24 reveals some insight:

> Seventy weeks have been decreed for your people and
> your holy city, to finish the wrongdoing, to make an end
> of sin, to make atonement for guilt, to bring in everlasting
> righteousness, to seal up vision and prophecy, and to anoint
> the Most Holy Place. (Daniel 9:24)

The seventy weeks aren't yet complete, even if the first sixty-nine weeks are. Verse 24 isn't yet fulfilled in any *real* sense. It describes a world free of injustice. This hasn't yet emerged, arguably for anyone, and certainly not "for your people and your holy city" (i.e., Hebrews and Jerusalem) to whom this prophecy is addressed.[109] It seems the seventieth week might not have immediately followed the sixty-ninth. Many Christians today see a pause between Daniel's sixty-ninth and seventieth weeks:

> Certainly we are living in the closing days of this age of grace—
> the period of time between the 69th and 70th weeks of Daniel's
> prophecy.[110] (Greene)

Unindicated pauses (aka "gaps") are common in prophecy (see appendix A.6.1). Notably, one exists in Daniel 9:25.

A Pause between the Seven and Sixty-Two Weeks

The seventy weeks are given in three parts: seven, sixty-two, and one. Three periods are created by two divisions, breaks, or pauses.

Figure 8. The three segments are created by two pauses (P1 and P2).

If there were no break between the seven and sixty-two weeks, then why did Daniel, in one of the Bible's most info-dense verses, write out the longer "seven weeks and sixty-two weeks" and not the shorter *sixty-nine weeks?*[111] This caught Isaac Newton's attention:

> We avoid also the doing violence to the language of Daniel, by taking the seven weeks and sixty-two weeks for one number. Had that been Daniel's meaning, he would have said sixty and nine weeks, and not seven weeks and sixty-two weeks, a way of numbering used by no nation.[112] (Newton)

We can't ignore Daniel's dividing the seven and sixty-two weeks. In Daniel 9:26, Messiah is cut off after "sixty-*two* weeks." It does not read *after sixty-nine weeks*, so we shouldn't read seven and sixty-two as simply sixty-nine. In fact, the number *sixty-nine* doesn't appear anywhere in this prophecy. The seven and sixty-two weeks are distinctly separate from each other.[113]

Some scholars assert the Hebrew text divides Daniel's seven and sixty-two weeks also by a punctuation mark called an *atnach*, a Hebrew equivalent to our semicolon.[114]

שָׁבֻעִים שִׁבְעָה וְשָׁבֻעִים שִׁשִּׁים וּשְׁנַיִם

Figure 9. Hebrew text from Daniel 9:25 (color added).

The above reads "weeks **seven;** and weeks sixty-two" (reading right to left). The atnach is the wishbone shape ⌃ under the word **seven**. According to Hebrew scholars, it indicates a break or pause between the seven and sixty-two weeks.

Other scholars claim the atnach to be a late addition, the oldest examples of which appear in the Hebrew Masoretic Text (MT). The oldest recovered punctuated copy of the MT (Aleppo Codex) dates to c. AD 925.[115] No earlier punctuated copy of Daniel 9:25 has been recovered, so we don't know precisely when this *atnach* originated.

In short, this book neither asserts nor excludes the atnach in Daniel 9:25 but rather ignores it. Asserting the *atnach* fully supports this book's thesis, and excluding it has no impact either way. The *atnach* suggests that Jews long considered Daniel's seven and sixty-two weeks as two distinct periods; we just don't know for how long. Also, note that Hebrew punctuation evolved over time, and punctuation is not inspired. For those seeking more detail on this *atnach*, see appendix A.6.2.

In short, the *atnach* isn't our reason for separating the seven and sixty-two weeks. Daniel separates them verbally, as Isaac Newton and many others have noted.

Daniel's Seventy Weeks do not elapse in unbroken sequence. They exist as three distinct periods. Daniel's wording directly indicate this. Those words will prove to be not only carefully chosen but also astoundingly precise.

Some Christians also separate the seven and sixty-two weeks: [116]

> There is a small gap between the seven weeks and the sixty-two weeks, in which there are years not accounted for, just as there is a gap between the sixty-ninth and the seventieth weeks.[117] (Greene)

Daniel indicates a pause between the seven and sixty-two weeks even more plainly than the pause before the final week. Interestingly, that pause does not void the Palm Sunday fulfillment (this will make more sense after a few pages). The point is that Scripture indicates a pause here, even though it does not openly state its duration.[118] Could its duration be of a *definable* time? Is it something confirmed even by Scripture itself?

The answer is *yes*.

Unannounced pauses in Bible prophecy are not rare. One example is the Ezekiel 26 prediction of Tyre's destruction. Its prophetic elements were all fulfilled, but by different people and at different times, separated by centuries. See also 2 Samuel 7:12–13; Psalm 110:1–3; Hosea 3:4–5; 5:15–6:1. To reject a pause because the Bible doesn't directly announce or measure it, would degrade the validity of these and many other prophecies which contain unindicated or unmeasured pauses.

Chapter 6 Key Points

- Daniel 9:25 may foretell advents (arrivals) of Messiah also before Jesus' Palm Sunday advent.

- Scripture indicates a pause between the seven and sixty-two weeks of Daniel 9:25 (P1 on figure 8).

*Every assertion that you have read to this point has also appeared somewhere else over the years. **The next chapter steps into new territory.***

But as for you, Bethlehem Ephrathah,
Too little to be among the clans of Judah,
From you One will come forth for Me to be ruler in Israel.
His times of coming forth are from long ago,
From the days of eternity.
(Micah 5:2)

7

Read this to me

THE SEAL

This chapter presents newly discovered keys to Daniel 9:25.

ANIEL'S PROPHETIC CLOCK STARTED when a decree to restore and rebuild Jerusalem issued. The Bible contains four such decrees, each from a Persian king. The one from Artaxerxes to **Nehemiah** (chapter 4) is the fourth of those. The first is from **Cyrus**, the second from **Darius**, and the third from the same Artaxerxes to the Jewish scribe **Ezra**.[119] Each of these four decrees mandated restoring a part, but not all, of Jerusalem.

Four Starting Points, Not One

Previously, scholars have chosen only one of these four decrees, asking: *Which decree to rebuild Jerusalem does Daniel indicate?* One decree is chosen, and the others are dismissed. Picking only one of these four scriptural decrees might be the only point of (prior) universal agreement and may help explain why this prophecy's full meaning has remained shrouded for centuries—"secret and sealed"—as Daniel 12:4, 9 foretold it would. As it turns out, this is one of two points where virtually all prior attempts at solution (no discovered exceptions) have gone off track.

Is there a reason to dismiss three of those four decrees? The short answer is no. Is there a reason more than one decree, or more correctly, more than one "issuing" of a decree is indicated? Actually, there is.

A careful reading of Daniel 9:25 shows the time span started not with a *dabar* (word), but when that *dabar* issued. Daniel left the point open for other Scripture to define.

Micah 5:2 (facing page) is among the most beloved of messianic prophecies. It predates Daniel. Micah wrote that Messiah's advents were set from "the days of eternity." These advents (lit. "goings forth," *plural)* reference more than just one event and *include* Messiah's origin in Bethlehem.

Remember, in the entire Bible, only Daniel 9:25 foretells the exact *timing* of Messiah's advents. And here, Micah indicates one Messiah with more than one advent, and one of those advents is his birth. *How can we know?* Because other Scripture confirms this.

When we take the universal question, "Which of the four decrees to rebuild Jerusalem does Daniel indicate?" and turn it slightly to, "*By whose decree was Jerusalem rebuilt?*" we find a direct answer in Scripture:

> And the elders of the Jews were successful in building through the prophecy of Haggai the prophet and Zechariah the son of Iddo. And they finished building following the command of the God of Israel and the decree of Cyrus, Darius, and Artaxerxes king of Persia. (Ezra 6:14)

Daniel's decree to restore and rebuild Jerusalem is the "command of the God of Israel." That decree issued via three kings, not one.[120] Maybe this is why Daniel, in an extremely info-dense passage, wrote "from the issuing of a decree" and not simply "from a decree" as so many have inferred.

Some claim Ezra 6:14 concerns building only the temple and not Jerusalem. This verse is part of the temple's construction narrative. Even though the word *temple* isn't mentioned in the text of this verse,[121] it is certainly implied by context, and this is not disputed.

But consider this: the temple is *part* of Jerusalem—a vital part. Rebuilding the temple equals rebuilding Jerusalem[122] just as repairing a car's engine equals repairing that car. Scripture confirms this view.

The Edict of Cyrus[123] mandates rebuilding the temple, but not explicitly Jerusalem. Yet two centuries before Cyrus' birth, the prophet Isaiah divinely foretold that Cyrus would order *Jerusalem* rebuilt:

> "It is I who says of Cyrus, 'He is My shepherd!
> And he will carry out all My desire.'
> And he says of Jerusalem, 'She will be built,'
> And of the temple, 'Your foundation will be laid.'" (Isaiah 44:28)

> "I have stirred him in righteousness,
> And I will make all his ways smooth;
> He will build My city and let My exiles go free,
> Without any payment or reward," says the LORD of armies.
> (Isaiah 45:13)

Cyrus decreed that Jerusalem be rebuilt. Insisting the temple can't count as Jerusalem would undermine Isaiah's validity as a prophet.[124] Equating the temple and Jerusalem preserves Isaiah's validity. Scripture equates building the temple with building Jerusalem. The temple is *part* of Jerusalem.

Ezra 6:14 indicates Jerusalem was rebuilt by the "command of God." This is the decree of Daniel 9:25. It issued via decrees from "Cyrus, Darius, and Artaxerxes." This gives several starting points for Daniel 9:25, not just one.

> Moreover, the Artaxerxes in Ezra 6:14 ruled five decades *after* the temple was built. He ordered the city wall rebuilt,[125] not the temple. The city wall is also a *part*, not the whole, of Jerusalem. By naming him here, Ezra 6:14 indicates building Jerusalem, not just the temple.
>
> Remember, Daniel's prophetic clock starts "from the *issuing* of a decree" and not "from a decree." Ezra 6:14 may indicate Daniel's "decree" (*dabar*, "word") to be the "command of the God of Israel,"[126] which issued via decree of each of these three kings.

Despite the countless interpretations published over the centuries, this is truly a new approach—a path not yet taken.[127] It has scriptural basis. But how can we know it's *correct?* At the very least, it must fit both Scripture and math. Daniel gives us hard numbers. Those numbers must work.

The four biblical decrees to restore and rebuild Jerusalem are from King **Cyrus**, King **Darius**, King Artaxerxes to **Ezra**, and King Artaxerxes to **Nehemiah**.[128] The years of those decrees are charted below.

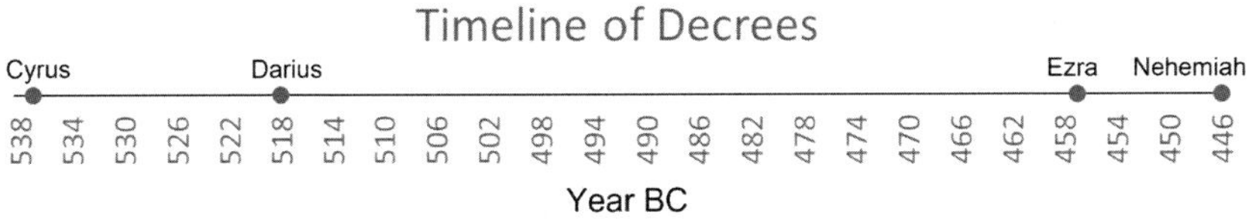

Figure 10. Four biblical decrees to rebuild Jerusalem and their BC years. The precise dates for each decree and advent will be identified. Note BC years count down as time passes.

Another common objection to the Edict of Cyrus is that it occurs too early to indicate Jesus. If he was crucified in AD 31 in his thirties, then sixty-nine weeks of years after Cyrus lands a good half-century before Jesus' birth. Yet on other points, Cyrus fits this prophecy remarkably well.[129] So before dismissing Cyrus, let's be sure we aren't missing something important.

Chapter 3 mentioned another solution starting with a decree to Ezra in 457 BC and ending sixty-nine weeks (483 solar years) later in AD 27—a plausible year of Jesus' baptism. This one is enlightening in unexpected ways.

Following that solution, but using sixty-nine weeks of *prophetic* years (360 days) instead, reaches AD 20, which is seven years before AD 27. Note that seven solar years is a standard Hebrew unit of time—a *sabbatical cycle*.

Now let's do the same with Cyrus. Starting in c. 537 BC and adding 483 *prophetic* years brings us to c. 61 BC. This is short of Jesus' birth by c. fifty-five to sixty years or roughly eight sabbatical cycles. Because seven sabbatical cycles equal one Hebrew *jubilee cycle* (49 years), we might consider it one jubilee cycle plus one sabbatical cycle. Note this too.

The previous chapter identified a pause between the seven weeks and the sixty-two weeks. What if that pause is not a single duration but is instead a structured progression? The decree of Darius (c. 518 BC) plus sixty-nine weeks of prophetic years reaches c. 42 BC. Adding a pause of *one jubilee cycle* (forty-nine years) extends the span to AD 8, when Jesus could have been around age twelve and entered the temple as the prophets foretold.[130]

This is a *hypothesis*, not a deduction. It's a proposal to explore. There may be four advents of Jesus, each with a pause between Daniel's seven and sixty-two weeks. Those pauses may be whole sabbatical and jubilee cycles.

But Hang On Now . . .

Some might object (actually, I would too) that pauses can make almost anything fit—an elastic variable can't give a valid solution. Also, even if the math works (as it must) we should also see scriptural basis for these pauses and their lengths, which cannot be *elastic*.

Scripture gives this basis. It notes decrees from three kings, notes one Messiah with plural advents (including his birth) and pauses between the seven and sixty-two weeks. If true, then this could be part of this prophecy's *recursive* structure, one reason it stayed "secret and sealed," as Daniel foretold. Looking ahead a bit, this *hypothesis* will yield fulfillments that are:

– precise to the day,
– historically verifiable, and
– confirmed in Scripture.

If even one is true, then this approach *might* not be arbitrary. If all three are true, *objectively* true, then we couldn't claim it to be arbitrary at all. We would then have to seriously consider its validity.

The New Key

A structured progression of pauses between the seven and sixty-two weeks links all four biblical decrees to these key advents of Jesus:

Decree:	Linked to	Advent:
Cyrus		His Birth (Nativity)
Darius		His First Temple Entry
Ezra		His Baptism
Nehemiah		His Triumphal Entry

Decree:	Cyrus	Darius	Ezra	Nehemiah
Start date	?	?	?	1 Apr 446 BC
Hebrew date	?	?	?	Nisan 6, Sun
Start JDN	?	?	?	1,558,612
7+62 weeks	173,880	173,880	173,880	173,880
Pause	1 Jubilee, and 1 Sabbatical	1 Jubilee	1 Sabbatical	Zero
+ Pause days	20,454	17,897	2,557	0
= Total span	194,334	191,777	176,437	173,880
End JDN	?	?	?	1,732,492
End date	?	?	?	Apr 22, AD 31
Event:	**Nativity**	**Temple**	**Baptism**	**Triumphal Entry**
Hebrew date	?	?	?	Nisan 10, Sun

Figure 11. Chronology table showing each decree, pause, and advent.

Pause 1: One Jubilee Cycle and One Sabbatical Cycle: (56 solar years* of 365.242 days/year, which is 20,454 days), for a total span of **194,334** days.

Pause 2: One Jubilee Cycle: (49 solar years,* which is 17,897 days), for a total span of **191,777** days.

Pause 3: One Sabbatical Cycle: (7 solar years,* which is 2,557 days), for a total span of **176,437** days.

Pause 4: Zero: for a total span of **173,880** days.

These are the pause spans, in units of sabbatical and jubilee cycles, calculated to the precise day. They are not elastic—they are fixed to the precise day. And, as will be shown, they are also confirmed in Scripture.

---

* Why use solar years and not prophetic years for calculating these pauses? This is defined by Scripture itself. The explanation is contained in a later chapter.

Road Map Chronological Chart

The below chart will serve as a chronological road map introducing each of the next chapters.

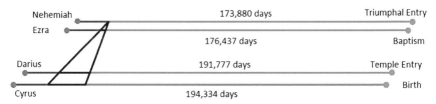

Figure 12. Timelines of decrees (left side), pauses (triangle), and advents (right side) for all four fulfillment strings of Daniel 9:25. This road map chart will appear in the chapter headers to help orient readers through time, as a type of chronological "you are here" signpost.

These Pauses Are Confirmed in Scripture

Daniel didn't openly write out the confirmation, but he did show us where to look—*at the four scriptural decrees to restore and rebuild Jerusalem.* To understand the pauses' confirmations, we must first know the historical events resulting from those decrees. Those are presented in the following chapters. The pauses' scriptural confirmations follow in context right after.

Remarkably, Scripture confirms pauses in *solar* years, not prophetic years. If it seems odd to use prophetic years alongside solar years for the pauses, keep in mind the usage is not only consistent and not arbitrary, but is also confirmed in Scripture. Those confirmations will be presented.

> Daniel 9:25 is one of the most information-dense passages in the Bible. Rarely if ever, is so much meaning packed into one verse. Yet in three spots, Daniel seems to be oddly wordy. He wrote ***issuing of a decree*** instead of *decree*, ***restore and rebuild***—instead of *rebuild*, and ***seven weeks and sixty-two weeks*** instead of *sixty-nine weeks*. These spots are remarkable for two reasons. First, they starkly contrast with the verse's extreme brevity. Second, expositors have traditionally (i.e., nearly always) inferred the simpler meanings (i.e., *decree, rebuild, sixty-nine*) in each case. But that's not how Daniel wrote this text. If Daniel intended the simpler meanings, he would have chosen the simpler wordings. And yet Daniel chose the more complex wording. Maybe for a reason? We always have warrant to seek meaning from the *exact wording* as it appears in the text.
>
> Daniel's word choice is careful, deliberate, and astoundingly precise. Evaluating his words *as he wrote them* will prove vital to a correct understanding, as will be shown. Assuming the simpler meanings has, in each case, obscured this prophecy's solution. This may seem like a bold statement now, but by book's end, you will see its validity.
>
> Understanding all of this requires first knowing the historical events mandated by those four scriptural decrees. Those will be presented in the next chapters.

Remember, Daniel wrote that we wouldn't fully understand this prophecy "until the end of time" (Daniel 12:4, 9). If Daniel had directly, openly specified these pause lengths, then this prophecy would have been quickly solved, and *the seal* of Daniel 12:4, 9 would have been broken far sooner than intended.

> Why are the pauses in solar years and not prophetic years? Both units are confirmed in Scripture. Scripture confirms Daniel's "weeks" as groups of seven 360-day periods (appendix A.3.3) that we today often call "prophetic years" (note that Daniel carefully avoided the word "year").
>
> Remember, the pauses between the seven and sixty-two weeks are 365.242-day *solar* years. The use of solar years and not 360-day prophetic years for these pauses isn't arbitrary, but rather is confirmed by Scripture and applied consistently. That confirmation, presented in a later chapter, requires first knowing the events resulting from the four biblical decrees.

Chapter 7 Key Points

- Ezra 6:14 indicates Daniel's decree (*dabar*) could be "the command of the God of Israel," which issued via four decrees from three Persian kings Cyrus, Darius, and Artaxerxes (2).

- The *issuing* of those four biblical decrees indicate the timing of four advents (arrivals) of Jesus.

- The pause between the seven and sixty-two weeks could be a progression of precisely complete sabbatical and jubilee cycles.

- The pauses are only solar years, never prophetic years. The seven and sixty-two weeks are only prophetic years, never solar years. Scripture will confirm this usage.

- This book will find the dates of each decree and advent and will verify them mathematically, to a surprisingly thorough extent.

- The solution will reveal a precise fulfillment of a large part of Old Testament prophecy and serve as new, direct evidence of God.

*You now hold the newly discovered keys to Daniel 9:25. Now let's see how they unlock **everything**.*

"It is I who says of Cyrus, 'He is My shepherd!
And he will carry out all My desire.'
And he says of Jerusalem, 'She will be built,'
And of the temple, 'Your foundation will be laid.'"
(Isaiah 44:28)

The **Shahbaz** flag of Cyrus the Great

You Are
Here
↓

The start of the first fulfillment

8

Read this to me

CYRUS

This chapter places the Edict of Cyrus between March 537 BC and March 536 BC. This is the starting point of the earliest fulfillment sequence of Daniel 9:25.

537 BC—Babylon

Persian King Cyrus ended the seventy-year Babylonian captivity: [131]

> "This is what Cyrus king of Persia says: 'The Lord, the God of heaven, has given me all the kingdoms of the earth, and He has appointed me to rebuild for Him a house in Jerusalem, which is in Judah. Whoever there is among you of all His people, may his God be with him! Go up to Jerusalem which is in Judah and rebuild the house of the Lord, the God of Israel; He is the God who is in Jerusalem. And every survivor, at whatever place he may live, the people of that place are to support him with silver and gold, with equipment and cattle, together with a voluntary offering for the house of God which is in Jerusalem.'" (Ezra 1:2–4)

This decree, often called the "Edict of Cyrus," mandated two key events. First, it allowed Jews to **return** to the land of Israel, and second, it allowed the **temple** to be rebuilt.[132]

Daniel's seven weeks and sixty-two weeks until Messiah started when that edict issued. The Jewish scribe Ezra dated this edict to the "first year of Cyrus king of Babylon."[133] As before, we need three elements to find the correct year.

The First Year of Cyrus, King of Babylon

A. Cyrus took the title "king of Babylon" in January 537 BC, six weeks after Ugbaru's (Darius the Mede's) death[134] (appendix A.8.1). Before this time, Daniel dated events to Darius the Mede, not to Cyrus.[135] Thus, to Jews, Cyrus began his accession year as "king of Babylon" in January of 537 BC.

B. Jews used the accession year (year zero) when exiled in Babylon (chapter 4 and appendix A.4.2). Cyrus falls in this period.

C. Jews advanced Cyrus' years in Nisan:

They reckoned his [Cyrus'] reign [...] from Nisan.[136] (Talmud)

Ezra followed Jewish scribal convention and dated Cyrus with the accession year and from Nisan. Thus, Cyrus' accession year began in January of 537 BC. Cyrus' *first* year started that spring, on the next Nisan 1, in 537 BC.

Cyrus, King of Babylon's Years, per Ezra

539	Oct. 12		Babylon Falls
BC	OND	AY	Darius M. king
538	JFM	AY	
	AMJ	1	Darius M. Year 1
	JAS	1	
	OND	1	Darius M. dies
537	JFM	AY	Cyrus takes king title
	AMJ	1	First year of Cyrus,
	JAS	1	king of Babylon,
	OND	1	per Daniel, Ezra, and
536	JFM	1	Jewish scribes
	AMJ	2	Cyrus' year 2

Figure 13. Jews began the first year of Cyrus in 537 BC. (Babylonians counted Cyrus' years differently.) The second column displays the months of quarter-years (e.g., JFM for Jan, Feb, Mar, etc.). Quarter-years are used simply for ease of display as they can show periods starting with Hebrew Nisan, Tishri, and Julian January. April is proxy for Nisan, the start of a foreign king's year (e.g., Cyrus). The yellow shaded area is the "First year of Cyrus king of Babylon" per Daniel and Ezra.

To Jews, the first year of Cyrus ran from Nisan 1 in 537 BC to Nisan 1 in 536 BC (appendix A.8.1). Parker and Dubberstein (*PDBC*),[137] authoritative for Babylon, identifies these dates as:

Start:	March 12, 537 BC [138]
End:	March 31, 536 BC

The precise date of Cyrus' edict will be identified and confirmed in a later chapter.

> How do we know Jews did not follow Babylonian scribal convention for dating Cyrus? See appendix A.8.1. For detail on Darius the Mede's identity, see appendix A.2.1.
>
> The Edict of Cyrus is surely one of the most prominent events in all Jewish history. Daniel was alive when it issued (Daniel 10:1). Intriguingly, Daniel doesn't mention this edict anywhere. This is extremely odd, yet Daniel 12:4, 9 suggest why this might be so.

Chapter 8 Key Points

- The Edict of Cyrus issued at some point between March 537 BC and March 536 BC.

- The Edict of Cyrus allowed Jews to **return** to the land of Israel and rebuild the **temple**.

- Judean dating method (ABC), derived in appendix D.1, appears below. This book applies it consistently, without exception:

    A. **Accession date** is obtained from the historical record.

    B. **First regnal day** (all kings) was counted to:
       1. first year (NAY, year one) when Jews were in the land, or
       2. accession year (AY, year zero) when Judah was outside the land (587 to 457 BC).

    C. **Month of advance** (when to count up to the king's next year)
       1. Tishri 1 for Judean kings (and Artaxerxes), or
       2. Nisan 1 for foreign kings (except Artaxerxes).

> Why is Artaxerxes Longimanus exceptional? See appendix A.14.1.

Five centuries later, a very pregnant couple slowly made their way toward Bethlehem.

The Nativity by Botticelli

But when the fullness of the time came, God sent His Son,
born of a woman, born under the Law (Galatians 4:4)

9

Read this to me

ORIGIN

This chapter finds a likely date of Jesus' birth, to be verified in the next chapter. This is the ending point of the first fulfillment sequence of Daniel 9:25 that started with the Edict of Cyrus and spanned 194,334 days (figure 11).

THE BIBLE DOES NOT state the day or year of Jesus' birth. As will be shown, the traditional date of December 25 is extremely unlikely. Some claim the early church used the nativity to co-opt the late December Roman holidays.[139] Others assume a Passover conception and a December 25 birth. These may explain *why* we celebrate Christmas on December 25, but neither indicates the true nativity date. Because other key events of Jesus' life occurred on Hebrew holidays, many scholarly estimates land in the spring or autumn.

The traditional year AD 1 is from sixth-century monk Dionysius Exiguus. He attempted to calculate the year of Jesus' birth but made errors. Dionysius numbered the years after Jesus' birth and labeled them "AD" (*Anno Domini*). Use of "BC" began two centuries later when the English monk Bede numbered the years *before Christ*. The BC/AD system reinforced a misconception that Jesus was born as BC became AD. Today, scholars place the nativity earlier. Most estimates span 7 BC to 1 BC.[140]

This chapter follows scriptural evidence to calculate a plausible nativity date, and the next chapter will verify it objectively. First, let's follow traditional evidence as far as we safely can.

> This chapter covers familiar territory for many readers. However, understanding it requires reading the prior chapters. This book is written to be read conventionally, each page in order. If you start this book here, you will miss its entire message.
>
> It's important to note that this chapter presents only one of many reasonable ways of interpreting the nativity evidence. Don't despair if you see it interpreted differently from what is familiar to you. This chapter's goal is *not* to exclude other approaches, nor is it to prove what *must* be concluded, but instead to show how this approach is supported by Scripture. The following chapters will then present a direct and surprisingly strong confirmation of this chapter's conclusion.

Forty-Six Years

> The Jews then said, "It took forty-six years to build this temple, and yet You will raise it up in three days?" (John 2:20)

This was spoken during the first recorded Passover of Jesus' ministry. Temple construction began in King Herod's eighteenth year (October 20 BC to October 19 BC).[141] The temple complex was still under construction forty-six years later, which was October AD 27 to October AD 28.[142] Passover in that year fell in April of AD 28.

> When He began His ministry, Jesus Himself was about thirty years old, being, as was commonly held, the son of Joseph, the son of Eli (Luke 3:23)

Passover of AD 28 couldn't have been more than one year after his ministry began (or it would have been his second Passover). So, Jesus was "about" thirty or thirty-one in April AD 28. This indicates a nativity date *loosely* between April 5 BC and April 3 BC. We will narrow this window as we go.

Herod's Death

Matthew's Gospel states that Jesus was born when Judea's King Herod the Great was still alive. According to Jewish historian Josephus, Herod died shortly after a lunar eclipse.[143] Modern astronomy identifies two possible eclipses. Of the two, history favors the one on March 13 in 4 BC.[144] It places Herod's death near the end of March in 4 BC. Thus, our nativity window now spans one year, from April 5 BC to March 4 BC. Scripture further narrows this window.

Not in Winter

Contrary to tradition, Jesus was not born in winter. A winter nativity is doubtful for two reasons: sheep and taxes. First, when Jesus was born, shepherds were staying out in the fields at night.

> In the same region there were some shepherds staying out in the fields and keeping watch over their flock at night. (Luke 2:8)

Sheep were not out at night in winter. Flocks were out at night in summer, when there was enough forage to compensate for the risk of overnight loss via predation, theft, straying, etc., *and* keeping them out all night was less work than taking them in and back out again. This was not the case in winter, even the mildest winter. Note that this has *nothing to do with air temperatures*, but everything to do with foliage, risk, and workload.

According to Scottish archaeologist Sir William Ramsay, sheep in Judea were pastured overnight only during the hot season because they would "not eat under the hot sun," yet "during the night they scatter and feed."[145] Staying in the field was more profitable than bringing sheep in for a short summer night and then back out again in the morning. Shepherds kept their flocks out overnight to increase profit and reduce workload. Sheep were simply out at night during summer, not winter.[146]

The second reason is money. Joseph and Mary traveled to Bethlehem for a census enrollment when Mary was heavily pregnant.[147] This indicates the enrollment was set for a specific time, and the couple had to travel whether it was convenient or not, because it certainly was not.

This census enrollment was in part for taxation.[148] No tax authority would have required travel in winter, which is the rainy season in Israel when roads can be treacherous.[149] Weather in early spring and late autumn is unpredictable. Because bad weather would reduce enrollment participation and thus reduce the ability to collect taxes, the authorities certainly did not plan this enrollment for winter.

This narrows the window of possibility to between late spring and early autumn of 5 BC. This span is bookended by the Hebrew festivals Pentecost (*Shavuot*) and Tabernacles (*Sukkot*), which all adult Jewish males were required to attend in Jerusalem.[150] Requiring people to be *both* in Jerusalem *and* somewhere else at the same time is impossible.[151]

Because Tabernacles (*Sukkot*, Tishri 15) is closely preceded by *Yom Kippur* (Tishri 10) and *Rosh Hashanah* (Tishri 1)—each a high Sabbath on which travel is forbidden—enrollment likely occurred before Tishri (October).

The weeks from Passover (April) to Pentecost (June) were devoted to the grain harvest.[152] This required labor in the field, so an enrollment before June in a non-sabbatical year such as 5 BC is extremely unlikely.[153]

Our window of possible nativity dates now runs from June to September in 5 BC. This window fits traditional evidence, including the earliest known nativity dating (appendix A.9.1) and other careful studies.[154] Fortunately, Scripture further narrows the window of possibility.

> Remember, this chapter doesn't *deduce* a nativity date but rather isolates one from scriptural evidence. That date will be verified in the next chapter.

John the Baptist's Conception

Jesus was conceived about six months after John the Baptist was conceived.[155] Scripture doesn't provide the date of either conception but does give clues to the timing of John's conception.

John's father Zechariah was a temple priest.[156] John was conceived after Zechariah completed his priestly duties at the temple.[157] Zechariah belonged to one of the twenty-four priestly watches who served in shifts according to a fixed duty roster.[158] Each shift lasted one week from Sabbath to Sabbath.[159]

Zechariah's watch *Abijah*[160] was "on shift" five times per year—twice alone and three times together with all other watches (i.e., "all hands on deck") during the three pilgrimage festivals that all Jewish men were required to attend. These were Passover (*Pesach*), Pentecost (*Shavuot*), and Tabernacles (*Sukkot*).[161] Their large crowds created plenty of work for all the priests.

> During the three pilgrimage festivals, all twenty-four watches were equally permitted to participate in the sacrificial service[162] (Talmud)

On duty, Zechariah entered the temple to burn incense. As he did:

> And the whole multitude of the people were in prayer outside at the hour of the incense offering. (Luke 1:10)

The "whole multitude" is from the Greek *pan to plethos*, (lit. "all the multitude"). *Plethos* is used thirty-one times in the Bible to indicate a large, dense crowd. Luke's wording most plausibly indicates one of the three pilgrimage festivals that all Jewish men were required to attend. A study presented in appendix A.9.2 suggests John may have been conceived after Pentecost, specifically on **June 5** in **6 BC**. This date for John's *conception* will be confirmed in the next chapter.

The Nativity

The angel Gabriel visited the Virgin Mary to announce Jesus' arrival when John's mother Elizabeth was six months pregnant.[163] Hebrew months are lunar. If John was conceived on June 5 in 6 BC, then Elizabeth's sixth month would have begun November 1 and ended November 30 of 6 BC.[164]

This frames a window of due dates for Jesus. We can't assume precision here—less than 5 percent of babies are born exactly on their due dates[165] and the Bible doesn't mention anything odd about Jesus' gestational term (aside from its beginning). So due dates provide only rough guidance. Due date is 266 days after conception.[166] The window of conception dates for Jesus gives this window of due dates:

Earliest due date:	July 23 in 5 BC
Latest due date:	August 22 in 5 BC

Bethlehem, Summer 5 BC

> And she gave birth to her firstborn son; and she wrapped Him in cloths, and laid Him in a manger, because there was no room for them in the inn. (Luke 2:7)

Right before Jesus' birth, Joseph couldn't find optimal quarters. The remark "there was no room for them in the inn" indicates their lodging was arranged in haste. It's a safe bet that given more time, Joseph could have found a better place for his pregnant fiancée somewhere in his ancestral village. It seems Joseph didn't have that time. Why would their lodging be arranged in haste? Why does Luke speak of *the* inn, a single location, yet doesn't explain why they didn't—or couldn't—consider the rest of Bethlehem? In the Hebrew culture, one possibility stands out above others.

One possible reason is that the couple arrived in Bethlehem as Sabbath began. At Friday sundown, anyone traveling had to stop and take whatever lodging was available where they stood *at that time.* At sundown, they were no longer able to search out a more suitable room.[167]

They couldn't travel again until Sabbath ended at sundown on Saturday. At that point, there were only two possibilities. Either Jesus was already born, or birth was imminent and movement wasn't practical. Arriving as Sabbath began, followed by a birth that Friday or Saturday night, fits the evidence best.[168] Sabbaths in this window are **July 29** and **August 5, 12,** and **19**.

Angels addressed the shepherds at night:

> for today in the city of David there has been born for you a
> Savior, who is Christ the Lord. (Luke 2:11)

The angels announced that Jesus was born "today." This indicates Jesus was born at night. Hebrew days began at sundown. *Today* can only mean that night or the following daytime, but not the previous daytime. Because his birth had already occurred and it was night, Jesus had to have been born *that* night, shortly before the angels' announcement.

Joseph and Mary arrived in Bethlehem, probably on a Friday at sundown. This suggests that Jesus was born on either that Friday night, or on the following Saturday night. *But which one?*

For centuries, scholars have supposed that Jesus was born on a Hebrew holiday. His other milestone events occurred on holidays: his triumphal entry on Nisan 10—the day Hebrews accepted Passover lambs,[169] his crucifixion on Passover,[170] his resurrection on the day of the *omer* offering,[171] and the Holy Spirit's outpouring on Pentecost.[172] Jesus' birth on a major holiday would fit the pattern.

Only one major holiday falls in this window. It's called "Tisha b'Av," the ninth day of the Hebrew month of Av. In 5 BC, it began on **Saturday, August 12** (appendix C.9) right after sundown, right after Sabbath ended.

Tisha b'Av

At first glance, Tisha b'Av (ninth of Av) seems the *least* likely day for Messiah to enter this world. It's an extremely dark date in Jewish history. In fact, there's no question it's the darkest—and by a wide margin.

Tisha b'Av is a major Jewish fast day. On Av 9, both the First and Second Temples were destroyed, in 587 BC and AD 70 respectively. Over the centuries, Jews have suffered a long list of catastrophes on Av 9 including expulsions, pogroms, and massacres.[173]

Tisha b'Av is not a happy holiday. Observant Jews don't schedule weddings for that day and keep their clothing modest. Men don't shave, and women don't wear (too much) makeup. Kids born to observant families on the ninth of Av don't have parties on their birthday. Nobody wishes anybody a "Happy Tisha b'Av." It's a day of deep humility.

Although some studies have also placed the nativity in the month of August,[174] this book is unaware of any Christian assertion that Messiah was born on Tisha b'Av. But in fact, *Jews have been saying this for centuries.* Jewish sages assert that Messiah was, or will be, born on Tisha b'Av:

- "Moshiach, the Divine emissary empowered to bring redemption to the world and the eternal Sanctuary to Jerusalem, was born on the Ninth of Av."[175] (Chabad.org)
- "Torah sages also teach that the Messiah will be born on Tisha B'Av as a sign that there is yet redemption in all the destruction."[176] (Arutz Sheva)
- "There is another tradition that on the day the Temple was destroyed, the Messiah was born. It is found in Lamentations Rabbah 1:51."[177] (Schwartz)

Note that Jewish tradition is *not* our basis for isolating August 12 in 5 BC. It simply lends unexpected endorsement to a nativity date isolated from scriptural and historical evidence. That date will be verified in the next chapter.

And yet, Scripture writes that at some point still in the future, Tisha b'Av will become a joyous, happy holiday for Jews:

> "The LORD of armies says this: 'The fast of the fourth, the fast of the fifth, the fast of the seventh, and the fast of the tenth months will become joy, jubilation, and cheerful festivals for the house of Judah; so love truth and peace.' (Zechariah 8:19)

Tisha b'Av is the fast of the fifth month. Some event will make Tisha b'Av a happy day for Jews, making up for the long list of tragedies suffered over the centuries. It has a lot of making up to do. Messiah could surely achieve this. It's fitting that on the darkest date for "your people and your holy city" was born the one who redeems everything in totality.

Messiah born on Tisha b'Av has both scriptural and traditional basis. The isolated (not yet proven) nativity date is:

Saturday (after sundown) on August 12, in 5 BC

This isolated date, August 12 in 5 BC, harmonizes with the earliest recovered historical nativity dating (appendix A.9.1).

Appendix C.9 calculates that the ninth of Av (Tisha b'Av) began at sundown on Saturday, August 12 in 5 BC. That moment marked the end of Sabbath and the beginning of Tisha b'Av (i.e., the nativity was not on the Sabbath, but shortly after it ended).

This nativity date will be verified in the next chapter, where the larger fulfillment begins to take form.

Chapter 9 Key Points

- Scripture does not record the nativity date but plausibly indicates the night of August 12 in 5 BC. This was a Saturday after sundown, after Sabbath had ended.

- The major Jewish holiday Tisha b'Av began at sundown on Saturday, August 12 in 5 BC.

- A set of supported assumptions indicates John the Baptist was conceived June 5 in 6 BC, about six months before Jesus' conception.

Then a shoot will spring from the stem of Jesse,
And a Branch from his roots will bear fruit. (Isaiah 11:1)

The next chapter will verify these dates.

Verifying the first fulfillment

194,334 days

10

Read this to me

ISRAEL

This chapter reconciles and then verifies the dates of the first fulfillment sequence of Daniel 9:25 from Cyrus' edict to Jesus' birth. It then verifies the verification.

CHAPTER 8 FRAMED A window for the Edict of Cyrus:

Earliest:	March 12, 537 BC
Latest:	March 31, 536 BC

Chapter 9 isolated a possible nativity date: **August 12** in **5 BC**. Chapter 7 set a required interval of **194,334** days (figure 11). *Do these fit?*

Math check: In review, to the 69 weeks of prophetic years, we must add the pause identified in chapter 7 of one jubilee cycle (49 solar years) plus one sabbatical cycle (seven solar years), creating a pause totaling 56 solar years.

69 weeks x 7 years/week x 360 days/prophetic year = 173,880 days
Pause: 56 solar years x 365.242 days/solar year = 20,454 days

173,880 + 20,454 = 194,334 days total span

Nativity:	JDN 1,719,821	August 12 in 5 BC
Minus:	-194,334	days
Renders:	JDN 1,525,487	July 22 in 537 BC

The calculated (not yet proven) date of Cyrus' edict, **July 22** in **537 BC**, does indeed fit our window of possibility. (For detail on JDN, see appendix A.5.1.) But is it *correct?*

> **Math check:** There are 532 Julian years from July 22, 537 BC, to *July 22*, 5 BC, which equals 194,313 days.
>
> $$532 \times 365.25 = 194{,}313 \text{ days}$$
>
> There are 21 days from *July 22*, 5 BC, until August 12, 5 BC. Thus, there are:
> $$194{,}313 + 21 = 194{,}334 \text{ days}$$
> from July 22, 537 BC, to August 12, 5 BC.
>
> Note, the italicized date *July 22*, 5 BC, is a *waypoint* in the calculation, marking a span of complete years. For example, to calculate the days from Jan 1, 2023, to Jan 10, 2024, we first calculate to *Jan 1*, 2024 (365 days) and then add the remaining nine days from then until Jan 10. These *waypoint* dates will appear *italicized* for clarity.
>
> The JDNs and math are confirmed in appendices A.5.1 and E.1. Both methods agree.

Verification

Captivity's end and Messiah's birth were both foretold in prophecy and both appeared suddenly. Another major prophetic event also appeared suddenly and in living memory. Its date is certain.

This Old Testament prophecy from Ezekiel has perplexed many to this day:

> Then you are to lie down on your left side and put the wrongdoing of the house of Israel on it; you shall bear their wrongdoing for the number of days that you lie on it. For I have assigned you a number of days corresponding to the years of their wrongdoing, 390 days; so you shall bear the wrongdoing of the house of Israel. When you have completed these days, you shall lie down a second time, but on your right side, and bear the wrongdoing of the house of Judah; I have assigned it to you for forty days, a day for each year. Then you shall direct your face toward the siege of Jerusalem with your arm bared, and prophesy against it. (Ezekiel 4:4–7)

Ezekiel spoke this during the Babylonian captivity. Ezekiel referenced a total of 430 days (390+40), and indicated that each day equals one year, so 430 years.[178] He also indicated these years to be atonement for wrongdoing. These atoning years plausibly began as the Babylonian captivity began.

> This may be the oldest surviving interpretation of Ezekiel 4. The Essenes (Dead Sea Scrolls) also considered Ezekiel's 430 years to begin with the Babylonian captivity.[179] As a side note, the Egyptian bondage also lasted 430 years, *to the exact day*.[180]

360 Years of Atonement Remain

Pay especially close attention right here: Ezekiel indicated 430 years. Seventy of those years were spent captive in Babylon[181] (appendix A.10.1) until the day Cyrus released them, so *360 years remained* on the date of Cyrus' edict, by calculation on July 22 in 537 BC:

$$430 - 70 = 360$$

This Became 2,520 More Years

According to the law of Moses, if Israel disobeys God's commandments, then God will send punishment. If Israel remains disobedient despite that punishment, then God multiplies the punishment by seven:

> If also after these things you do not obey Me, then I will punish you seven times more for your sins. (Leviticus 26:18)

We know Jews remained disobedient because Daniel tells us so:

> Just as it is written in the Law of Moses, all this disaster has come on us; yet we have not sought the favor of the LORD our God by turning from our wrongdoing and giving attention to Your truth. (Daniel 9:13)

As promised, God put a "curse" and "oath" on Israel. Again, Daniel tells us:

> Indeed, all Israel has violated Your Law and turned aside, not obeying Your voice; so the curse has gushed forth on us, along with the oath which is written in the Law of Moses the servant of God, because we have sinned against Him. (Daniel 9:11)

Note "the oath" and "the curse" are two separate items. The oath is plausibly the curse's multiplication by seven, as promised in Leviticus 26, part of the law of Moses.[182] Multiplying 360 years by seven gives us 2,520 years:

$$360 \text{ x } 7 = 2,520$$

2,520 *prophetic years* of 360 days each equals **907,200** days:

$$2,520 \text{ x } 360 = 907,200$$

What happened 907,200 days after the Edict of Cyrus?

Cyrus' Edict:	JDN 1,525,487	July 22 in 537 BC
Plus:	+ 907,200	days
Renders:	JDN 2,432,687	**May 15, 1948 AD**

> **Math check:** There are 2,484 years from July 22, 537 BC to *July 22*, 1948 AD. (Subtract 1 to account for no "year zero" between 1 BC and AD 1.) In this span, 2,118 are Julian years and 366 are Gregorian. The switch from Julian to Gregorian—when October 4, 1582 Julian led directly to October 15, 1582 Gregorian—left an artificial gap of 10 nominal days. There are 68 days between May 15 and *July 22*, 1948. Listed:
> - Julian Years: 2,118 x 365.25 = 773,599.5 days,
> - Gregorian Years: 366 x 365.242 = 133,678.6 days,[183]
> - Julian to Gregorian transition = 10 days to be subtracted, and
> - May 15, 1948, to *July 22*, 1948 = 68 days to be subtracted.
>
> Thus, there are 773,599.5 + 133,678.6 − 10 − 68 = 907,200 days
> from July 22, 537 BC. to May 15, 1948 AD.
>
> The JDNs and math are confirmed in appendices A.5.1 and E.1. Both methods agree.

May 15, 1948 is significant by any standard.

Hatikvah (The Hope)

> Therefore say, 'This is what the Lord GOD says: "I will gather you from the peoples and assemble you from the countries among which you have been scattered, and I will give you the land of Israel."' (Ezekiel 11:17)

For centuries, this seemed the unlikeliest of promises. How could any nation, after nineteen centuries of exile, be gathered back into its own land as a free people? For two millennia, Jews lived dispersed, yet never forgot their promised return to *Eretz Israel*,[184] a hope spoken every Passover for nineteen centuries: *"Next year, in Jerusalem!"* Against all odds, this hope never died.

The Hope (*Hatikvah*) never died, despite repeated efforts of kings, emperors, and dictators to kill it. The early 1940s were the darkest of years. The Holocaust took the lives of six million Jews (and a similar number of other peoples, whom we should also remember). Despite facing hell on earth, Jews kept a hope of survival and restoration. This hope was voiced in the poem and song *Hatikvah*, which ends:

> Our hope is not yet lost, the hope of two thousand years
> To be a free nation in our land, the land of Zion and Jerusalem

Traditionally, this was considered a type of Jewish anthem. Yet for centuries, there was no Jewish state. Then suddenly, God's promise was kept.

May 14, 1948—Tel Aviv, British Mandate Palestine

David Ben-Gurion **proclaiming the State of Israel** on May 14, 1948. (GPO)

At 4:00 p.m. on May 14, a lively crowd gathered at the Tel Aviv Museum of Art to witness a momentous event. The meeting wasn't widely advertised. Instead, messengers hand carried invitations to select guests, urging them to keep the time and place secret. The Jewish organizers feared the British authorities would shut the meeting down or that Arab activists might disrupt it. May 14 was the very last day of the British Mandate over Palestine. When it expired at midnight, Britain would no longer be in charge. Everyone's imaginations raced in anticipation of what would happen next.

Of course, the meeting wasn't kept secret. Word spread quickly, and the room filled. Everyone expected a major announcement but couldn't agree on what it might be. As Zionist leader David Ben-Gurion rose to speak, a brand-new radio station began airing its first-ever live broadcast. Through it, the nation and the world heard:

> WE DECLARE that, with effect from the moment of the termination of the Mandate being tonight, the eve of Sabbath, the 6th Iyar, 5708 (15th May, 1948), until the establishment of the elected, regular authorities of the State [...] to be called "Israel." [185] (Israel Ministry of Foreign Affairs, bolding added)

This was huge. No other nation ever lost its land and language, spent two millennia scattered and oppressed, and then overnight regained everything. It's never happened anywhere else in history—not even close. Yet the Bible directly foretold this to happen—figuratively overnight. And it happened when the British Mandate expired eight hours later—literally overnight.

> Who has heard such a thing? Who has seen such things?
> Can a land be born in one day?
> Can a nation be given birth all at once?
> As soon as Zion was in labor, she also delivered her sons.
> (Isaiah 66:8)

On May 15, 1948, at 12:01 a.m. Jerusalem time, Israel was reborn.

> Israel *declared* independence on May 14 but *achieved* it on May 15. Many refer to May 14 as the date of Israel's rebirth, but that was only the announcement date. Britain still held authority over Palestine on May 14. Then, at midnight on May 15, Israel legally re-emerged as a nation, and a war of independence began. By war's end, Israel had secured her land almost to her modern borders. The old city of Jerusalem and Temple Mount fell under Jordanian control. But Israel was truly back in her land as a free people—as God promised centuries ago—*right on time.*

Verifying the Verification

So how can we know if this *really* verifies the dates of the nativity and the Edict of Cyrus? How can we know this isn't just a forced backfit or supreme fluke? Does Ezekiel's prophecy even fit with Daniel's? *How can we know?*

Look at the dates. Israel was reborn on May 15, 1948. The key question is if this date is truly linked to the nativity date via Cyrus' edict or not.

In chapter 9, we calculated John the Baptist's conception on June 5 in 6 BC (JDN 1,719,387). Due date is 266 days after conception.[186] This would place John's due date on **February 26** in **5 BC** (JDN 1,719,653). Of course, due dates are no guarantee, but in this case the Bible makes extra effort to indicate the time of John's birth:

> Now the time had come for Elizabeth to give birth, and she gave birth to a son. (Luke 1:57)

Luke could have written *Elizabeth gave birth to a son,* but he added, "Now the time had come for Elizabeth to give birth." This text is either redundant, or it means exactly what it says: that John was *born on time.*[187]

Jesus' Birth	JDN 1,719,821	Aug 12, 5 BC
John's Birth	-JDN 1,719,653	Feb 26, 5 BC
Difference:	**168**	days

> **Math check:** From February 26 to August 12 there are 3 days remaining in February (5 BC was indeed a leap year, they were odd-numbered in the BC era), 31 in March, 30 in April, 31 in May, 30 in June, 31 in July, and 12 in August. Thus, there are:
>
> 3 + 31 + 30 + 31 + 30 + 31 + 12 = 168 days
> from to February 26, 5 BC, to August 12, 5 BC.
>
> The JDNs and math are confirmed in appendices A.5.1 and E.1. Both methods agree.

John was born 168 days before Jesus was born.[188] What happened 168 days before **Israel** was born?

Israel:	JDN 2,432,687	May 15, 1948
Minus:	- 168	days
Renders:	JDN 2,432,519	**Nov. 29, 1947**

November 29, 1947 is significant by any standard.

> **Math check:** From November 29 to May 15, there is 1 day remaining in November, 31 in December, 31 in January, 29 in February (1948 was a leap year), 31 in March, 30 in April, and 15 in May. Thus, there are:
>
> 1 + 31 + 31 + 29 + 31 + 30 + 15 = 168 days
> from November 29, 1947, to May 15, 1948.
>
> The JDNs and math are confirmed in appendices A.5.1 and E.1. Both methods agree.

November 29, 1947—New York[189]

On November 29, 1947, the United Nations approved General Assembly Resolution 181, the "United Nations Partition Plan for Palestine." This landmark UN action enabled the establishment of a legitimate Jewish state. It legally *prepared the way* for Israel's rebirth. The parallel to John the Baptist's preparing the way for Jesus is plain to see.[190]

Jesus' birth is linked via Cyrus' edict to Israel's rebirth, which is linked via John to Jesus' birth. Each link is precise to the day.

So, is this just a huge fluke or backfit? Is the link between Daniel and Ezekiel just coincidence? It's not, but don't take my word for it. If it were a fluke or backfit, then such a precise result certainly wouldn't happen *twice* like that. Surely, taking the exact same approach and applying the exact same method to a different biblical decree couldn't possibly yield such an extremely improbable result yet again.

But it does.

A Tel Aviv crowd celebrates approval of the **United Nations Partition Plan for Palestine** on November 29, 1947. (GPO)

Chapter 10 Key Points

- The nativity date is linked to the date of Cyrus' edict by the seven weeks and sixty-two weeks of Daniel 9:25 plus the pause of one jubilee cycle and one sabbatical cycle, proposed in chapter 7.

- This is verified by Ezekiel's prophecy of 430 years of atonement—70 in Babylon with the remaining 360 multiplied by seven, per Leviticus 26. This gives a span of 907,200 days from the Edict of Cyrus to the date of Israel's rebirth.

- The verification is confirmed by the 168-day span between John the Baptist's and Jesus' birth dates, matched by the 168-day span from the UN Partition of Palestine to Israel's rebirth.

The song *Hatikvah* is now Israel's official national anthem.

Now we go back in time to Jerusalem in 520 BC—to a small band of returned exiles, struggling to scratch out a living in their ruined city.

11

Read this to me

DARIUS THE GREAT

This chapter isolates a plausible date for the decree of Darius, to be verified in a later chapter. This is the starting point of the second fulfillment sequence of Daniel 9:25, from Darius' decree to Jesus' first temple entry.

SHORTLY AFTER KING CYRUS ended Israel's captivity, a small group of Jews returned to Jerusalem and started clearing the temple foundation. Neighboring Samaritan tribes opposed them,[191] and in 522 BC, persuaded the short-reigning Persian King Bardiya to halt *Jerusalem's* construction. Jews then stopped *temple* construction.[192]

Later that same year, Persia crowned a new king, Darius the Great (*not Darius the Mede*). Two years later, in September of Darius' second year, Jews resumed temple construction.[193]

520 BC—Jerusalem

Tattenai, the king's regional governor, learned that Jews had restarted temple construction. This violated a royal decree. Breaking a Persian king's command was a capital offense, yet the Jewish builders insisted they had permission from former King Cyrus. Before punishing them, Governor Tattenai reported the situation to the new king Darius and asked for orders.[194] Meanwhile, the Jews kept building.

King Darius ordered a search for Cyrus' edict in Babylon. It was eventually found, but in the summer palace at Ecbatana in Media.[195] Darius confirmed Cyrus' edict by issuing this decree of his own:

"Now as for you, Tattenai, governor of the province beyond the Euphrates River, Shethar-bozenai, and your colleagues, the officials of the provinces beyond the River, stay away from there. Leave that work on the house of God alone; let the governor of the Jews and the elders of the Jews rebuild that house of God on its site. Furthermore, I issue a decree concerning what you are to do for these elders of Judah in the rebuilding of that house of God: the full cost is to be paid to those people from the royal treasury out of the taxes of the provinces beyond the Euphrates River, and that without interruption. And whatever is needed, bulls, rams, and lambs for burnt offerings to the God of heaven, and wheat, salt, wine, and anointing oil, as the priests in Jerusalem order, it is to be given to them daily without fail, so that they may offer acceptable sacrifices to the God of heaven and pray for the lives of the king and his sons. And I issued a decree that any person who violates this decree, a timber shall be pulled out of his house and he shall be impaled on it; and his house shall be turned into a refuse heap on account of this. May the God who has caused His name to dwell there overthrow any king or people who attempts to change it, so as to destroy that house of God in Jerusalem. I, Darius, have issued this decree; it is to be carried out with all diligence!" (Ezra 6:6–12)

Darius' decree ordered the **temple** built, but not a **return** to Israel.

Eager to avoid impalement, Governor Tattenai "carried out the decree with all diligence."[196] This shows that Darius' decree issued before the temple's completion. Scripture doesn't record the date but does provide clues.

Construction restarted in September of Darius' second year. Several events had to have occurred before Darius' decree issued. Even if Darius gave Governor Tattenai's request top priority, his decree would not have issued before the end of Darius' second year. This places the earliest possible issue date at roughly the start of Darius' third year.[197]

> Babylon is 545 miles from Jerusalem, so travel time alone would be at least a month or two.[198] Then, after a failed search, those orders had to travel another 280 miles to Ecbatana. This certainly consumed the remainder of Darius' second year.

The temple was completed shortly before the end of Darius' sixth year:

> Now this temple was completed on the third day of the month
> Adar; it was the sixth year of the reign of King Darius. (Ezra 6:15)

Our window of possibility spans Darius' years three through six. Luckily, we have another vital clue. The Bible falls almost silent during this same window. This near silence is remarkable, as Haggai, Zechariah, and Ezra all diligently dated their many writings to before and after this window. Yet, over those same four years, Scripture is *almost* silent.

Almost. A single event breaks this long span of silence.

> In the fourth year of King Darius, the word of the LORD came to
> Zechariah on the fourth day of the ninth month, which is Chislev.
> Now the town of Bethel had sent Sharezer and Regemmelech
> and their men to seek the favor of the LORD, speaking to the
> priests who belong to the house of the LORD of armies, and to
> the prophets, saying, "Shall I weep in the fifth month and fast,
> as I have done these many years?" (Zechariah 7:1–3)

Note that "weep in the fifth month and fast" refers to Tisha b'Av (Av 9)—the *only* holiday of the fifth month when Jews weep and fast. This passage is dated to Darius' fourth year. This falls within the window of possibility. Although certainly not proven, this date will be verified in a later chapter (as we verified the date of Cyrus' edict and Jesus' birth). To find the Julian calendar date, we apply Judean dating method (ABC). The first question is: when did Darius become king?

A. In 522 BC, Darius accused the freshly enthroned King Bardiya of being an impostor. Darius killed Bardiya and seized the Persian throne on September 29 of 522 BC.[199]

> The Bible refers to Persian King Cambyses (Cyrus' son) as Xerxes (Ahasuerus) and to his successor, Bardiya, as Artaxerxes (Ezra 4:6–7).[200] Darius, Xerxes, and Artaxerxes are throne names[201] which recur during the Persian Achaemenid dynasty.

B. Zechariah applied the accession year. As detailed in appendix A.4.2, Jews used the accession year when in Babylon (587–457 BC). The decree of Darius falls during this period.

C. Zechariah advanced Darius' years from Nisan (appendix A.11.1).

Darius' Years by Quarter

	Months	Years	Event
522	JAS	AY	Darius' Accession
BC	OND	AY	
521	JFM	AY	
BC	AMJ	1	*Nisan advance*
	JAS	1	
	OND	1	
520	JFM	1	
BC	AMJ	2	
	JAS	2	Temple Build Start
	OND	2	
519	JFM	2	
BC	AMJ	3	
	JAS	3	
	OND	3	
518	JFM	3	
BC	AMJ	4	
	JAS	4	Tisha b'Av
	OND	4	
517	JFM	4	
BC	AMJ	5	
	JAS	5	
	OND	5	
516	JFM	5	
BC	AMJ	6	
	JAS	6	
	OND	6	
515	JFM	6	Temple Completed

Figure 14. Temple reconstruction per years of King Darius. Tisha b'Av in the fourth year of Darius fell on August 14 in 518 BC. The abbreviations JFM, AMJ, etc., are the calendar months of each quarter. Quarters are displayed simply for clarity of presentation. April 1 is proxy for Nisan 1.

Tisha b'Av (Av 9) in the fourth year of Darius fell on:

August 14 in 518 BC.

Av 9 in 518 BC fell on August 14. This is calculated in appendix C.11.

Chapter 11 Key Points

- Darius' decree allowed Jews to rebuild the **temple.**

- Darius' decree may have issued on Tisha b'Av in the "fourth year of King Darius," identified as August 14 in 518 BC. The date will be verified in a later chapter.

We now turn to Jerusalem in AD 8, when Jesus was about twelve years old.

12

Read this to me

TEMPLE

> This chapter isolates plausible dates of Jesus' first temple entry to be verified in the next chapter. This is the end point of the second fulfillment sequence of Daniel 9:25 from Darius' decree to Jesus' first temple entry.

J ESUS' FIRST TEMPLE ENTRY was foretold in prophecy[202] yet the Bible doesn't explicitly identify the event itself. Luke 2:22–38 places Jesus at the temple as an infant, long before any age of maturity. But from his infancy to his baptism as an adult, the Bible is *almost* silent.

Almost. A single event breaks this long span of silence.

AD 8—Jerusalem

Luke places Jesus in the temple at twelve years old[203] but does not claim it to be his *first* temple entry. If Jesus was born on Av 9 in 5 BC, then he turned twelve on Av 9 in AD 8. On the day *after* his twelfth birthday, Jesus reached an age of responsibility, as recorded in the Jewish Talmud:

> A boy who is twelve years and one day old, his vows are
> examined[204] (Talmud)

The oddly precise "twelve years and one day old" is a threshold age of maturity, when a Jewish boy gains responsibility for his word. The basis for "twelve years and one day old" is beyond our scope, yet we know Jesus was in the temple already at age twelve, not thirteen.[205]

> The Bible does not indicate a single age of maturity. Many modern readers are familiar with *bar mitzvah* (Hebrew for "son of the law") attained by Jewish boys at age thirteen, with or without a ceremony. This is just one of many Hebrew threshold ages listed in the Talmud.[206]
>
> Note that this advent of Messiah has nothing to do with a *bar mitzvah*, but rather Jesus' first-ever temple entry at an age of responsibility. This event was foretold by the prophets Haggai and Malachi. We may exclude age thirteen and later (i.e., *bar mitzvah*) because Luke placed Jesus in the temple already at age twelve, not thirteen.[207]

Window of Possibility—Earliest

Jesus could have entered the temple on Av 10 in AD 8, the day after he turned twelve. Historical evidence detailed in appendix A.12.1 places Av 10 in that year exceptionally early, on July 4. Therefore, Jesus' first-ever temple entry could have occurred no earlier than July 4 in AD 8.

Window of Possibility—Latest

Luke 2:41–51 places Jesus in the temple after the festival of Passover and Unleavened Bread. In AD 9, this ended on April 7. This is the latest possible date because any later temple entry could not have been his first.

The window of possibility for Jesus' first-ever temple entry is:

Earliest:	July 4, AD 8
Latest:	April 7, AD 9

> Scripture does not explicitly identify any event as Jesus' first-ever temple entry at an age of maturity. However, because the adult Jesus often entered the temple, there had to have been a *first* entry, recorded or not.

Chapter 12 Key Points

- The prophets Haggai and Malachi foretold that Messiah would enter the temple.

- Jesus entered the temple for the first time as an adult at some point between July AD 8 and April AD 9.

Can we verify this?

Jesus' Age at Key Events

From	Age			to	Event
Aug	5 BC	0	4 BC	Aug	Birth
Aug	4	1	3	Aug	
Aug	3	2	2	Aug	
Aug	2	3	1 BC	Aug	
Aug	1 BC	4	AD 1	Aug	
Aug	AD 1	5	2	Aug	
Aug	2	6	3	Aug	
Aug	3	7	4	Aug	
Aug	4	8	5	Aug	
Aug	5	9	6	Aug	
Aug	6	10	7	Aug	
Aug	7	11	8	Aug	
Aug	AD 8	12	9	Aug	Temple
Aug	9	13	10	Aug	
Aug	10	14	11	Aug	
Aug	11	15	12	Aug	
Aug	12	16	13	Aug	
Aug	13	17	14	Aug	
Aug	14	18	15	Aug	
Aug	15	19	16	Aug	
Aug	16	20	17	Aug	
Aug	17	21	18	Aug	
Aug	18	22	19	Aug	
Aug	19	23	20	Aug	
Aug	20	24	21	Aug	
Aug	21	25	22	Aug	
Aug	22	26	23	Aug	
Aug	23	27	24	Aug	
Aug	24	28	25	Aug	
Aug	25	29	26	Aug	
Aug	26	30	AD 27	Aug	Baptism
Aug	27	31	28	Aug	
Aug	28	32	29	Aug	
Aug	29	33	30	Aug	
Aug	30	34	AD 31	Aug	Triumphal Entry

Figure 15. Chart of Jesus' age at the advents foretold by Daniel 9:25. August is proxy for Av 9. The exact date of his baptism will be identified in a later chapter.

If I forget you, Jerusalem,
May my right hand forget its skill.
(Psalm 137:5)

Israeli soldiers at the Western Wall (*Kotel*) of the Temple Mount in
the Old City of Jerusalem on **June 7, 1967**. (David Rubinger / GPO)

Note again, all mathematical statements of this book (including the appendices and
endnotes) have been audited and confirmed correct (see appendix E.1).

13

Read this to me

TEMPLE MOUNT

> This chapter reconciles and verifies the second fulfillment sequence, from Darius' decree to Jesus' first temple entry. It then verifies the verification.

THE WINDOW OF POSSIBILITY for Jesus' first temple entry is:

Earliest:	July 4, AD 8
Latest:	April 7, AD 9

Chapter 11 identified a possible date for Darius' decree: **August 14, 518 BC** (JDN 1,532,449). Chapter 7 (figure 11) identified a total span of 191,777 days. What date is 191,777 days after Darius' decree issued?

Darius:	JDN 1,532,449	August 14 in 518 BC
Plus:	+ 191,777	days
Renders:	JDN 1,724,226	September 3, AD 8

September 3, AD 8, does indeed fit the window of possibility for Jesus' first temple entry. The Hebrew date is Tishri 15. This is the first day of Tabernacles (*Sukkot*), a major holiday and high (annual) Sabbath. All adult Jewish males were required to attend Tabernacles in Jerusalem. Joseph was alive at the time and should have attended. Jesus, having just come of age, went along to attend his first pilgrimage festival and entered the temple.

Evidence that Tishri 15 in AD 8 fell extremely early, on September 3, is presented in appendices A.12.1 and C.12.

Math check: There are 525 Julian years from August 14, 518 BC, to *August 14*, AD 8. (Subtract 1 because there is no "year zero" between 1 BC and AD 1.)

$$525 \times 365.25 = 191{,}756.25 \text{ days}$$

It's important to note here that the remainder (0.25) must be rounded up, not down, to give the correct span of **191,757 days**. The reason is that rounding depends on the actual number of leap days in the span, and not necessarily on the numerical value of the remainder (numbers after the decimal). In this span, we catch an extra leap year (517 BC and AD 8 were both leap years).

For example, January 1, AD 8, to January 1, AD 9, is one year, and $1 \times 365.25 = 365.25$, but because AD 8 is a 366-day leap year, the remainder (0.25) must be rounded up, not down to get the correct result.

Conversely, for example, January 1, AD 9, to January 1, AD 12, is three years, and $3 \times 365.25 = 1{,}095.75$. Yet, because there is no leap year in the span, the remainder (0.75) must be rounded down, not up, to give the correct number of 1,095 days. This is why rounding depends on whether you catch or miss actual leap days and not necessarily on the numerical value of the remainder.

There are twenty days from *August 14*, AD 8, to September 3, AD 8. Thus, there are:

$$191{,}757 + 20 = 191{,}777 \text{ days}$$
from August 14, 518 BC to September 3, AD 8.

The JDNs and math are confirmed in appendices A.5.1 and E.1. Both methods agree.

Verification

How can we know these dates are correct? Chapter 10 verified the dates of Jesus' birth and Cyrus' edict by confirming the 907,200 days (Ezekiel 4) between Cyrus' edict and Israel's 1948 rebirth as a nation. Here, we apply the exact same method.

In summary, Ezekiel 4 foretells 430 prophetic years of atonement, seventy years during the Babylonian captivity or, in this case a separate period of seventy overlapping years, sometimes called the *desolation* of Jerusalem. Scripture indicates these seventy years of desolation started with Jerusalem's 587 BC destruction and ended with Darius' decree.[208] This leaves 360 more years of atonement.

The seventy years of "desolation" (Jeremiah 25:11–12) ended with the decree of Darius. This is demonstrated in appendix A.13.1.

Again, due to Israel's continued unrepentance, we multiply those 360 years by seven,[209] rendering 2,520 prophetic years of 360 days each, totaling 907,200 days. These start on the date of Darius' decree: August 14, 518 BC (JDN 1,532,449). This is exactly the same method used in chapter 10.

Darius:	JDN 1,532,449	August 14 in 518 BC
Plus:	+ 907,200	days
Renders:	JDN 2,439,649	**June 7, 1967 AD**

The day 907,200 days after Darius' decree is June 7, 1967. This date is significant by any standard.

> **Math check:** There are 2,484 years from August 14, 518 BC, to *August 14*, 1967. (Subtract 1 to account for no "year zero" between 1 BC and AD 1.) In this span, 2,099 years are Julian and 385 years are Gregorian. The switch from Julian to Gregorian—when October 4, 1582 Julian led directly to October 15, 1582 Gregorian—left an artificial gap of 10 nominal days.[210] There are 68 days from June 7 to *August 14* in 1967. Listed:
>
> - Julian years: 2,099 x 365.25 = 766,659.8 days,
> - Gregorian years: 385 x 365.242 = 140,618.2 days to be added,
> - Julian to Gregorian gap = 10 days to be subtracted, and
> - June 7 to *August 14* in 1967 = 68 days to be subtracted.
>
> Thus, there are 766,659.8 + 140,618.2 – 10 – 68 = 907,200 days
> from August 14, 518 BC, to June 7, 1967 AD.
>
> The JDNs and math are confirmed in appendices A.5.1 and E.1. Both methods agree.

On June 7, 1967, the Old City of Jerusalem and Temple Mount returned to Israel.

For centuries, Jerusalem sat in foreign hands. Then, at the climax of Israel's Six-Day War, and precisely 907,200 days after Persian King Darius issued his decree to rebuild the temple, Israel returned. On June 7, 1967, Israeli soldiers entered Jerusalem's old walled city and stood atop the Temple Mount as a truly sovereign nation for the first time in two millennia.[211]

Verifying the Verification

June 7, 1967 is linked to the dates of Darius' decree and Jesus' first temple entry. Can we confirm this? In chapter 10, we verified that Jesus' birth, Cyrus' edict, and Israel's rebirth were linked via the number of days between John's and Jesus' births with the same number of days between the UN partition of Palestine and Israel's rebirth. Here we take the exact same approach.

Look at the dates of Jesus' first temple entry and Israel's return to the Temple Mount. Jesus could have entered the temple as an adult on July 4, AD 8 (JDN 1,724,165) at age "twelve years and one day."[212] This is sixty-one days before his first temple entry on September 3 (JDN 1,724,226). Jesus could have entered the temple **sixty-one days** before he actually did.

What happened sixty-one days before June 7, 1967? That date, **April 7, 1967** (JDN 2,439,588) is historically significant. A proverbial fuse was lit.

Early that morning, Syrian army units in the Golan Heights attacked Kibbutz Gadot, an Israeli farming settlement. This provoked an unprecedented Israeli response. Israel's army retaliated massively, triggering a major military engagement. Israel sent tanks against Syrian positions. Syria mobilized tanks in return. Both sides exchanged artillery across the entire Israeli-Syrian border. By afternoon, Israeli planes were bombing Syrian forward positions. Syria then scrambled a squadron of modern MIG-21 fighter jets. Israeli Mirage fighter jets then shot down six Syrian MIGs and chased the rest deep into Syria.[213] As darkness fell, fighting stopped. These events occurred on a single day: April 7, 1967.

This full-bore battle made global news. It was not a typical border skirmish but easily the largest Israeli military engagement after the 1956 Sinai Campaign and before the 1967 Six-Day War. The press echoed major Israeli newspaper *Ma'ariv's* verdict: "This was not an 'incident,' but a real war." [214]

The April 7 battle set world events into motion. Politically, it thrust Egyptian President Nasser, the populist leader of the Arab world, into the unbearable role of Israel's second-biggest enemy. But only briefly.

Nasser quickly upped his bellicose rhetoric toward Israel. Syria and other Arab states echoed, and this goaded Nasser even more. On April 7, the Arab world began an unstoppable spiral toward war with Israel.

April 7 was a point of no return. On that day, war became inevitable. The April 7 battle led directly to the 1967 war and Israel's reestablishing its ancient ownership over the old city of Jerusalem and the Temple Mount, as it did—**61 days later.**

Similarly, Jesus didn't enter the temple the day after his twelfth birthday. But he could have entered it at that age of maturity, according to the Talmud's oddly precise "twelve years and one day," on Av 10 in AD 8. This date potentiated his first ever temple entry, as he did—**61 days later.**

> The Temple Mount is currently (2024) administered by the *Islamic Religious Endowments Authority* yet remains within Israel's sovereign territory.

At this point, we have set Ezekiel's prophecy into the framework of Daniel's and shown it was fulfilled precisely to the day—not once, but twice. As promised, we have demonstrated by concrete example that Daniel's Seventy Weeks is indeed a chronological key to other prophecy. And we aren't done yet—*not even close.*

Chapter 13 Key Points

- The date of Jesus' first temple entry is linked prophetically to the date of Darius' decree by Daniel's Seventy Weeks. The span between them is the seven weeks and sixty-two weeks of Daniel 9:25 plus the pause of one jubilee cycle, as proposed in chapter 7.

- These two dates are verified by Ezekiel's prophecy of 430 years: 70 in desolation and the other 360 multiplied by seven (Leviticus 26). Applying the prophetic year gives a span of 907,200 days from Darius' decree. That span ends on June 7, 1967 AD, the date of the Temple Mount's return to Israel.

- The verification is verified by the sixty-one-day spans before Jesus' first temple entry and Israel's recapturing Jerusalem's Temple Mount. In AD 8, Jesus could have legally first entered the temple on Av 10 but didn't until sixty-one days later. Similarly, the 1967 war nearly started on April 7. Sixty-one days later, Israel recaptured the old city of Jerusalem and Temple Mount.

On May 15, 1967, just days before the Six-Day War, The song "Jerusalem of Gold" (*Yerushelayim Shel Zahav*) debuted at a festival marking the 19th anniversary of Israel's independence. It was a soulfully deep love song to the Old City of Jerusalem.

This haunting, hopeful song quickly became wildly popular. Its lyrics such as *"We've returned to the cisterns, the market, and the plaza"* and *"The shofar sounds from the Temple Mount,"* quickly dominated the airwaves. Those lyrics would also very quickly prove astoundingly prescient.

Because only days after their release, events of the Six-Day War validated those lyrics for all the world to see. The song, in essence, foretold events of millennial importance only days prior—events that were also foretold by the prophets, centuries prior.

"Jerusalem of Gold" remains beloved by Israel to this day. It is now considered Israel's unofficial "second national anthem."

Rabbi Shlomo Goren sounds a shofar at the Western
Wall (*Kotel*) at the Temple Mount on **June 7, 1967.**
(David Rubinger/GPO)

*Now, let's go back in time again, to eighty years after Cyrus ended the Babylonian
captivity, back to Judah in 457 BC—to a colony adrift.*

14

EZRA

This chapter finds the date of Ezra's mission to Jerusalem. This is the start point of the third fulfillment sequence of Daniel 9:25 and is verified in a later chapter.

For Jews, the first decades of freedom after captivity were not a wild success. Most remained in Babylon. They had grown comfortable in the land of their exile and felt little urge to leave it.[215] These were still Babylon's golden years. Even long after it fell to Persia, Babylon remained a dynamic cosmopolitan center. Like modern New York or London, it was simply the place to be. Why leave?

Jewish response to the Edict of Cyrus in 537 BC was underwhelming, to put it kindly. One group did return quickly to establish a toehold around Jerusalem. They were surrounded by rivals, most notably Samaritans, who were often openly hostile.[216] Life was hard and stayed hard for decades.

The little Jewish colony struggled in scarcity. Despite having a temple and prophets, Jews were slowly losing their identity. Markets traded on the Sabbath. Jews married foreigners, adopting their strange customs while neglecting their own. The Torah (Mosaic law) faded from everyday life.[217] If this continued, the returnees would no longer maintain a Jewish culture. Jews might have simply morphed into yet another Samaritan-ish tribe.

Jews were growing complacent, squandering their new freedom. This drifting away was sorely felt, even in Babylon, and most notably by one man in particular.

457 BC—Babylon

Ezra was a supremely learned Jewish scribe and priest from Babylon. He was an undisputed authority on the Torah and is credited with restoring it to Israel. In fact, Ezra might be the most significant Old Testament figure many today have scarcely heard of. At some point, Ezra made requests to Persian King Artaxerxes. The king granted them all in this decree: [218]

"Artaxerxes, king of kings, to Ezra the priest, the scribe of the Law of the God of heaven, perfect peace. And now I have issued a decree that any of the people of Israel and their priests and the Levites in my kingdom who are willing to go to Jerusalem, may go with you. Since you are sent on the part of the king and his seven advisers to inquire about Judah and Jerusalem according to the Law of your God which is in your hand, and to bring the silver and gold, which the king and his advisers have voluntarily given to the God of Israel, whose dwelling is in Jerusalem, with all the silver and gold which you find in the entire province of Babylon, along with the voluntary offering of the people and of the priests, who offered willingly for the house of their God which is in Jerusalem; with this money, therefore, you shall diligently buy bulls, rams, and lambs, with their grain offerings and their drink offerings, and offer them on the altar of the house of your God which is in Jerusalem. And whatever seems good to you and your brothers to do with the rest of the silver and gold, you may do according to the will of your God. Also the utensils which are given to you for the service of the house of your God, deliver in full before the God of Jerusalem. And the rest of the needs of the house of your God, for which it may be incumbent upon you to provide, provide for them from the royal treasury.

"I myself, King Artaxerxes, issue a decree to all the treasurers who are in the provinces beyond the Euphrates River, that whatever Ezra the priest, the scribe of the Law of the God of heaven, may require of you, it shall be done diligently, up to a hundred talents of silver, a hundred kors of wheat, a hundred baths of wine, a hundred baths of anointing oil, and salt as needed. Whatever is commanded by the God of heaven, it shall be done with zeal for the house of the God of heaven, so that there will not be wrath against the kingdom of the king and his sons. We also inform you that it is not allowed to impose tax, tribute, or toll on any of the priests, Levites, singers, doorkeepers, temple servants, or other servants of this house of God.

"And you, Ezra, according to the wisdom of your God which is in your hand, appoint magistrates and judges so that they may judge all the people who are in the province beyond the Euphrates River, that is, all those who know the laws of your God; and you may teach anyone who is ignorant of them."
(Ezra 7:12–25)

Note that this decree mandated a **return** to the land of Israel. It did not order **temple** construction—the temple was already built at that time.

Ezra was permitted to take as many Jews with him to Jerusalem as would go. They volunteered in droves. Hundreds of extended families joined this mass return from Babylon to *Eretz Israel*—the land of Israel.

Ezra departed on Nisan 1 of Artaxerxes' seventh year.[219] The Bible records the precise date, so we don't need to frame any windows. But which BC year was this? Over the centuries, scholars have asserted 458 or 457 BC.

Ezra was a scribe. Judean scribal convention places Nisan in Ezra's "seventh year of King Artaxerxes" in 457 BC (appendix A.14.1). In that year, Nisan 1 daytime fell on:

$$\text{March 27, 457 BC.}^{220}$$

Nisan 1 in 457 BC is calculated as March 27 in appendix C.14 and confirmed by *PDBC*. Note this date does *not* harmonize with Nehemiah's dating of Artaxerxes' twentieth year to 446 BC. The two men indeed applied Judean dating method, but at different times. Nehemiah's and Ezra's dates are reconciled in appendix A.14.2.

We may exclude 458 BC for a few reasons. First, Elephantine Papyrus AP6 (appendix A.14.1) indicates that Nisan in the seventh year of Artaxerxes fell in 457 BC. Second, Nisan 1 in 458 BC was Saturday, April 8 (daytime). This is a Sabbath, when travel would have broken the Law of Moses.[221] (Note that the seven-day cycle of weekdays has continued unaltered since ancient times—see appendix E.2). Third, 457 BC will be confirmed in a later chapter.

Why start a journey two weeks before Passover? According to Mosaic law, it is indeed permitted to be on a journey during Passover (Numbers 9:13).

Although this wasn't the *first* return after the exile, it was certainly the *definitive* one. Prior to Ezra, the few Jews around Jerusalem lacked leadership and weren't observant. Ezra restored the Torah (Mosaic law) and the center of Judaism to Jerusalem. Ezra returned the heart of Judaism and "leading men from Israel"[222] from Babylon, back to *Eretz Israel*—the land of Israel.

> when Torah was forgotten from the nation of Israel, Ezra ascended from Babylonia to Eretz Yisrael and reestablished it.[223] (Talmud)

When Ezra's multitude arrived four months later, Jerusalem was no longer a struggling little backwater village writing off to Babylon to ask about Scripture and law. Babylon would now write off to Ezra in Jerusalem. When Ezra and the returnees settled in, Judah was once again restored to her land. This was a restoration in the truest sense. It was a restoration of the law, the people, and the spirit of Jerusalem.

This is significant, because from 457 BC onward, the center of Judaism was again established in Jerusalem. Jews were now truly **back in the land**.

How do we know? Because at this point in time, Jews resumed not only Torah observance but tellingly, also many pre-exilic Hebrew customs, including their traditional calendar.[224]

Chapter 14 Key Points

- Artaxerxes' decree to Ezra allowed Jews to **return** to the land of Israel.

- Ezra departed Babylon on Wednesday, March 27 in 457 BC.

- Upon Ezra's arrival in Jerusalem, the center of Judaism was restored to the land of Israel.

- At this point in time, Jews resumed their traditional calendar.

We now turn to Roman Judea in AD 27, when Jesus was "about thirty years old."

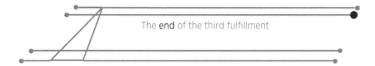

The **end** of the third fulfillment

15

Read this to me

BAPTISM

This chapter identifies the window of possible dates for Jesus' baptism and then reconciles it to the date of Ezra's return. This is the end point of the third fulfillment sequence of Daniel 9:25 and will be verified in the next chapter.

JOHN THE BAPTIST BAPTIZED Jesus.[225] The Bible doesn't give the date but does record that *John's* ministry started in the "fifteenth year" of Tiberius Caesar.[226] To find this year, we apply Judean dating method (appendices A.4.2 and D.1) as used throughout this book. So, the first question is: *When did Tiberius become Caesar?*

A. In AD 12, Tiberius became "co-regent" with authority equal to Caesar Augustus "in the provinces," including Judea.[227] When Augustus died in AD 14, Tiberius immediately began his sole reign.[228] These two starting points, AD 12 and AD 14, evenly split scholarly opinion. Appendix A.15.1 shows Luke counted Tiberius' years from **AD 12**. This will be verified in the next chapter.

B. Jews did not apply an accession year in that era. Luke counted Tiberius' first day to his "year one."

C. Tiberius was a foreign king. Jews advanced his years at Nisan.

Figure 16 shows that John the Baptist began his ministry in AD 25 or 26. Note that Luke's "fifteenth year" of Tiberius refers directly to *John's* ministry, not Jesus' baptism. Scripture does not record the baptismal date.[229] Obviously, it was after John's ministry started, but we aren't told *how long* after.

Tiberius' Years **per Luke**

From		Year		To
Jan	AD 12	1	12	Apr
Apr	12	2	13	Apr
Apr	13	3	14	Apr
Apr	14	4	15	Apr
Apr	15	5	16	Apr
Apr	16	6	17	Apr
Apr	17	7	18	Apr
Apr	18	8	19	Apr
Apr	19	9	20	Apr
Apr	20	10	21	Apr
Apr	21	11	22	Apr
Apr	22	12	23	Apr
Apr	23	13	24	Apr
Apr	24	14	25	Apr
Apr	25	15	26	Apr

Figure 16. Tiberius' fifteenth year (Luke 3:1–2) marks the start of ***John's*** ministry. April is proxy for Nisan 1.

The first Passover of Jesus' ministry was in AD 28 (chapter 9). Thus, Jesus was baptized sometime between the Passovers of AD 27 and 28. These Passovers fell on April 11 and April 29, respectively.

Earliest:	April 11, AD 27
Latest:	April 29, AD 28

Reconciliation

Ezra's decree issued on **March 27, 457 BC** (JDN 1,554,590). Adding seven and sixty-two weeks (173,880 days) plus the pause (figure 11) of one sabbatical cycle (2,557 days) gives a span of 176,437 days. Does this land in the window of possibility?

Ezra:	JDN 1,554,590	March 27, 457 BC
Plus:	+ 176,437	days
Renders:	JDN 1,731,027	**April 18, AD 27**

Math check: There are 483 Julian years from March 27, 457 BC, to *March 27*, AD 27. (Subtract 1 because there is no "year zero" between 1 BC and AD 1.)

$$483 \times 365.25 = 176,415.75 \text{ days}$$

Note that the decimal (0.75) here must be rounded down, not up, to give the correct span of **176,415 days**. The reason is that rounding depends on whether you catch or miss actual leap days and not necessarily on the numerical value of the remainder (numbers after the decimal). Here, we miss leap days at both ends of the span. Both 457 BC (February 29, outside the span) and AD 28 are leap years.

For an illustrating example, January 1, AD 9, to January 1, AD 12, spans three years, and 3 x 365.25 = 1,095.75. Yet, because there is no leap year in the span—both AD 8 and AD 12 (February 29, outside the span) are leap years—the remainder (0.75) must be *rounded down, not up*, to give the correct span of 1,095 days. This is why rounding depends on whether you catch or miss actual leap days and not necessarily on the numerical value of the remainder.

There are 22 days from *March 27* to April 18 in AD 27. Thus, there are:

$$176,415 + 22 = 176,437 \text{ days}$$
from March 27, 457 BC to April 18, AD 27.

The JDNs and math are confirmed in appendices A.5.1 and E.1. Both methods agree.

April 18, AD 27, does fall in the window of possibility for Jesus' baptism. That day was Nisan 21 (appendix C.15), a major holiday and one of seven "high Sabbaths" (aka "annual Sabbaths") in the Hebrew year.[230]

This allows ample time for the many recorded events after Jesus' baptism and before his first Passover in AD 28. April 18 in AD 27 fits scriptural evidence. This is shown in appendix A.15.2. Luke writes that Jesus began his ministry at "about thirty years old."[231] In fact, he was exactly thirty, as most cultures count age today.[232]

Why 30 and not 32 (5 BC to AD 27)? When adding BC and AD years, 1 must be subtracted, because there is no "year zero" between 1 BC and AD 1.
Okay, why not 31? Jesus did turn thirty-one in AD 27—but later, in August. On his baptismal date, Jesus was still 30 years old (figure 15).

Chapter 15 Key Points

- John the Baptist's ministry began in AD 25 or 26.

- Jesus was baptized by John on April 18 in AD 27, seven weeks and sixty-two weeks (173,880 days) plus one sabbatical cycle (2,557 days) after Ezra departed Babylon on March 27 in 457 BC.

The two dates of Jesus' (1) baptism and (2) triumphal entry will both be verified in the next chapter. As noted earlier, these two verifications work in tandem.

Then after the sixty-two weeks, the Messiah will be cut off and have nothing, and the people of the prince who is to come will destroy the city and the sanctuary. And its end will come with a flood; even to the end there will be war; desolations are determined. (Daniel 9:26)

Siege and Destruction of Jerusalem by David Roberts, depicting Rome's destruction of Jerusalem and the temple in the summer of AD 70, an event foretold in Daniel 9:26.

Note again, all mathematical statements of this book (including the appendices and endnotes) have been audited and confirmed correct (see appendix E.1).

Verifying the third and fourth fulfillments

16

Read this to me

JERUSALEM

> This chapter verifies both the third and fourth fulfillment sequences, ending with Jesus' baptism and triumphal entry, respectively.

CHAPTERS 5 AND 15 calculated these dates for Jesus' baptism and triumphal entry:

Baptism:	April 18, AD 27	JDN 1,731,027
Triumphal Entry:	April 22, AD 31	JDN 1,732,492

Jesus' AD 27 baptism and AD 31 triumphal entry harmonize with historical and scriptural evidence (appendix A.16.1). But are those dates *correct*? Can we verify them as we verified the nativity with Israel's 1948 rebirth and Jesus' first temple entry with the 1967 return of the Temple Mount to Israel?

Those two fulfillment strings were verified by the prophecy in Ezekiel 4 (chapter 10) that referenced 430 years of iniquity in two parts: 390 for Israel (Northern Kingdom) and 40 for Judah (Southern Kingdom). Israel's 390-year segment is beyond our scope. Judah's 40 years is our focus here. A common view is that these are the four decades from Jesus' crucifixion to Jerusalem's destruction, in which Judah rejected him as Messiah. But is that view *correct*?

Forty *prophetic* years after Jesus' triumphal entry reach into AD 70, when Rome destroyed Jerusalem and the Second Temple, an event significant by any standard. Ezekiel's prophecy references forty years, and Daniel's Seventy Weeks references the temple's destruction.

Is this just coincidence? Now that we've seen God's penchant for precision, we might expect an exact chronological fit. Even if the math works

Three Proofs of God | 87

perfectly (as it must), we should also find scriptural support. Here is our start. First, is this scriptural? Forty years? Jerusalem and the temple destroyed?

Is forty years scriptural? The Bible often associates the number forty with trial, probation, and judgment. A thorough reading shows no other number to be as closely linked to these themes in Scripture.

For example, Noah's deluge lasted forty days. Moses lived forty years in Egypt, forty more with the Midianites, and stayed forty days on Mount Sinai. Moses sent spies into Canaan for forty days. Hebrews wandered the desert forty years. Goliath taunted Israel forty days. The three kings of united Israel each ruled forty years. Jonah gave Nineveh forty days to repent. After his baptism, Jesus spent forty days in the wilderness and remained on earth forty days after his resurrection. We have already read that Ezekiel lay on his right side forty days to bear the punishment of Judah, one day for each of forty years of sin.

You see the pattern. Forty signifies, by overwhelming precedent, a period of probation and trial. But does the number forty fit here? Each advent of Jesus recorded in the Bible was followed by a forty-day period. Mary and Joseph waited forty days[233] after Jesus' birth to present him in the temple.[234] After his baptism, Jesus was tempted in the wilderness for forty days.[235] After his resurrection, Jesus appeared to his disciples for forty days.[236] If forty-day periods followed Jesus' advents, then it's not a stretch to consider a forty-year period after Jesus himself. It's not proven, but a pattern does exist.

Finally, although forty isn't in Daniel's prophecy, it's certainly in Ezekiel's, which speaks of bearing the "wrongdoing of the house of Judah" for "forty days, a day for each year."[237] Judah rejected Jesus and was crushed forty prophetic years later. Could those be the forty years of Judah's iniquity? If Jesus is Messiah, then they certainly might be.

Is the link between Jesus' rejection and Jerusalem's destruction scriptural? Jesus foretold Jerusalem's destruction right after his triumphal entry, so we can't dismiss a connection. Moreover, Jesus said Jerusalem's destruction would result from its people not recognizing the *time of his coming*:

> and they will level you to the ground, and throw down your children within you, and they will not leave in you one stone upon another, because you did not recognize the time of your visitation. (Luke 19:44)

Finally, Daniel 9:26 reads that "Messiah will be cut off" before "the city and the sanctuary" are destroyed. Daniel links Messiah's rejection and Jerusalem's destruction directly in this prophecy. So yes, the destruction of Jerusalem forty prophetic years (40 x 360 = 14,400 days) after Messiah does have a scriptural basis. But is it *true*? First, what are these dates?

Trimphal Entry:	JDN 1,732,492	April 22, AD 31
Plus:	+ 14,400	days
Renders:	JDN 1,746,892	Sept. 24, AD 70

> **Math check:** There are 39 Julian calendar years from April 22, AD 31, to *April 22*, AD 70. This equals 14,245 days. Eight days remain in April, 31 in May, 30 in June, 31 each in July and August, and 24 until September 24. Thus, there are:
>
> 14,245 + 8 + 31 + 30 + 31 + 31 + 24 = 14,400 days
> from April 22, AD 31, to September 24, AD 70.
>
> The JDNs and math are confirmed in appendices A.5.1 and E.1. Both methods agree.

Forty prophetic years after Jesus' triumphal entry is September 24, AD 70. The Hebrew date is Tishri 1, the major holiday *Rosh Hashanah*, a high (annual) Sabbath.[238] This is interesting but not conclusive. The key question is: was Jerusalem destroyed *on that day*?

Tishri 1 falls *after* the ninth of Av, when the Second Temple was destroyed. But we know the city took longer to conquer. Jerusalem fell in stages from July to September in AD 70. Daniel's prophecy foretells the destruction of both the *city* and sanctuary (see page 86). So, on what day was Jerusalem the *city* destroyed?

Jerusalem's destruction was a climax of the First Jewish-Roman War. The Bible is silent on these events, but we have an excellent source in Jewish historian Flavius Josephus, an eyewitness from start to finish.

> Ancient historians Tacitus, Suetonius, and Cassius Dio also gave written accounts of Jerusalem's destruction but in far less detail than did the eyewitness Josephus.

Josephus wrote that Jerusalem fell completely into Roman hands on September 3, AD 70.[239] That is the last dated event before Jerusalem's destruction in Josephus' narrative. But even after September 3, the city was not yet destroyed, not even yet pacified. Romans still met armed resistance.

> Caesar gave orders that they should kill none but those that were in arms and opposed them[240] (Josephus)

Then, after resistance ended, the Roman army destroyed Jerusalem.

> as soon as the army had no more people to slay [. . .] Caesar
> gave orders that **they should now demolish the entire city**[241]
> (Josephus, bolding added)

Jerusalem was destroyed well after it fell to Rome. The calculated date of September 24 in AD 70 is Tishri 1, *Rosh Hashanah,* a high (annual) Sabbath and one of the highest holy days in Judaism. Roman historian Cassius Dio's account plausibly indicates destruction on Rosh Hashanah:

> Thus was Jerusalem destroyed on the very day of Saturn, the day
> which even now the Jews reverence most.[242] (Cassius Dio)

Dio's "day of Saturn" that Jews "reverence most" surely indicates a Sabbath and quite possibly Rosh Hashanah, a high Sabbath. But Dio, unlike Josephus, wasn't Jewish, so we won't treat his words as conclusive.[243] But we do have a fit precise to the year for a triumphal entry in AD 31—forty prophetic years before Jerusalem's destruction. So, what about the earlier date?

War Starts in AD 66—The Point of No Return

Jesus was baptized four years before his triumphal entry. The Jewish-Roman War started in AD 66—four years before Jerusalem's destruction.

Can we pinpoint the day the war *started?* Remarkably, we can.

By spring of AD 66, ethnic tensions in Judea were boiling over. In the coastal town of Caesarea, tit-for-tat reprisals between Jews and Gentiles burst into active hostility.

Jerusalem was also caught up in a vicious cycle of provocation. Making everything worse, Roman Governor Gessius Florus was a callously abusive ruler who never quite knew when to back off. His excesses fueled the spiral of violence between Jews and Romans.[244]

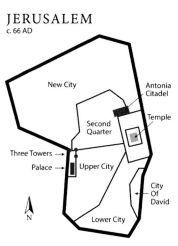

JERUSALEM
c. 66 AD

That summer, a spirit of rebellion gripped Jerusalem. People split into two main factions. One, the "rebels," fought internally almost as bitterly as they would later fight the Romans. The other faction was a "Peace Party" of families connected to the government, non-Jews, property owners, and pacifists.

By August AD 66, the two factions were in open conflict. The Peace Party held the upper city, palace, and citadel. Rebels held the lower city and the temple.[245] Josephus provided this sequence of events:

August 25, AD 66: Rebels took the upper city and burned the homes of Peace Party leaders who fled into the palace for protection.[246]

August 26: Rebels besieged the citadel. Two days later, the citadel defenders fled to the palace. The rebels then besieged the palace.[247]

Undated: A rebel group under Manahem allowed all Jews in the palace to surrender peacefully but would not accept any Roman surrender.[248]

September 15: The abandoned Roman soldiers could not defend the palace, so they withdrew to three adjacent towers. Rebels then took the palace and besieged the towers, but could not take them.[249]

September 16, a Tuesday: Manahem's rebels killed the Jewish high priest and several Peace Party leaders. Manahem began behaving as top leader of Jerusalem's rebels. A rival rebel group under Eliezer killed Manahem.[250]

"The sabbath day": The besieged Roman soldiers negotiated with Eliezer for safe passage out of the city in return for surrendering their weapons. The instant they were disarmed, the defenseless Romans were slaughtered by Eliezer's rebels. Josephus wrote: "this murder was perpetrated on the *sabbath day*." (italics added)[251]

At exactly the same time, and over fifty miles away, all Jews in the coastal town of Caesarea were massacred—not only on the same day, but even during the *same hour*.

> NOW the people of Caesarea had killed the Jews that were among them on the **very same day and hour** [when the soldiers were killed], which one would think must have come to pass by the direction of Providence; insomuch that in one hour's time above twenty thousand Jews were killed, and all Caesarea was emptied of its Jewish inhabitants.[252] (Josephus, bolding added)

There was no turning back. Rome would never tolerate her soldiers being murdered so treacherously. To Jews, having twenty thousand kinsmen ruthlessly massacred was equally odious. Moreover, both atrocities occurred *simultaneously*, each unprovoked by the other. At that point, neither side could back down. There would be war. Josephus confirmed this directly:

> such occasions were afforded for a war as were **incurable**[253]
> (Josephus, bolding added)

To the eyewitness Josephus, this was the *incurable* point—the point of no return. Starting that Sabbath, the war was on. This "sabbath day" is our critical date. But when was this Sabbath?

The last dated event in Josephus' narrative was Tuesday, September 16, AD 66. The next Sabbath fell on Saturday, September 20.

Jesus' triumphal entry occurred forty prophetic years before Jerusalem was destroyed, so we might expect some significant event to have occurred forty prophetic years (14,400 days) before the Jewish-Roman War began on September 20, AD 66. *What is that date?*

War Start:	JDN 1,745,427	Sep. 20, AD 66
Minus:	-14,400	days
Renders:	JDN 1,731,027	**April 18, AD 27**

> **Math check**: There are 39 Julian years from April 18, AD 27, to *April 18*, AD 66, equaling 14,245 days. There are 12 days remaining in April after *April 18*. May, June, July, and August have 31, 30, 31, and 31 days respectively. There are 20 days until September 20 in AD 66. Thus, there are:
>
> 14,245 + 12 + 31 + 30 + 31 + 31 + 20 = 14,400 days
> from April 18, AD 27 to September 20, AD 66.
>
> The JDNs and math are confirmed in appendices A.5.1 and E.1. Both methods agree.

April 18, AD 27, is the date of Jesus' baptism.

Just let that sink in for a moment. That's the **exact same date** calculated previously using a **completely different approach**. Jesus was baptized on April 18, AD 27, forty prophetic years before the first Jewish-Roman war started, and the precise number of days after Ezra's mission foretold by Daniel 9:25— both events indicate the *exact same date in history*. This astoundingly precise fit provides solid confirmation from two independent lines of evidence.

This means that *all four* fulfillment sequences of Daniel 9:25 are now verified in harmony with the dates of Jeremiah's foretold captivity and desolation (appendices A.10.1 and A.13.1) and period of atonement in Ezekiel 4. Moreover, all are *confirmed* to the precise day. This resolves not only four key advents of Messiah but also four important Old Testament prophecies. In short, **everything** fits.

At this point, a *single method* has produced many precise synchronizations, each verified with mathematical precision, as promised. Remember, Daniel urged us to *know and understand* this text, not to just believe it, but to *figure it out*. This suggests we might be correctly interpreting Daniel 9:25.

Those Pauses

At this point, the biggest remaining question is surely about the pauses between the seven and sixty-two weeks, as proposed in chapter 7.

As presented in chapter 6, Daniel indicated pauses by separating his seventy weeks into three sections. The pause between the first (seven weeks) and second (sixty-two weeks) sections is now our focus. As promised in chapter 7, we have shown they provide a solution that is:

  – precise to the day and
  – historically verifiable.

It was also promised that these pauses are **confirmed in Scripture**. The next chapter presents that confirmation.

Chapter 16 Key Points

- Jesus' April 18, AD 27, baptism is verified by the September 20, AD 66, start of the First Jewish-Roman War. These two dates are forty prophetic years apart, precisely to the day. This in turn verifies the date of Ezra's Nisan 1 departure on March 27 in 457 BC.

- Jesus' AD 31 triumphal entry and Jerusalem's AD 70 destruction are forty prophetic years apart. This in turn confirms Nehemiah's decree issuing in 446 BC.

Okay, so how exactly are those pauses confirmed in Scripture?

It is the glory of God to conceal a matter,
But the glory of kings is to search out a matter.
(Proverbs 25:2)[254]

17

Read this to me

THE PROGRESSION

> This chapter presents the scriptural confirmation of the pauses between the seven weeks and sixty-two weeks of Daniel 9:25.

SCRIPTURE DOESN'T DIRECTLY DISCLOSE the pauses' lengths (chapter 7), but it does *confirm* them. Those pauses (figure 11) in solar years are:

	Years	=	Jubilee	+	Sabbatical
Cyrus	56		49		7
Darius	49		49		
Ezra	7				7
Nehemiah	0				

The four scriptural decrees to restore and rebuild Jerusalem mandated these events:

1. **Cyrus** (537 BC) – **Temple** construction and Jews' **return** to the land of Israel

2. **Darius** (518 BC) – **Temple** construction but no return

3. **Ezra** (457 BC) – No temple construction but a **return** to the land of Israel

4. **Nehemiah** (446 BC) – Neither temple construction nor return

Charting reveals a possible connection:

	Years	=	Jub	+	Sab	Temple	Return
Cyrus	56		49		7	X	X
Darius	49		49			X	
Ezra	7				7		X
Nehemiah	0						

A quick glance shows there *might* be a link between the temple and forty-nine years, and also between the return and seven years. If this connection is true, then (1) it should have scriptural support, and (2) the math must work perfectly. Let's start in Scripture. Is there a scriptural link between the decrees, and a return to Israel and the temple?

In Daniel 9:25, the decrees' purpose is "to *restore* and *rebuild*." At first glance, it's remarkable to see two similar words here instead of one. Expositors today often paraphrase this using one word, usually "rebuild," aiming to capture Daniel's intent but missing his wording. For centuries, people have overlooked this conflation, assuming it didn't merit much investigation. But what if it does? After all, in one of the Bible's most info-dense verses, we find *two* words here, not one.

Daniel's wording is *lehashib* for "to restore" and *welibnot* for "and rebuild."

To Restore—*lehashib*

Daniel's Hebrew for "to restore," *lehashib*, refers generally to restore, make restitution, turn back, reverse, bring back, or recall. Notably, it appears in the book of Jeremiah. Importantly, Daniel directly referred to Jeremiah's writings right before presenting the Seventy Weeks Prophecy:

> in the first year of his reign, I, Daniel, observed in the books the number of the years which was revealed as the word of the LORD to Jeremiah the prophet for the completion of the desolations of Jerusalem, namely, seventy years. (Daniel 9:2)

Jeremiah mentioned seventy years here:

> For this is what the LORD says: 'When seventy years have been completed for Babylon, I will visit you and fulfill My good word to you, to bring you back to this place. (Jeremiah 29:10)

Jeremiah's "to bring you back" is from the Hebrew *lehashib*, which refers to a return from Babylon to Israel. So yes, there is a scriptural connection between the return to Israel and Daniel's description of the decrees. It's not yet proven (the math must also work), but a scriptural connection does exist.

And Rebuild—*welibnot*

Daniel's Hebrew for "and rebuild," *welibnot*, appears in this exact form only one other time in Scripture:

> and give my son Solomon a perfect heart to keep Your commandments, Your testimonies, and Your statutes, and to do them all, and to build the temple for which I have made provision. (1 Chronicles 29:19)

Here, "and to build" is also *welibnot*. That specific wording, in that form, appears nowhere else in the Bible. It concerns building the temple in Jerusalem. So there is a possible connection between the temple and Daniel's description of the decrees. Again, this is not yet proven (the math must also work), but a scriptural connection here also exists.

Lehashib and *welibnot* is, after all, the exact wording Daniel chose.

Confirmations

The four scriptural decrees to restore and rebuild Jerusalem mandated specific historical events. Daniel's exact wording, as defined by Scripture itself, may be associated with the temple and the return to the land of Israel. But are those truly linked with those pauses? Specifically, is a return to Israel connected with seven solar years? And is the temple connected with forty-nine solar years? In short, *does the math work?*

Note there were two biblical mass returns to Israel. The first is "Joshua's Conquest" (c. 1400 BC), when Israel reentered the land of Jacob's birth. The second definitive return occurred with Ezra in 457 BC.[255]

There were also two temples. The First Temple, aka "Solomon's Temple," was known to Daniel. The Second Temple was entered by Jesus.

Let's start with the temple. Does a connection exist between the temple and one jubilee cycle (forty-nine *solar* years) in the Bible? Yes—twice in fact. One exists for each the First *and* the Second Temples.

The First Temple—Forty-Nine Years

The First Temple was completed in the eleventh year of Solomon.[256] But God's desire for the temple dates to the reign of Solomon's father King David.

David wanted to build God's temple.[257] God forbade David from constructing it[258] but did allow him to prepare it. God gave David the plans for the temple's location, structure, furnishing, and operation.[259] Moreover, David procured the site, financing, and materials.[260] The temple started with David.[261] Scripture indicates the timing of God's desire for the temple:

> 'Since the day that I brought My people Israel from Egypt, I did not choose a city out of all the tribes of Israel in which to build a house so that My name would be there, but I chose David to be over My people Israel.' (1 Kings 8:16)

This verse connects two ideas we humans might not normally associate. But there it is—in God's own words. God verbally connects the *time* ("Since the day") of his desire for a temple *in Jerusalem* to his choice of David to rule over "My people Israel." The theology is beyond our scope; the chronology is our focus. When did King David's reign "over My people Israel" begin? [262]

> 1 Kings 8:16 teaches that God established the House of God and the House of David *simultaneously.* This is affirmed in 2 Chronicles 6:5–6.

When King Saul died, David was named king over the House of Judah.[263] Saul's son Ishbosheth was also named king by his father's supporters. For two years, both men claimed the crown.[264] Then, Ishbosheth died[265] and David was made king over "My people Israel." [266] David reigned forty years total. He reigned over a united Israel for **thirty-eight** of those years—from Ishbosheth's death to his own natural death, when his son Solomon became king.[267]

The temple was completed in Solomon's **eleventh** year.[268] So the temple project lasted forty-nine (solar) years from the start of David's unified rule until temple construction was complete:

$$38 + 11 = 49 \text{ years}$$

Herod's Temple—Forty-Nine Years

The Second Temple was renovated several times over its history. Its final form, Herod's Temple, was entered by Jesus, fulfilling prophecy that Messiah would enter the temple.[269] The time from the start of Herod's Temple's construction until Jesus' crucifixion is also forty-nine years.

> The Jews then said, "It took forty-six years to build this temple, and yet You will raise it up in three days?" (John 2:20)

These words "**forty-six years**" were spoken in AD 28, during the first recorded Passover of Jesus' ministry (chapter 9).[270] Jesus was crucified in AD 31, **three years** later (chapter 5). This totals forty-nine (solar) years:

$$46 + 3 = 49 \text{ years}$$

Although Herod's Temple physically stood until AD 70, its function ceased about four decades prior (appendix A.17.1). This doubly connects the forty-nine-year pause (one jubilee cycle) associated with the temple.

> These spans display symmetries: the First Temple span starts with God's desire for a temple, and the Second Temple span ends with God's abandoning the temple. Similarly, the First Temple span ends with construction completion and the Second Temple span starts with temple construction commencement.

What about a connection between Hebrews' return to the land of Israel and one sabbatical cycle (seven years)? Again, this holds for both the first and second return. Let's start with the first—Joshua's conquest.

Joshua's Conquest—Seven Years

The exodus from Egypt and return to Israel were not instant events. God required the Hebrews to wander the desert forty years before entering the promised land. As they took possession of it, they forcibly displaced much of its population. This conquest phase lasted seven years. We can confirm this by tracking the birthdays of a man named Caleb. The Bible presents this sequence of events:

1. After the exodus, Hebrews camped at Kadesh Barnea.

2. Caleb was forty years old at Kadesh Barnea.[271]

3. The time from Kadesh Barnea to crossing the Zered brook was thirty-eight years.[272]

4. Immediately after crossing the Zered, Israelites crossed the nearby Arnon River.[273] This is the START of the conquest,

the point at which they entered land allotted to the tribe of Reuben,[274] **thirty-eight years after Kadesh Barnea.**

5. Israel "waged war a long time"[275] until Joshua took the whole land, divided it among the tribes, and "the land was at rest from war."[276] This is the END of the conquest.

6. Caleb turned eighty-five years old when the land was divided,[277] meaning this was **forty-five years after Kadesh Barnea** (see #2).

We can conclude that there were:

– **thirty-eight years** from Kadesh Barnea to conquest START

– **forty-five years** from Kadesh Barnea to conquest END.

Thus, there were seven years (solar years) from the conquest's START to END:

$$45 - 38 = 7 \text{ years}$$

Ezra's Return—Seven Years

The connection between Ezra's return and seven years started with King Artaxerxes and ended with Ezra's mass return to Jerusalem in the seventh year of Artaxerxes (chapter 14). Remarkably, Artaxerxes' accession parallels King David's, in that both took the throne alongside a rival. Just as David at first briefly shared the kingship with Ishbosheth, so did young Artaxerxes at first briefly share power with the would-be usurper Artabanus (chapter 4).

> Historians date the start of Artaxerxes' reign in August 465 BC, but also note seven months of the usurper Artabanus which ended in March 464 BC.[278]

The failed usurper Artabanus died in March **464 BC**.[279] Only at this point was Artaxerxes truly king, and able to decree Ezra's return to Jerusalem—as he did seven years later—in March of **457 BC** (chapter 14). That return restored the center of Judaism to Jerusalem. This was the first return since Joshua and the last before the modern era. This gives us start and finish dates, exactly seven years (solar years) apart:

$$464 \text{ BC} - 457 \text{ BC} = 7 \text{ years}$$

> These spans also display symmetries: the first return span starts with Israel's entering the land, and the second return span ends with Israel's departing to enter the land. Similarly, the First Temple span starts with David's rival to the crown deposed, while the second return span starts when Artaxerxes' rival was deposed.

The Bible links the seven-solar years (one sabbatical cycle) with the **return** in both the decrees from Cyrus and to Ezra and also links forty-nine solar years (one jubilee cycle) with the **temple**—also twice. So, these durations are each *doubly connected* in Scripture.

Solar Years, Not Prophetic Years

These pauses are not prophetic (360-day) years; they are solar years. This point is defined by Scripture itself. Specifically, kings' years, Caleb's birthdays, etc., referenced in Scripture are truly *solar* and not prophetic. The Bible confirms the pauses as solar years, not prophetic years.[280]

> We have applied prophetic years only to prophetic periods and never to pauses. We have applied solar years only to pauses and never to prophetic periods. The usage is consistent and the reasons are scriptural, not arbitrary.

To sum it up, Daniel referenced decrees to restore and rebuild Jerusalem. Four appear in Scripture.[281] Three of them mandated temple construction and/or mass return to Israel. Even though the Bible doesn't indicate the lengths of these pauses, it does show us where to look, and we find connections to forty-nine and seven solar years, respectively—each *twice*.

> It's unlikely that these are coincidences for two big reasons. First, each of these four pauses of seven and forty-nine carry the *exact same units*—namely *solar* (365.242 days) years. Second, note the sheer size and scope of each larger fulfilment string, and the extreme unlikelihood that four separate fulfillments would fit precisely to the day using the *same* method, each over spans of *hundreds of thousands* of days—at prohibitively slim odds (appendix A.19.1). What follows will confirm these synchronizations to an extent far beyond what was promised.

Verification

How can we know the return and temple are linked to these pauses? How can we know this isn't a backfit or fluke? How do we go from these synchronizations to the promised *confirmations*? An intriguing fact emerges when we put pencil to paper and graph each pause length versus the BC years of their respective decrees.

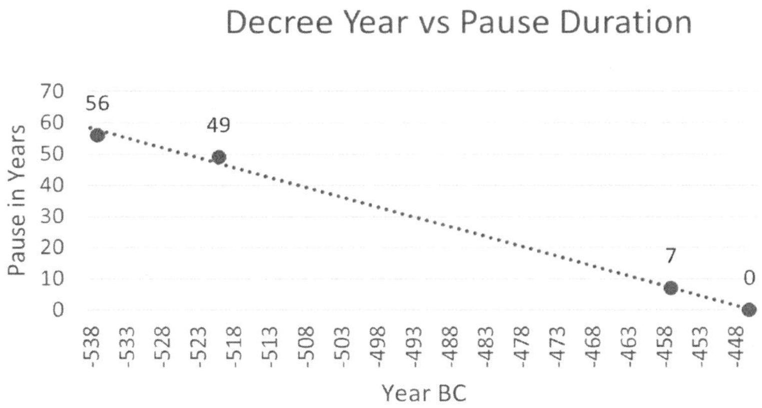

Decree Year vs Pause Duration

Figure 17. BC years of each decree vs. pause lengths in solar years.

The pause years correlate mathematically with their decree years. Four points correlating this tightly indicates some type of underlying connection.[282] This is an unexpected and positive surprise.

The correlation is too strong to dismiss.[283] Remember, Daniel said nothing about *when* the decrees would issue, so this correlation is *not* an artifact of our method,[284] but shows a link between the pauses and the decree years, in the *same units*. God didn't promise us any such correlation, but he gave it to us. It's an elegant symmetry that exceeds expectations.

So, we now see that the scriptural connections of seven and forty-nine to the pauses of Daniel 9:25 are confirmed mathematically. The next chapter shows they are confirmed yet again scripturally.

Chapter 17 Key Points

- Daniel's words describing the decrees are linked to the **temple** and a **return** to the land of Israel.

- The pauses' lengths are each doubly confirmed in Scripture.

- Scripture confirms these pauses as solar, not prophetic years.

- These pauses correlate with the BC years of their respective decrees. The correlation is strong and completely unexpected.

- These pauses are confirmed in Scripture.

These pauses are confirmed both scripturally and mathematically. We now turn our attention back to the solution as a whole.

Who has ascended into heaven and descended?
Who has gathered the wind in His fists?
Who has wrapped the waters in His garment?
Who has established all the ends of the earth?
What is His name or His Son's name?
Surely you know!
(Proverbs 30:4)

An Absolute Chronology of Important Dates

Daniel 9:	7 weeks and 62 weeks plus pauses			
Decree from	**Cyrus**	**Darius**	**Artaxerxes**	**Artaxerxes**
Issue Date	22 Jul 537 BC	14 Aug 518 BC	27 Mar 457 BC	1 Apr 446 BC
Hebrew Date	Av 15	Av 9	Nisan 1	Nisan 6
Start JDN	1,525,487	1,532,449	1,554,590	1,558,612
7+62 weeks	173,880	173,880	173,880	173,880
Pause	1 Jubilee and 1 Sabbatical	1 Jubilee	1 Sabbatical	Zero
+Pause (days)	20,454	17,897	2,557	0
=total span	194,334	191,777	176,437	173,880
End JDN	1,719,821	1,724,226	1,731,027	1,732,492
End Date	**Aug 12, 5 BC**	**Sep 3, AD 8**	**Apr 18, AD 27**	**Apr 22, AD 31**
Event	**Nativity**	**In Temple**	**Baptism**	**Palm Sunday**
Hebrew Date	Av 9	Tishri 15	Nisan 21	Nisan 10
Ezekiel 4:	(430 - 70) = 360 x 7 = 2,520 prophetic years x 360 = 907,200 days			
Start Event	**Cyrus**	**Darius**		
Start Date	22 Jul 537 BC	14 Aug 518 BC		
Hebrew Date	Av 15	Av 9		
Start JDN	1,525,487	1,532,449		
+907,200 days	907,200	907,200		
End JDN	2,432,687	2,439,649		
Date (Gregorian)	**May 15, 1948**	**June 7, 1967**		
Event	**Israel's Rebirth**	**Temple Mount**		

Figure 18. Master chronological chart for Daniel 9:25 and Ezekiel 4,

Note again, all mathematical statements of this book (including the appendices and endnotes) have been audited and confirmed correct (see appendix E.1).

18

HIGH SABBATHS

> This chapter confirms the entire solution to Daniel 9:25 in a scriptural context.

T HE SOLUTION SHOWN IN figure 18 reconciles four decrees to restore and rebuild Jerusalem with four advents of Jesus by identifying the pauses between Daniel's "seven weeks and sixty-two weeks." How can we know these are real and not just chosen to achieve a desired result?

Road Map Chronological Chart
(from chapter 7)

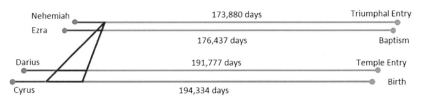

Figure 12. (from chapter 7) Roadmap timeline of each decree, pause, and advent, matching **figures 11** and **18**.

> To review chapter 6, Daniel breaks his seventy weeks into seven, sixty-two, and one. Two pauses create these three segments. A pause before the final week is widely asserted. Our focus here is on the pause between the seven and sixty-two weeks.

These specific pauses enable fulfillments over a span of twenty-four centuries—*precise to the day*—using a uniform solution method—*four times*. These pauses are confirmed in Scripture and *mathematically correlate* with their respective decree years (figure 17), an elegant symmetry that exceeds expectations. How can we know this isn't just a backfit or extreme fluke?

Intriguingly, even conclusively, these pauses place each advent of Jesus on a *biblically referenced Hebrew holiday:*

1. **Nativity**—on Av 9, the major fast day Tisha b'Av (chapter 9)

2. **Temple entry**—on Tishri 15, the first day of Tabernacles (*Sukkot*), a high Sabbath (chapter 13)

3. **Baptism**—on Nisan 21, the seventh day of Unleavened Bread, a high Sabbath (chapter 15)

4. **Triumphal entry**—on Nisan 10, the day God instructed Hebrews to accept the Passover lamb[285] (chapter 5)

High Sabbaths (John 19:31), aka annual Sabbaths, are major Hebrew holidays, similar to weekly Saturday Sabbaths, except that high Sabbaths can fall on any day of the week. There are seven high Sabbaths in a Hebrew year, and a similar number of other major holidays (e.g., Tisha b'Av) referenced in Scripture. The odds that any one of Jesus' advents would randomly fall on a major Hebrew holiday are slim. That all four would are prohibitively unlikely—conservatively one in four hundred thousand.[286] We can't dismiss this as randomness. God didn't promise that Messiah's advents would land on major Hebrew holidays, but they do. This is yet another elegant symmetry that exceeds expectations.

All Saturdays are Sabbaths, but not all Sabbaths are Saturdays. There are also seven high (annual) Sabbaths in the Hebrew year, six of which can fall on any day of the week (Leviticus 23). These were established at Sinai (c. 1450 BC). Uniquely, some of them memorialize *future* events (other cultures' holidays memorialize *past* events) meaning many Hebrew holidays predate the events they commemorate. The Bible presents them as "a shadow of what is to come."[287]

Also, consider the entire solution to Daniel 9:25. Each fulfillment sequence displays a unified theme:

1. Cyrus—Nativity—1948   Birth
2. Darius—Temple entry—1967   Confirmation
3. Ezra—Baptism   Spirit
4. Nehemiah—Triumphal entry   Completion (*shalam*)

1. Cyrus/Nativity/1948: Each created something new overnight: Judah's freedom, Messiah's birth, and Israel's rebirth. The common theme is *birth*.

2. Darius/Temple entry/1967: Darius confirmed Cyrus' edict. Messiah confirmed prophecy as he entered the temple. In 1967, Israel returned to the Temple Mount and confirmed to the world that the young nation would indeed survive. The common theme is *confirmation*.

3. Ezra/Baptism: Ezra restored the law, people, and spirit to Jerusalem, re-establishing it as the center of Judaism. At Jesus' baptism, the Holy Spirit descended upon him.[288] The common theme is *spirit*.

4. Nehemiah/Triumphal entry: Nehemiah rebuilt Jerusalem's walls and established its security. Jesus entered Jerusalem triumphantly as Messiah. The common theme might be roughly described as *completion* but is much better captured by the Hebrew word *shalam*.[289]

This uniformity of theme for each fulfillment sequence is also a pleasant surprise. Remember, Daniel didn't describe any aspect of these advents except for their *timing*. God didn't promise thematic consistency, but he gives it to us. It's yet another elegant symmetry that exceeds expectations.

Required Scope and Time Limit

The scope of Daniel's prophecy is "for your people and your holy city" (Daniel 9:24). Note that each fulfillment concerns the Hebrew people and Jerusalem, as that verse requires. Each fulfilling event fits this scriptural scope without any forcing.

Also, don't forget that Messiah had to arrive before AD 70—the only time after Daniel's lifetime that Jerusalem *and* the temple were both destroyed (Daniel 9:26). All advents of Messiah fell before AD 70 as the text requires.

> If we have a correct understanding of the teachings of [Daniel 9]
> we can then see readily how all prophecy, **without any forcing**,
> falls right into place and is intimately linked with this the great-
> est of all time prophecies.[290] (Ironside, bolding added)

Can We Be Sure That We're Sure?

This book has demonstrated that Jesus is the promised Messiah of Daniel 9:25. How confident can we be in this conclusion? Knowing the truth of something requires addressing objections to it. The next chapter tests these results. To truly know the conclusion is valid, you need to see those tests with your own eyes.

And don't be afraid to look. This book's thesis is built on verifiable evidence. The mathematical statements appearing in this book have been audited and shown to be correct. The discovered fulfillment conforms to a face-value reading of Scripture.

Again, **don't take my word for it**—or anyone else's. (This is a highly contentious topic with fiercely guarded—and conflicting—opinions.) Check the math, the sources, the chronology. All are verifiable. You *can* get to the bottom of it. Compare this book with others on this subject and be sure to check their sources as well. Never let anyone make a key claim without providing evidence, even for claims you already accept. Challenge everything, not only claims you haven't accepted.[291]

Only then can you "understand" and "know" as Jesus and Daniel both urge us directly in Scripture, right in this spot.

Those words are truly meant for us—for you, for the Church, and for the world—*for a time such as this.*

Chapter 18 Key Points

- This solution places Messiah's advents on major Hebrew holidays.

- This solution displays unified themes for each of the four ful-fillment strings. The placement and symmetry are completely unexpected and pleasant surprises.

- The fulfilling events all fall within this prophecy's scriptural scope: "for your people and your holy city" (Daniel 9:24).

- Messiah's advents fall before Jerusalem and the temple were destroyed (AD 70) as required by Daniel 9:26.

Can we accept these results as valid? Have we broken any rules?

19

TRIPLE-CHECK

> This chapter applies basic scientific method to test the solution's validity.

JESUS FULFILLS DANIEL 9:25 precisely to the day. But to be *sure* of this, we must test our evidence, methods, and results.

Could This Be Due to Random Chance?

One basic test of scientific method is the *null hypothesis*. Put simply, is there a relationship between Daniel's prophecy and Jesus' advents *at all?* Could those advents have happened as Daniel foretold purely due to chance?

The odds are calculated in appendix A.19.1 at roughly one in ten undecillions. That's unimaginably slim—one chance in one followed by thirty-seven zeros (there aren't that many grains of sand on Earth). We may exclude the null hypothesis—this fulfillment cannot be dismissed as random chance.

Are There Other Possible Results?

Scientific method requires us to consider *alternate explanations*. In other words, could someone interpret the evidence as pointing to a different conclusion of equal validity?

People have certainly tried. The hundreds of solutions to Daniel 9:25 proposed over the centuries are, by definition, *alternate explanations*. Yet a careful examination of those reveals none as deep, precise, and verifiable as this one. So the answer is no, unless an equally valid one appears.

Is This a Huge Backfit?

No, but don't take my word for it. If it were, then other solutions must also be possible. If one person can backfit, then so can another. So again, the answer is no until a different yet equally valid solution appears.

A common objection to Bible prophecy is that you could allegedly "get anything you want."[292] This must be addressed before accepting this or *any* prophetic solution. This thesis overcomes the objection. *How so?* Getting *anything you want* means you must also be able to get *something else*. For centuries, people have sought a solution to Daniel 9:25 but have found none that presents the same depth, breadth, and precision. Unless one is found, we can know we aren't just getting *anything we want*.

Some hold Daniel 9:25 to be inspired text yet insist it indicates someone other than Jesus. *Could it?* Daniel identifies Messiah only by the *time* of his coming. What are the odds that someone else shared Jesus' exact chronological fingerprint? Those odds are calculated in appendix A.19.2 conservatively at one in almost six hundred thousand. We may dismiss the possibility that Daniel 9:25 points to anyone other than Jesus.[293]

Scientific method also requires challenging the context of our evidence. Key questions include:

- Was Daniel 9:25 written with an agenda?
- Was Daniel 9:25 written *after* the Gospels?[294]
- Are these prophecies self-fulfilling?
- Were the Gospels edited to fit Daniel 9:25?
- Most intriguingly: *why wasn't this discovered before?*

Was Daniel 9:25 written with an agenda? One fact makes the question moot. Daniel was written *before* the events it foretells (next section). In this context, any human bias or agenda would be inconsequential.

Was Daniel 9:25 written *after* the Gospels? Daniel was written before Jesus' birth. The oldest recovered copy of Daniel dates to c. 125 BC.[295] Another Dead Sea Scroll, dated to c. 100 BC, directly refers to Daniel 9:25.[296] One Jewish interpretation of Daniel's Seventy Weeks predates 146 BC.[297] This makes it certain that Daniel 9:25 predates Jesus' birth. Moreover, any claim that any part of these prophecies (Daniel, Ezekiel, and Jeremiah) were written *after* the events they collectively foretell isn't credible, as two of those events occurred in the twentieth century.

Are these prophecies self-fulfilling? For self-fulfillment, the fulfilling criteria must be known at the time of fulfillment. That is certainly not the case here because the solution to Daniel 9:25 remained "secret and sealed" for centuries. Showing only now, in the twenty-first century, how prophecies of Daniel, Jeremiah, and Ezekiel are not only fulfilled but also interconnected, removes any possibility of self-fulfillment.

Were the Gospels edited to fit Daniel 9:25? We know they weren't because they make no Daniel 9:25 argument anywhere. In fact, the Gospels never directly mention Daniel 9:25. This raises a key question: *why not?*

Why wasn't this discovered before? During Jesus' ministry, anyone could have made a Daniel 9:25 case for Jesus' messiahship, but none is found in the New Testament. Had the Gospel writers seen its fulfillment in Jesus, then they, especially Matthew, would have mentioned it. They certainly had every motivation to, but no such claim is found.

After all, seeing the promised Messiah was a hope of generations[298] and Jesus lived during a time of high messianic expectation.[299] Many knew Jesus was Messiah yet nobody made the connection with Daniel's prophecy. Just consider this for a moment: Daniel 9:25 is purely chronological and it pointed to this era, so a case—strong or weak—might have been made for *anyone at that time*. A case for Jesus would have been extremely strong. How on earth did *everyone* miss that? Isn't that exceedingly odd?

> The earliest known *Christian* interpretation of Daniel's Seventy Weeks was written by church father Irenaeus in c. AD 180, long after the biblical era.[300]

But exactly this was foretold—by Daniel himself. Daniel 12:4 reads, "keep these words secret and seal up the book until the end of time." In other words, Daniel's prophecies won't be fully understood until the time of the end. It doesn't read "until the time of Messiah." And that's what happened—the fulfillment remained hidden, even as he stood in plain sight. To stress the point, the angel repeated:

> And he said, "Go your way, Daniel, for these words will be kept secret and sealed up until the end time. (Daniel 12:9)

The Bible tells us *twice* that Daniel's Seventy Weeks would stay "secret and sealed" *until the end time*—not before.[301]

> Scripture wasn't divided into chapters and verses until the Middle Ages. The seal of Daniel 12 is thus not limited to that chapter. Note also that Jesus confirmed that *his time* wasn't understood (Luke 12:56; 19:44). Although the Gospels don't directly refer to Daniel 9:25, they do contain an intriguing *indirect* reference (appendix A.19.3).

Evidence that Daniel 9:25 is fulfilled far outweighs evidence that it isn't. Put simply, Daniel's numbers not only fit, they also make **everything** related to them fit, both historically and scripturally. This indicates that Daniel's testable prediction is **true**. It identifies Jesus as the promised Messiah. It makes a robust case that a predictive prophecy is truly fulfilled.

Why favor *this* solution over *other* solutions? Any valid solution must at least meet a *basic standard* of fulfilling all aspects of a prediction.

This book shows scriptural, mathematical, and historical evidence producing a complete solution, within its scope and term, and without forcing. It not only meets the *basic standard* of fulfilling Daniel 9:25 in all aspects, but also exceeds it by going beyond what was promised, expected, or even imagined. In contrast, other solutions fall short of this *basic standard*.[302]

> Be aware that the mere *existence* of any solution (including this one) doesn't automatically grant it validity. Take for example a hypothetical court case with a defendant who is 100% guilty. No matter how strong the prosecutor's case, the defense attorney will still present an opposing argument. It's the jury's job to weigh all evidence and reach a verdict, just as readers should weigh all Daniel 9:25 evidence for this solution versus other solutions.

The solution rests on verifiable evidence. It never required accepting or rejecting anything on faith alone. It never appealed to authority or popularity.[303] It never changed its methods and never tortured the historical record. It consistently interpreted Scripture at face value. In short, we have followed hard evidence to reach this conclusion: Daniel 9:25 is a *true prediction*.

> Readers still in doubt should see appendix A.19.4 before moving on.

Chapter 19 Key Points

- Daniel 9:25 links four biblical decrees to restore and rebuild Jerusalem to four key advents of Jesus.

- Daniel 9:25 is truly fulfilled, to an extent that far exceeds prior expectation. It is a **true prediction**.

*Was this the work of God? This true prediction violates the laws of nature. Humans simply cannot foretell the future like that. But **something** certainly did. This is evidence for God, but taken alone, isn't yet proof. We haven't formally proven God's existence, at least not yet.*

So can we?

20

Read this to me

THE FINAL WORD

I S THIS PROOF OF God? For centuries, people have sought exactly this. Thomas Aquinas and René Descartes are just two of many who tirelessly attempted irrefutable proof of God using traditional Aristotelian logic. Atheists have tried this same approach to prove God's nonexistence.[304] Although this type of logic allows irrefutability in theory, it doesn't achieve it in real-world praxis.[305] Traditional logic is conveyed in words, whose contexts and definitions are often inexact and always open to dispute.[306] That's unlikely to change.

Such attempts have led to a popular assumption that proof must be irrefutable. But this is not how proof typically works. *Why not?* Let's start in the only practical field that does allow irrefutable proof: mathematics. Its logic is expressed in numbers and can be irrefutable in praxis.

For example, we can irrefutably prove[307] that $2x+2y=2(x+y)$. Proof in math derives from math itself. It doesn't require measurement or observation. In math, we can achieve proof to the exclusion of alternate conclusions. Correctly formed, its proofs can be irrefutable.[308]

But when we take the first tiny step away from the ideal world of pure math, we must leave irrefutable proof behind. *Why?* Even in adjacent fields such as physics and chemistry, we must collect our evidence from measured observation and apply relevant natural laws. This introduces uncertainty. For example, no measurement is without a margin of error, however tiny, even under optimal conditions. Additionally, we don't fully know all the laws of physics and chemistry—we are still making discoveries.[309]

These are just two reasons why irrefutable proof outside math isn't achievable. We can get extremely close to irrefutable, close enough for every practical purpose, but proof here can never be irrefutable. Even if the strongest objections are incredibly weak, we still can't dismiss them without a hearing. Proof here might be established beyond *reasonable* doubt, but proof outside of math cannot exist beyond *all* doubt.[310]

In the physical sciences, the conclusion that best explains all evidence is often deemed "proven" even though it isn't irrefutable. For example, notice how scientific consensus occasionally changes. "Proven" ideas can be disproven by new evidence. The twentieth century provides two big examples.

First, the universe was once thought to be eternal, steady-state, and without beginning. Now consensus favors the Big Bang model with a definite beginning. Second, our theory for the atom's structure shifted from the nineteenth-century plum pudding model to today's Rutherford-Bohr model with its familiar nucleus and orbiting electrons. Both shifts required much debate and challenge. Both changed their fields fundamentally.

In the past, people could refer to the plum pudding atom or the steady-state universe as "proven," but a careful scientist would have added that those theories simply *best explained the evidence* at that time. This is a rational standard of proof used by competent scientists to this day. But scientific consensus isn't permanent. New evidence can overturn "proven" ideas yet again.

> Why do we expect this book's thesis to not change? Unlike scientific evidence, Scripture doesn't change (Matthew 24:35). Why go to this detail to define a standard of proof? Because that standard is often manipulated, especially in a debate context, where one side holds the other to a high standard of proof while using a lower standard for themselves. Standards of proof should be well-defined and consistent.

And those two scientific examples are from fields where experimental conditions can be tightly controlled and results reliably replicated. Our everyday real world is a far messier place.

Webster's defines *proof* as: "that degree of evidence which convinces the mind of any truth or fact."[311] Even the strongest evidence must be judged by "the mind." If it judges that the evidence establishes fact, then the fact is proven—to that mind. Proof (not *Truth* but *proof!*) is subjective and works one mind at a time. This accurately describes observed human behavior.

Irrefutable proof of God may be impossible, but by the same irrefutable standard, so is proof of our own history. In theory at least, no one can *prove* we weren't all created just five minutes ago, along with intact memories and the appearance of age.[312] For irrefutable proof, we are limited to math.

But real-world proof is very possible. After all, juries do reach verdicts—sometimes quickly—and people do accept facts (such as we were *not* all created just five minutes ago). This type of proof requires us to judge the evidence one way or the other—sometimes easy, sometimes not so easy.

This real-world standard of proof is *beyond a reasonable doubt*. A doubt is reasonable if objective evidence supports it. If no such evidence exists, then that doubt is not reasonable and may be dismissed.[313] The definition of *reasonable* lies with the reader, therefore proof (outside math) can never be claimed as universally irrefutable.

> Ironically, irrefutable proof of God's existence would make faith unnecessary. Faith is the necessary bridge from evidence to accepted fact (Hebrews 11:1). This is true for all questions outside math—both sacred and secular. Until God's existence (or any fact) is proven with pure math alone, then faith remains essential.

A prophecy was fulfilled. You, and only you, may decide if the evidence proves to you that God exists. Let nobody tell you what to decide. Remember, we cannot claim irrefutable proof of God beyond every possible doubt.

But we can get extremely close.

The True Prediction

So how to approach Daniel's *true prediction?* This book has demonstrated its fulfillment. It has shown that randomness cannot explain it, that it points only to Jesus, and is confirmed in Scripture. Two other prophecies are precisely fulfilled when set in Daniel's framework, and the dates of key events fit scriptural, physical, and historical evidence. All of it can be objectively verified (and is therefore *reproducible*). Daniel foretold, centuries in advance, the precise dates of Jesus' key advents. In short, *everything* fits.

French philosopher and genius mathematician **Blaise Pascal** anticipated this exact type of evidence. He judged its weight to be *infinite*.

> If one man alone had made a book of predictions about Jesus Christ, as to the time and the manner, and Jesus Christ had come in conformity to these prophecies, this fact would have infinite weight.[314] (Pascal)

Blaise Pascal

Daniel 9:25 provides Pascal's evidence exactly. It truly predicted the precise dates of Jesus' advents. Its fulfillment breaks the laws of nature and is thus not of human origin. "This fact" of "infinite weight" allows us to draw some firm conclusions.

Three Proofs of God

First—A Supernatural Entity Exists

Natural law forbids *true predictions*—defined as foretelling the exact dates of unique human action, centuries in advance, not by calculation or pattern, but by revealed truth.[315] Humans simply cannot provide the type of *true prediction* that Daniel provided. Any entity that can provide such a *true prediction* operates above natural law and is, by definition, *supernatural*.

Either the supernatural exists or the supernatural does not exist. The two options are mutually exclusive and collectively exhaustive.[316] Put plainly, it's either one or the other and nothing outside of, or between the two.

> If a *true prediction*, as defined previously, exists, then a supernatural entity must exist. Daniel 9:25 provides a *true prediction*. Therefore, a **supernatural entity exists.**

This argument is *deductive,* meaning that if the premises are true, then the conclusion is true. Rejecting the conclusion now requires greater evidence to the contrary (appendix A.20.1). This argument can also be written in a different yet also deductive form.[317]

A supernatural entity exists. But how can we know if this supernatural entity, the source of Daniel's *true prediction*, is indeed the God of the Bible?

Second—God of the Bible

The argument is in *four* parts (the fourth part is in the third proof). First, Daniel, Ezekiel, and Jeremiah form a single framework of predictive prophecy, fulfilled precisely to the day and verified with exacting precision. They are true prophets, and each named the biblical God as their source.[318] Because other verifiable aspects of their prophecies are true, we have no reason to dismiss their stated source. In both Scripture as in law, they give objective evidence that the prophetic source is, as claimed, the God of the Bible.[319]

Second, Daniel correctly foretold the promised Messiah's advents. Messiah is a recurring theme of the Old Testament. Daniel verified the promised Messiah in harmony with the rest of the Old Testament. This is further evidence that the source of Daniel's prophecy is the God of the Bible.

Third, John the Apostle wrote we will know God when we know Jesus:

Jesus said to him, "I am the way, and the truth, and the life; no one comes to the Father except through Me. If you had known Me, you would have known My Father also; from now on you know Him, and have seen Him." (John 14:6–7)

It's remarkable that God's existence is demonstrated by identifying Jesus as Messiah. The above verse is true in a broader context than ours *but is also true in ours.* Together, these show that the source of Daniel's *true prediction,* this proven supernatural entity, is indeed the God of the Bible.

Third—God, Creator of the Universe

Again, more unexpected evidence emerges from the solution itself. It seems this prophecy's Creator actually cared enough to sign his creation.

Decrees - 91 years

Pauses - 56 years   Advents - 35 years

Consider the entire solution to Daniel 9:25. The four decrees, from Cyrus in 537 BC to Nehemiah in 446 BC, span **ninety-one solar years**, start to finish. Also consider the advents of Jesus from his birth in 5 BC to his triumphal entry in AD 31. These span **thirty-five solar years.**

There is no "year zero" between 1 BC and AD 1, so we subtract one, to get 35.

Also, the pauses for the temple (forty-nine) and return (seven) total **fifty-six solar years.** We have no reason to expect these spans to be noteworthy, but they absolutely are. These span lengths bear a distinct signature:

Advents: Thirty-five years are **five weeks** of years $35 \div 7 = 5$
Pauses: Fifty-six years are **eight weeks** of years $56 \div 7 = 8$
Decrees: Ninety-one years are **thirteen weeks** of years $91 \div 7 = 13$

Five, eight, and thirteen are **Fibonacci numbers**, the basis of the golden ratio (aka "phi," "divine section"). This is highly significant and unexpected. Remember, Daniel foretold Messiah would arrive a certain time after these decrees, but not the timing of the decrees themselves. So, we can't expect Fibonacci numbers to appear. But they do appear—precisely, in sequence, and *in the same units* (weeks of years) used in Daniel's prophecy.

Why is it significant? It's beyond our scope here to fully present Fibonacci numbers. But in short, Fibonacci numbers are "fascinatingly prevalent"[320] in natural patterns. There are many examples, such as the natural arrangement of leaves and seeds, the proportions of animal bodies, and the spiral patterns of seashells. They are a common rule in the natural world.[321]

> The decree span (thirteen weeks) equals the pause span (eight weeks) plus the advent span (five weeks). Fibonacci numbers must display this equality. Intriguingly, this equality also exists *precisely to the day:*
> Pauses (20,454 days) + Advents (12,671 days) = Decrees (33,125 days).[322]

We know Fibonacci numbers didn't just evolve by natural selection because they also appear in *nonliving* forms (e.g., storms, ocean waves, and the fractal structures of snowflakes). Fibonacci numbers are also in the Bible, including Noah's ark, the ark of the covenant, Ezekiel's Temple, and New Jerusalem.[323] To those, we can now add the Seventy Weeks of Daniel. This is the fourth reason that this prophecy originates from the God of the Bible.

And here's something truly amazing. Natural structures typically display *two* adjacent Fibonacci numbers. Yet, true to form, Daniel exceeds nature by displaying *three*. This is yet another unexpected and positive surprise confirming that we have reached a correct understanding.

We observe Fibonacci numbers at every scale: from the microscopic, to the immense starry arms of spiral galaxies.[324] They are a distinctive hallmark signature of structures *everywhere in the universe.*

The universe made by God the Creator.

The heavens tell of the glory of God;
And their expanse declares the work of His hands. (Psalm 19:1)

For since the creation of the world His invisible attributes,
that is, His eternal power and divine nature, have been clearly
perceived, being understood by what has been made, so that
they are without excuse. (Romans 1:20)

We started right where Jesus urged us to look (Matthew 24:15). We followed Daniel's direction to *know and understand.* We applied Jesus' standard of *everything* (Luke 24:44). We now end up here, right where the Bible proclaims evidence of God is to be found—in his creation.

We have followed not only scriptural evidence but also scriptural guidance. If the evidence presented to you in this book establishes for you that God exists, then this is, by definition, *proof of God.*[325]

Now What?

If this is new to you, and you want to know more about God, then be patient with yourself. *Seek Jesus.* Find out who he is, why he came, and the priceless gift he offers freely to all who *believe and receive* him.

> But as many as received Him, to them He gave the right to become children of God, to those who believe in His name (John 1:12)

> Despite the amount of material covered, we have unpacked only one sentence from the Bible. This book does *not* present Christianity, but it does establish the *Truth* of Christianity. To know Jesus, you must hear the *gospel* (good news). The Bible tells us that "faith comes from hearing, and hearing by the word of Christ." (Romans 10:17) Don't be distracted by the rituals of man. Focus on Truth, not its packaging.

Start in the Bible. The book of Luke is an excellent place. Luke literally wrote it to someone who also wanted to learn more about Jesus.

And don't be intimidated by the Bible's size. You've already covered a big chunk of it, even some of its most challenging parts. You got this. You have an excellent head start—you just need to actually start.

When ready, seek those who gladly offer to help when you simply express a curiosity. Find a Bible study group. These are almost always social and welcoming, especially to the newly curious. (If not, then find a different one.) You shouldn't feel any pressure, judgement, or unease. Remember, the Church is full of real people, just like you, with all their faults and mistakes. You have just as much human dignity as anyone else there, including the ones giving the sermons. You do fit in. You do belong. Just don't expect dramatic epiphanies or Hollywood magic—this is real Life, not media fantasy.

You now see factually that God exists, that Jesus is Messiah, and that Scripture is reliable. These are all good and important, but knowing all this with your head isn't quite enough. You must accept God also in your heart.

God promised to reveal himself to those who truly seek him. It's one of the most repeated promises in the Bible.[326] This includes **you**, no matter who you are, where or when you were born, or the life you've lived. For you, the Way is clear, the Door is open, the Light is on.

And if all this is very familiar to you, then you might suspect there is far more to Daniel's Seventy Weeks than presented here—and you'd be right. For centuries, people have viewed Daniel 9 as a master key to prophecy.

We have now seen this to be literally, concretely true. And this master key unlocks much more (appendix A.20.2).

> Does this book contradict Judaism? *Absolutely not.* Quite the opposite in fact. It shows the Old Testament to be *true*, just as it shows the New Testament to be *true*. It shows God's covenants remain *valid*, that *Messiah is real*, and his name is *Jesus*.

Key Points of this Book

It is established beyond a reasonable doubt that:

- God exists,
- Jesus is the promised Messiah, and
- Scripture is reliable.

> If you found enlightenment here, please write a review on Amazon and tell others.[327] Let them know this book indeed delivers new, objective evidence of God. Most people will stop when the reading gets challenging *unless* someone trusted has told them that it does indeed provide new, objective evidence of God. Your clear endorsement is by far the most vital motivation for someone to actually read it. Please let them know—for their sake, and for *His* sake.
>
> It's important to spread this message personally. Share this book, and the website threeproofsofgod.com. It's up to you, not somebody else (Matthew 28:19-20).

And we now have evidence that, according to Daniel 12, *the seal* is, just perhaps, ready for breaking.

The Best News of All

As Daniel urged us directly, we now "know and understand" that the promises of Daniel 9:25 are true to a depth and extent beyond what Scripture promised or what humans even imagined.

That's yet another reason we can expect the wonderful promises of the prior verse, Daniel 9:24, to also be kept *beyond our expectations*. Here we have seen God's capability far exceed human imagination. That's **excellent** news—those promises in Daniel 9:24 describe the **Kingdom of God**—the coming world that Jesus spoke about so often as he walked among us. And it's coming—it's here, **and** it's coming. Can you share this message?

He came as foretold.
As foretold, he will come again.

Soli Deo Gloria

APPENDIX A
DETAILS

A.1.1[*] A Note to Believers

Some may object to a reason-based approach to the Bible.[328] But God tells us to use reason: "Come now, and let us debate your case" and "Bring forward your evidence" (Isaiah 1:18; 41:21), to "test the spirits to see whether they are from God" (1 John 4:1), to "examine everything; hold firmly to that which is good" (1 Thessalonians 5:21), and to "make a defense to everyone who asks you to give an account for the hope that is in you" (1 Peter 3:15).[329]

The Bereans were "noble-minded" because they examined the Scriptures "to see whether these things were so" (Acts 17:11). Scripture deems reasoned inquiry "noble-minded," certainly not improper.

Moreover, the Bible urges us to "know and understand" (Daniel 9:25) and "understand" (Matthew 24:15) this specific passage—not just "believe" but *understand*. We are told to use reason right here in this spot—directly and from the highest authority.

A.2.1 Who Was Darius the Mede?

Discussions of Darius the Mede (DM) usually focus on either his *existence* or his *identity*. Some claim him fictional, noting a lack of reference to this name in historical sources. Others assert that he is a real person whom Daniel gave the throne name "Darius." Leading contenders for DM are Cambyses II, Cyaxares II, Cyrus, Gobryas, Gubaru, and Ugbaru.

Of these, Cambyses and Cyrus are easily dismissed. "Darius the Mede" was "the son of Ahasuerus, of Median descent" (Daniel 9:1). Yet Daniel references "Cyrus the Persian" (Daniel 6:28) whose father was Cambyses I, a Persian. Cambyses II's father was Cyrus. Daniel references years of Cyrus *after* those of DM.[330] Cambyses II replaced his father Cyrus, also a Persian, as emperor nine years after Babylon's fall.

Cyaxares, Gobryas, Gubaru, and Ugbaru are also historical figures. Later historians may have conflated their names, as Josephus remarked:

> but when Babylon was taken by Darius [...] he was sixty-two years old. He was the son of Astyages, and had another name among the Greeks.[331] (Josephus)

His "name among the Greeks" might have been Cyaxares (former consensus for DM, who isn't excluded) or Gobryas. Greek historian Xenophon identified the general who took Babylon as **Gobryas**. The names Gobryas, Gubaru, and Ugbaru may have been used interchangeably by historians for centuries, as they took care to match their various sources.

---

* The first number of the appendix locators refers to the corresponding chapter. The second number is sequential within its chapter.

The Babylonian Chronicle named **Ugbaru**, governor of Gutium (in Media), as the commander who took Babylon.[332] The chronicle also announced his death, an honor reserved for royalty. Most conclusively, both the Bible and the Babylonian Chronicle state that *somebody* (not Cyrus) appointed governors in Babylon right after the Persian takeover. This complete change of government happened only once in that era. The Bible attributes this to **Darius the Mede**. The Babylonian Chronicle attributes it to **Ugbaru**.[333]

> Ugbaru appears three times in the chronicle, each with a different spelling. One is best read "**Gubaru**" yet it refers with near-certainty to the same person Ugbaru. A different Gubaru appears in the Babylonian Chronicle years later as a satrap who could not have been DM.[334] For more detail, see appendix A.8.1.

This summary doesn't present the full body of evidence. Consensus identifies Darius the Mede as **Ugbaru**[335] but isn't dominant. This book follows, but only for ease of presentation.

Because here's the rub—in our context, *it doesn't matter*. DM's *identity* doesn't alter this book's thesis. The key is his *existence*. The point is that there *was indeed* a vassal king in Babylon under Cyrus, who reigned shortly after Babylon's fall. His throne name was Darius the Mede, no matter if he were Ugbaru, any of the others, or even someone else.[336]

A.3.1 "know and understand"

Therefore when you see the ABOMINATION OF DESOLATION which was spoken of through Daniel the prophet, standing in the holy place—let the reader understand— (Matthew 24:15)

Jesus directly indicated an "ABOMINATION" via "Daniel the prophet" and urged us to understand its meaning.[337] Daniel mentions the abomination in three places: Daniel chapters 9, 11, and 12. Chapter 9 is the first and principal mention.[338] *How can we know?*

In Matthew 24:15, Jesus referred to *future* events.[339] Daniel 11 describes events that occurred before Jesus.[340] Daniel 12 briefly references the abomination to define the timing of events during Daniel's seventieth week. In other words, Daniel 12 isn't really *about* the abomination, but rather recalls it from chapter 9.

Daniel 9 presents the abomination during the seventieth week of Daniel. So Jesus referred to Daniel's Seventy Weeks, found in Daniel 9:24–27. But how do we know Jesus referred to more than just the abomination? Because Matthew 24:15 doesn't leave it at that.

Intriguingly, it adds: "let the reader understand."[341] The remark is significant. In the Gospels, only a handful of verses directly tell the reader to "understand" them.[342] This rare red-flag callout grabs us by the lapels to signal something especially important.[343] This is one instance. In fact, Daniel 9 is the *only* Old Testament prophecy the Gospels directly urge us to understand.[344] Jesus referred to the *reader,* which might have seemed odd to those listening to him speak at the time, because Jesus' words weren't yet written. But Daniel's words were already written. Jesus urged *the reader of Daniel* to understand it.

This suggests that Jesus meant more than just the abomination because when we turn to Daniel 9, we see Daniel used the same red-flag callout to *understand* something. Daniel wrote, "So you are to know and understand" (i.e., pay close attention here) and then presented the "seven weeks and sixty-two weeks" in that same sentence.

> Note that Scripture wasn't divided into chapters and verses until the Middle Ages. Jesus' reference to Daniel 9:27 doesn't exclude the rest of Daniel 9. Note also that Daniel placed this callout in the middle of that prophecy, not its beginning. Here, Daniel focused us on the seven and sixty-two weeks; surely also the rest of the prophecy, but with absolute certainty the seven and sixty-two weeks.

In summary, Jesus called out Daniel 9, and Daniel called out the seven and sixty-two weeks. This makes the Seventy Weeks of Daniel the only biblical text that two different sources explicitly urged us to *understand*.

A.3.2 Messiah the Prince—*mashiach nagid*

"Messiah the Prince" (Hebrew: *mashiach nagid*) in Daniel 9:25, also translated "Anointed One, the ruler" (NIV) refers to someone chosen to rule.[345]

Mashiach is Hebrew for *anointed*. It appears over thirty-five times in Scripture and refers to people sanctified by pouring oil on them (1 Samuel 10:1) or chosen by God for a purpose (Isaiah 45:1). Objects could also be anointed (Genesis 31:13; Leviticus 8:10) but the anointed one in Daniel 9:25 is by context a person, not an object.[346]

Daniel combines *mashiach* with *nagid* to indicate a person of extremely high importance. How do we know? *Nagid* is a title of authority. It appears over forty times in Scripture as prince, ruler, leader, or officer. *Nagid* is prominently applied to kings in the line of David.[347] It's also used in a general sense (Job 31:37; Proverbs 28:16) but *nagid* relates most prominently to David and to rulers in the Davidic line.[348]

Daniel 9:25 is the only verse combining *mashiach* with *nagid*[349] or any title of worldly authority (e.g., *adon, melek, nasi, shalit*). There are cases where *mashiach* is a possessive object (e.g., "the Lord's anointed," 1 Samuel 24:6) or verb ("anoint him as ruler," 1 Samuel 9:16; 10:1; 1 Chronicles 29:22) but only Daniel 9:25 combines *mashiach* with a title of authority to form a compound title.[350] This happens only once in Scripture—right here.

Contrast this with Isaiah 45:1, which names Persian Emperor Cyrus as God's "anointed" using a form of *mashiach* but doesn't include any title of authority. This is remarkable because Cyrus was one of the greatest emperors of world history, yet the Bible doesn't include a title of "ruler." Thus, Daniel's Messiah is more significant than Cyrus, and *nagid* could connect him to the Davidic line. Here again, the Bible interprets itself. Indeed, many read Daniel's *mashiach nagid* as Israel's promised Messiah.[351] How do we identify him? In a word, chronologically. He's the one who shows up right on time.

> Overwhelmingly, the earliest Christian writers saw the Seventy Weeks fulfilled in Jesus, though their calculations varied greatly.[352] The Talmud and some prominent Jews (e.g., Rashi) have also interpreted this prophecy as messianic.[353]

A.3.3 The Prophetic Year

The 360-day prophetic year is a cornerstone of much scholarly prophetic interpretation, yet some scholars reject its use. These objections appear succinctly in this critique:

Nothing corresponds to a 360-day year. It is longer than the standard Jewish year (of 12 lunar months), which is 354 days, and is shorter than a solar year or a Jewish leap year (which is 13 lunar months). Such a year could not have been used in biblical times because the festivals, which are at least in part agricultural, would have gotten out of sync with the seasons. **What can this "biblical year" be other than an invention? When you set your own intervals, you can make anything come out.** (Anon, coloring added)

Each objection can be addressed. There is indeed basis for a 360-day period. True—it's neither a solar nor lunar year, and observing a 360-day calendar year would cause holidays to drift out of season. But the issue is not the use of a 360-day year on calendars. At issue is its use in *prophecy*, so objections one and two are moot. The key question is if this 360-day period is indeed valid or instead just an arbitrary "fudge factor."

The 360-day prophetic year is neither arbitrary nor invented. It is the only value established explicitly in the Bible. Specifically, every time the Bible references an exact number of days *and* the equivalent number of months or "years," that equivalency is *always* to a 360-day "year" and *never* to any other length—*without exception*. For example, the great flood started "in the second month, on the seventeenth day of the month" (Genesis 7:11). The ark rested on land "at the end of 150 days" "in the seventh month, on the seventeenth day of the month" (Genesis 8:3–4). If five months are 150 days, then twelve months are 360 days.[354] And Scripture provides even more direct and precise examples.

Daniel and Revelation measure the duration of events foretold for the seventieth week of Daniel. The reign of Antichrist is set for "a time, times, and half a time" or 3½ times (Daniel 7:25), and for "forty-two months" (Revelation 13:5). The great tribulation (Daniel 12:7) is for "time, times, and half a time" or 3½ times. The woman's exile is "1,260 days" and "a time, times, and half a time," or 3½ times (Revelation 12:6, 14). The holy city is trampled (Revelation 11:2) for "forty-two months." The two witnesses (Revelation 11:3) speak for "1,260 days." These events [3½ times = 42 months = 1,260 days] are reconciled only by a period of 360 days. This 360-day period was awkwardly named the "prophetic year."

> The 360-day period has scriptural basis. However, using the word "year" in its name "prophetic year" has caused much confusion. Daniel 9:25 never used the word "year."

Moreover, in Daniel 7:25's "time, times, and half a time," the word for "time" is the Aramaic *iddan*.[355] This word *iddan* appears here in the Greek Septuagint as *kairos* (G2540).[356] Revelation 13:5 measures this same span as "forty-two months." Forty-two months are 3½ years, so "time, times, and half a time" are 3½ "years." But Daniel didn't write *year*. He wrote *"time"* instead. We understand "time" to resemble, but not necessarily equal, a year. How long exactly is this unit that Daniel calls a "time"?

Scripture provides a measurement. Revelation 12:14 describes a woman in the wilderness for "time, times, and half a time," where "time" is also *kairos* (G2540) as in Daniel 7:25. Revelation 12:6 measures this same span as 1,260 days. By calculation, a "time" (*kairos*) is exactly 360 days. If "time" were a familiar solar year, then three and a half of them would be 1,278 days, not 1,260. How do we know this 360-day period applies specifically to the "seven weeks and sixty-two weeks" of Daniel 9:25?

We know because the above events are foretold to occur during Daniel's seventieth week. It's in the *same prophecy*, thus in the *same units*. A length other than 360 days would create scriptural disparity. Here, Scripture defines its own terms; the Bible interprets itself.

It may still seem odd to use the 360-day prophetic year because *that is simply not a year*. But consider how the Bible carefully avoids the word "year." Look closely at the above verses, including Daniel 9:25. Note a conspicuous absence. They refer directly to days and months but not to years, even though they imply something similar to years (*iddan, kairos*). These verses indicate a period similar but not identical to a familiar solar year.

Daniel might have left yet another linguistic clue by using the Hebrew *shabuim* for "weeks." Hebrew ascribes gender to nouns. *Shabuim* is a masculine-sounding plural of the singular *shabua*. The normal Hebrew plural of *shabua* is the feminine-sounding *shavuot*, not the masculine *shabuim*. Altering the plural's gender suggests that Daniel may have intended an alternate or nonobvious meaning—in other words, weeks of seven unconventional years.[357] Seven prophetic years of 360-days each could fit this indication.

The Bible establishes a basis for the 360-day "prophetic year." But we also require this 360-day period to actually *work*, that is, to produce an accurate and meaningful result. This book will demonstrate that many times over.

A.3.4 The Anderson/Hoehner Solution

> With highest respect to Sir Robert Anderson and Dr. Harold Hoehner, the known technical errors of their solutions to Daniel 9:25 are summarized here. Their works remain worthy advances, key waypoints to the present discoveries.

According to **Sir Robert Anderson** (1881), the prophecy started on Nisan 1 of Artaxerxes' twentieth year, or March 14, 445 BC, and ended on Nisan 10, or April 6 in AD 32. Anderson asserted these dates are 173,880 days—sixty-nine weeks of prophetic years—apart.[358] In summary, the Anderson start date is impossible, the end date is incorrectly converted, and the time span is off by two days. The Anderson dates cannot be adjusted into viability.

Anderson's required date for Nisan 1—March 14—is earlier than any Nisan 1 in the Persian era[359] (except for 537 BC,[360] see figure 21). Parker and Dubberstein, authoritative for Persia, place Nisan 1, 445 BC, on April 13.[361]

Anderson's end date is misaligned with the Hebrew date. Anderson put Nisan 1 of AD 32 on March 28, impossibly *before* the new moon on March 29.[362]

Anderson's period started March 14, 445 BC, and ended on April 6, AD 32. The respective JDNs (Julian Day Numbers, see appendix A.5.1) are 1,558,960 and 1,732,842. The time span is 173,882 days—overshot by two. This was not apparent in Anderson's calculations— he used Julian calendar dates but added *Gregorian* calendar leap years—despite having addressed the issue directly.[363] This incorrectly mixed the Julian and Gregorian calendars. A valid calculation would use either Gregorian dates with 116 Gregorian leap days or Julian dates with 119 Julian leap days.

According to **Dr. Harold Hoehner** (1977), the prophecy started on Nisan 1, or March 5 of 444 BC, and ended Nisan 10, or March 30 in AD 33. Hoehner asserted these are 173,880 days—sixty-nine weeks of prophetic years—apart.[364] In summary, the start date is impossible and the time span is off by four days. The Hoehner dates cannot be adjusted into viability.

Dr. Hoehner's date for Nisan 1—March 5—is earlier than any Persian Nisan 1, without exception (figure 21). Parker and Dubberstein place Nisan 1 in 444 BC on April 3.[365]

Dr. Hoehner's required period ran from March 5, 444 BC, to March 30, AD 33. The respective JDNs (appendix A.5.1) are 1,559,316 and 1,733,200—a difference of 173,884—overshot by four days. In his calculation, Hoehner correctly noted that *Julian* March 5, 444 BC, and *Julian* March 5, AD 33, are 476 Julian years apart, but then multiplied those 476 Julian years by 365.242—the number of days in the *Gregorian* year.[366] This incorrectly mixed the Julian and Gregorian calendars. A valid calculation would use either Gregorian dates and 365.242 days per year or Julian dates and 365.25 days per year.

> Despite missing some technical details, Anderson and Hoehner still deserve immense credit for advancing our understanding. Their *interpretation* will prove valid.

A.4.1 Commands, Decrees, and Words

In Daniel 9:25, *decree* is from the Hebrew *dabar* meaning "word." *Dabar* appears over 1,400 times in Scripture: 829 times as *word* and thirty-six times as *decree, command,* or *message*. Significantly, *dabar* is a basic word used in many contexts. It neither requires nor excludes a human or divine source. It is general, not specific.[367] Here are the original words used for each of the four biblical decrees (chapter 7) to restore and rebuild Jerusalem:

1. Cyrus	*kol*	(Ezra 1:1)	proclamation
2. Darius	*taim*	(Ezra 6:12)	decree (Aramaic)
3. Ezra	*taim*	(Ezra 7:13)	decree (Aramaic)
4. Nehemiah	*iggerot*	(Neh. 2:9)	letters

Scripture might have indicated one of these four decrees by using the word *dabar*, but it doesn't.[368] So we can't exclude any of them based on language alone. The point remains open for other Scripture to define.

Note Daniel 9:25 writes "issuing of a decree" (*motsa dabar*) instead of just "decree" (*dabar*). Two verses prior, in Daniel 9:23, the angel announced that at the beginning of Daniel's prayer, "a command was issued" (*yatsa dabar*—*yatsa* relates to *motsa*) from God.[369] This is an example of *dabar* referring to a divine word in Daniel 9.

> The decrees from Darius and to Ezra use the Aramaic word *taim*. Although only small parts of the Old Testament are in Aramaic,[370] they do refer to three of these decrees. (Ezra 6:3 refers to Cyrus' decree also as *taim*.) Biblical Aramaic reference to those three decrees exclude direct comparison with Daniel's *dabar*.[371]

Looking ahead a bit, we will see that Scripture defines Daniel's "from the issuing of a decree to restore and rebuild Jerusalem" as the issuing of each of these four scriptural decrees, including the one to Nehemiah.

A.4.2 Did Nehemiah Count Artaxerxes' Years from Zero or One?

> Don't be intimidated by this topic. It's far simpler than scholars often portray. The key question is simply if Nehemiah started counting the king's years at *zero* or at *one*.

Babylonian and Persian scribes used the accession year (year zero). Historians and Bible scholars traditionally apply the accession year to Persian King Artaxerxes' reign. This assumption is so dominant that it's rarely questioned.[372]

An ancient papyrus (AP6) from a Jewish colony in Egypt was dated to the "accession year" of Artaxerxes.[373] This shows that Jewish scribes used the accession year for Artaxerxes, and by *assumption*, so did Nehemiah. This book accepts the validity of this evidence.

But the *assumption* might not be valid. AP6 was created in December 465 BC, when most Jews were still in Babylon. At that time, all Jews—both scribes and nonscribes—used the accession year to date kings' years, in step with the rest of Babylon.

This section will show that Jews used Babylonian dating while in Babylon, and then immediately resumed their traditional dating methods upon returning to Jerusalem. Scripture shows that this was neither the first nor the only time Jews made such a change. Nehemiah wrote his account years *after* Ezra's mass return to Jerusalem. Nehemiah did not use the accession year (year zero), but instead counted Artaxerxes' first day as king to his **first** year, per Jewish tradition. *How do we know?*

Although historians count Artaxerxes' years using an accession year (year zero), only Nehemiah's count matters here. Nehemiah's date is written in first person, from Nehemiah himself. The following evidence shows Nehemiah applied the traditional Judean nonaccession year (year one). First, *how can we know the nonaccession year was traditional for Jews?*

If Jews traditionally used the nonaccession year (year one), then we would see:

1. Jewish and Babylonian references to the same event, dated to the same king, with the Jewish count one year higher (+1) than the Babylonian

2. A shortage of biblical events dated to a king's "accession year" (year zero)

Jewish and Babylonian Dates for the Same Event

Babylonians captured Judean King Jehoiachin in 597 BC. That event was recorded in both the Babylonian Chronicle and in the Bible:

> In the **seventh year** [of Nebuchadnezzar], the month of Kislimu, the king of Akkad mustered his troops, marched to the Hatti-land, and encamped against the city of Judah and on the second day of the month of Adar he seized the city and **captured the king** [Jehoiachin].[374] (Babylonian Chronicle, bolding added)

> At that time the servants of Nebuchadnezzar the king of Babylon went up to Jerusalem, and the city came under siege. And Nebuchadnezzar the king of Babylon came to the city, while his servants were besieging it. Then Jehoiachin the king of Judah went out to the king of Babylon, he, his mother, his servants, his commanders, and his officials. And the king of Babylon took him prisoner in the eighth year of his reign. (2 Kings 24:10–12)

Jehoiachin's capture is recorded by Babylonians in Nebuchadnezzar's **seventh** year and by Jews in his **eighth**.[375] We know Babylonians used the accession year. This suggests Jews may have used the nonaccession year as it accounts for the one-year difference.

Shortage of Accession-Year References

More evidence comes from Scripture. If Jews used the accession year, we would expect to see Jews dating at least some events to a king's "accession year." *Do we?* Not really.

The Bible dates approximately one hundred unique events to a king's year, but not a single event explicitly to a king's "accession year." This isn't just a curious under-representation; it's a total and significant absence, as the chart shows.

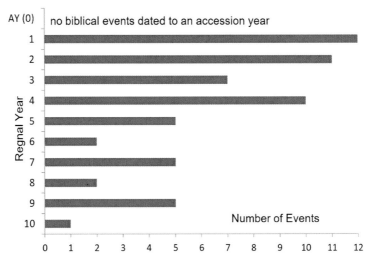

Count of Biblical Events Dated to Kings' Numbered Years

Figure 19. Tally of biblical references to each numbered regnal year. No events are explicitly dated to any king's *accession year* (AY).

> Scripture dates twelve events to the "first year" of a king's reign, eleven to the second year, seven to the third, and so on. No event is dated explicitly to a king's "accession year" (AY). The graph shows the results of a simple Bible search of "the accession year of," "the first year of," "the second year of," and so on, until "the tenth year of."[376] All references not to a king's years were omitted. Results are tallied by year number. No reference to "accession year of" or even "accession" was found. Searches of the ASV, ESV, KJV, NASB, NIV, and NKJV confirm the result.[377] No search for a Hebrew term is possible because its Hebrew equivalent never appears in Scripture. We conclude there is no biblical event dated *explicitly* to a king's "accession year."

If Jews used the accession year, we would expect to find at least some events dated explicitly to an "accession year," but we don't. This doesn't prove Jews never used it but is evidence that the accession year was, at best, the exception and not the rule. But we can find indirect evidence of three exceptions. As is so often the case, the exceptions help define the rule.

Exceptions That Define the Rule

The Bible does date three events *indirectly* to an accession year. These aren't explicit but rather paraphrased descriptions of an accession year.

1. **"in the year that he became king"** (562 BC) King Evil-merodach:

   > Now it came about in the thirty-seventh year of the exile of Jehoiachin king of Judah, in the twelfth month, on the twenty-seventh day of the month, that Evil-merodach king of Babylon, in the year that he became king, released Jehoiachin king of Judah from prison; (2 Kings 25:27)

2. **"in the beginning of his reign"** (530 BC) King Cambyses, biblical throne name Ahasuerus/Xerxes:

   > Now in the reign of Ahasuerus, in the beginning of his reign, they wrote an accusation against the inhabitants of Judah and Jerusalem. (Ezra 4:6)

3. **"in the days of"** (522 BC) King Bardiya/Smerdis, biblical name Artaxerxes (he reigned only a few weeks, so his *only* year was an accession year):

   > And in the days of Artaxerxes, Bishlam, Mithredath, Tabeel, and the rest of his colleagues wrote to Artaxerxes king of Persia; and the text of the letter was written in Aramaic and translated from Aramaic. (Ezra 4:7)

Note each reference *describes* an accession year. If Jews followed traditional dating, they would have written "in year one" as they did elsewhere in Scripture. But here, they didn't. These three passages paraphrase "accession year" without using a specific word for it. This is remarkable and allows us to draw two conclusions.

First, Jews never used any standard term for "accession year" in Scripture. They not only paraphrased it, but they did so in (at least) *three different ways*. In contrast, Babylonian scribes routinely used a specific term for "accession year."[378] This suggests Jews traditionally didn't apply the accession year, because they didn't use a standard name for it.

Second, these three exceptions occur within a relatively short forty-year window. The Old Testament's other four thousand years fail to explicitly date any event to a king's accession year. These three exceptions falling in quick sequence stick out like a proverbial sore thumb. It seems Jews used the accession year *only* during this brief period. What makes this period of time different?

These events occurred when the center of Judaism was outside the land of Israel. Jews were removed to Babylon right after Jerusalem's destruction and returned with Ezra, decades later. We know this because Scripture shows that Jews started using the accession year precisely when they were removed from Judah to Babylon. *How do we know?*

Confirmation in Jeremiah 52 and 2 Kings 25

Jeremiah records events before, during, and after Jews' removal from Judah to Babylon. First, Jeremiah 52:12 records a Babylonian officer approaching Jerusalem in the "nineteenth year of King Nebuchadnezzar." Jeremiah used the nonaccession year here because he dated a *later* event to the "eighteenth year of Nebuchadnezzar" (Jeremiah 52:29). This downcount can be explained by his switching abruptly from nonaccession to accession year between those two verses. *Why the sudden change?* This is found between these two verses, in Jeremiah 52:27, "So Judah was led into exile from its land."[379]

How can we be sure? Because 2 Kings 25 shows the same progression. Verse 8 uses the nonaccession year. Then Judah was led out of its land in verse 21. Finally, verse 27 reflects accession-year dating. Scripture provides a confirmation.

When the people of Judah were deported to Babylon, their dating method switched from nonaccession to accession year in harmony with their Babylonian host culture. Therefore, taken together, we have scriptural evidence supporting this rule:

> Jews used the nonaccession year (year one) when the center of Judaism was in the land of Israel, and the accession year (year zero) when the center of Judaism was in Babylon, from 587 BC to 457 BC.

When did the center of Judaism return to Jerusalem? The short answer—presented in chapter 14—is with Ezra's 457 BC return. Historical evidence indicates that Jews resumed their own traditional calendar at that time.[380]

> *Why* did Jews change dating systems like that? It might be due to practicality. Jews may have simply adopted Babylon's method for the same reason we set our watches forward two hours when flying from Denver to Atlanta. Jews simply adopted their host country's use of the accession year (year zero). In this context, any Jewish scribe would have used the accession year to date events during the Babylonian captivity to ensure all Jews would correctly understand exactly *when* something happened. That's the whole point of recording a date.

Nehemiah's decree issued years *after* Jews were reestablished in Jerusalem and resumed their traditional dating methods. Thus, Nehemiah used the nonaccession year (year one). This places Nisan of King Artaxerxes' twentieth year in **446 BC** (figure 6).

A.5.1 The Julian Day Number

Astronomy provides an excellent tool for measuring long time spans. The **Julian Day Number** (JDN) is designed to help the calculation of long time spans—even millions of days—quickly and precisely. It's easy because it's so straightforward. The JDN is simply a **continuous count of days**. It starts at zero on January 1, 4713 BC,[381] and counts up each day, one by one, to the present time and beyond. Each day in history has an actual number, a unique and permanent JDN.[382] We're almost up to day number 2.5 million now. JDNs are available on some astronomy websites, including NASA's.[383]

> Websites often display JDN as a half day (x.5) because calendar days advance at midnight, but JDNs advance at noon, GMT. Thus, for Judah, always round JDNs **up, not down**. When using JDNs, double-check to note Julian or Gregorian calendars and BC or AD years. Note, JDNs shouldn't be confused with "ordinal date," which is the sequential count of days within a single year and is often mislabeled "Julian date."

JS Brown

February 15, 2020

Dear Mr. Brown,

Below are the Julian Day Numbers (JDN) corresponding to each of the requested calendar dates. Note that the listed JDN corresponds to noon UT on each given date. Thus, the span of time elapsing between any two dates equals the numerical difference between the respective JDN values, in units of days. Note also that, by convention, dates falling prior to October 5, 1582 CE are presented as Julian Calendar dates, and dates falling after October 5, 1582 CE are presented as Gregorian calendar dates.

Date			JDN	Date			JDN
25 Jul	606	BCE	1,500,287	3 Sep	8	CE	1,724,226
16 Aug	587	BCE	1,507,249	18 Apr	27	CE	1,731,027
22 Jul	537	BCE	1,525,487	22 Apr	31	CE	1,732,492
14 Aug	518	BCE	1,532,449	20 Sep	66	CE	1,745,427
27 Mar	457	BCE	1,554,590	24 Sep	70	CE	1,746,892
1 Apr	446	BCE	1,558,612	29 Nov	1947	CE	2,432,519
5 Jun	6	BCE	1,719,387	15 May	1948	CE	2,432,687
26 Feb	5	BCE	1,719,653	7 Apr	1967	CE	2,439,588
12 Aug	5	BCE	1,719,821	7 Jun	1967	CE	2,439,649
4 Jul	8	CE	1,724,165				

Sincerely,
Dr. Geza Gyuk
Senior Associate
Kavli Institute for Cosmological Physics

William Eckhardt Research Center (ERC) - Suite 499, 5640 South Ellis Avenue, Chicago, IL 60637

Figure 20. Julian Day Numbers (JDN) of key dates, which are all verifiable online. Note that the astronomer Dr. Gyuk was provided a list of dates and asked simply to list their corresponding JDNs with no leading knowledge of this book's context or thesis. JDNs are verifiable via some astronomy websites, including NASA's.

To find the number of days between any two dates, just look up their respective JDNs and subtract. The numerical difference is the exact number of days in between. It's really that simple. The JDN is a *huge* time-saver. This book uses it alongside longhand arithmetic as a double check. Fortunately, astronomy websites accurately convert JDNs to and from Julian calendar dates for all dates in recorded history.

> For example, July 4, 1776, is JDN 2,369,916, and December 2, 2022, is JDN 2,459,916. We know the USA was exactly 90,000 days old on December 2, 2022, because:
>
> 2,459,916 – 2,369,916 = 90,000 days
> from July 4, 1776, to December 2, 2022.
>
> Internet-sourced JDNs are indeed reliable for Julian calendar dates, but not for Hebrew calendar dates. To obtain a correct JDN, a biblical-era Hebrew date must first be converted to the Julian calendar before referencing its JDN.

A.5.2 Nisan in AD 31 Began in April, Not March

The modern Hebrew (Hillel II) calendar is algorithmic. It contains fixed cycles of leap years and set month lengths. It was adopted c. AD 359 and is still used today,[384] most notably by internet date converters. Using those for biblical Hebrew dates is probably the *single most common mistake* in biblical chronology.

In the biblical era, the Hebrew calendar was natural, not algorithmic. Eyewitness observation of the moon and natural springtime (appendix B) determined new months and leap years (intercalations). The Talmud records calendrical rules used in that era.

The modern Hebrew (Hillel II) calendar places Nisan 1 in AD 31 on March 13. But this was far too early for Nisan 1. The lunar month starting March 13 would have been a leap month *Adar II*. In AD 31, Nisan started on April 12. *How do we know?* Because in the biblical era, leap-year decisions were governed by the equinox.

> On account of three things we intercalate a month into the year: on account of the grain's ripening [...] the tree fruits ripening [...] and on account of the season [equinox][385] (Talmud)

> This book does not ascribe scriptural authority to the Talmud but does cite it as a reliable historical source of Jewish culture and thought in the era of our study.

Jews observed the equinox to keep holidays from drifting out of season. Remember, twelve Hebrew months held only 354 days, so the leap month *Adar II* was inserted every two or three years to keep holidays in their proper season (appendix B). In AD 31, when Jews viewed the crescent on March 13, the temple would have intercalated (declared the leap month *Adar II*). We know this because the Talmud requires the Festival of *Sukkot* (Tabernacles), which begins on Tishri 15, to fall after the autumn equinox.[386]

In AD 31, the autumn equinox fell on September 25.[387] Without intercalation, *Sukkot* (Tishri 15) would have fallen on September 20 or 21, *before* the equinox. That would have violated the above Talmudic rule. Thus, Jews almost certainly intercalated AD 31, pushing the start of Nisan to April. That Talmudic rule requires Nisan 1 to fall **after March 17** in the New Testament era in a normal year (without famine).

> Famine years were not intercalated to avoid delaying the grain harvest.[388] There is no record of famine in AD 31 Judea. Note Jews were fully capable of calculating the equinox for making leap month (intercalation) decisions. Note also, the earliest historically observed Babylonian/Persian (figure 21) date for Nisan 1 in the *Old Testament Era* is March 21 (ignoring the one outlier).

A.6.1 Pauses in Prophecy

Prophecy can contain pauses, even ones that aren't explicitly mentioned. This example was written seven centuries before Jesus' birth:

> For a Child will be born to us, a Son will be given to us;
> And the government will rest on His shoulders;
> And His name will be called Wonderful Counselor, Mighty God,
> Eternal Father, Prince of Peace. (Isaiah 9:6)

Christians consider this messianic and see a pause between "a Son will be given to us" and "the government will rest on His shoulders." To some, this pause is about thirty years. To others, it's two thousand years and counting. Another example:

> And He came to Nazareth, where He had been brought up; and as was His custom, He entered the synagogue on the Sabbath, and stood up to read. And the scroll of Isaiah the prophet was handed to Him. And He unrolled the scroll and found the place where it was written: "THE SPIRIT OF THE LORD IS UPON ME, BECAUSE HE ANOINTED ME TO BRING GOOD NEWS TO THE POOR. HE HAS SENT ME TO PROCLAIM RELEASE TO CAPTIVES, AND RECOVERY OF SIGHT TO THE BLIND, TO SET FREE THOSE WHO ARE OPPRESSED, TO PROCLAIM THE FAVORABLE YEAR OF THE LORD." And He rolled up the scroll, gave it back to the attendant, and sat down; and the eyes of all the people in the synagogue were intently directed at Him. Now He began to say to them, "Today this Scripture has been fulfilled in your hearing." (Luke 4:16–21)

Here is the Isaiah passage Jesus read from:

> The Spirit of the Lord GOD is upon me,
> Because the LORD anointed me
> to bring good news to the humble;
> He has sent me to bind up the brokenhearted,
> To proclaim release to captives
> And freedom to prisoners;
> To proclaim the favorable year of the LORD
> And the day of vengeance of our God;
> To comfort all who mourn (Isaiah 61:1–2)

Jesus stopped reading right after "favorable year of the LORD." Jesus announced he would fulfill the purposes he read *at that time*, but not those purposes he didn't read. There is a pause between the favorable year and the day of vengeance. This pause continues beyond today. So yes, there is precedent for pauses in prophecy, even unindicated ones.[389]

A.6.2. The *Atnach*

The *atnach* (aka *etnachta*, *'atnah*) is a major Hebrew cantillation mark (*ta'amim*). Cantillation marks depict the vocal inflection and melody of Hebrew scriptural text, which can literally be sung. *Atnach* in Hebrew means "pause" and it signals a pause in the text.

Cantillation marks are part of the general Hebrew punctuation system called *nikkud*. The current Tiberian nikkud was standardized by the Masoretic copyists who in c. AD 925 produced the Masoretic Text (MT), the oldest recovered copy of the Old Testament with full punctuation. It contains over thirteen thousand atnachs.

Some claim the Masoretes added the atnach to Daniel 9:25 where it didn't exist before.[390] But that claim is a stretch. First, we know the Masoretes drew upon the older Babylonian nikkud to create the Tiberian nikkud. The Babylonian nikkud already had a type of atnach,[391] so we know the Masoretes didn't invent it from scratch.

> Cantillation—singing the Scriptures—goes far back in time. By tradition, Moses (c. 1450 BC) taught Torah cantillation long before cantillation marking.[392] We aren't sure how old cantillation marking is, but the Talmud refers to it during the times of King Solomon (c. 950 BC) and of two notable first-century AD Jewish figures.[393] Note that this book does not ascribe scriptural authority to punctuation. The intent here is *historical*—that is, finding traditional Hebrew interpretations of Daniel 9:25, even though we can't know how far back in time they existed.[394]

What about this specific atnach in Daniel 9:25? Could it have been added or moved to where it didn't exist before? No direct evidence supports that claim.[395] The key point here is that a claim of late addition bears a burden of proof.[396]

> Most Hebrew texts, both ancient and modern, aren't punctuated. The earliest recovered copies of Daniel, among the Dead Sea Scrolls, show "no major disagreements" with the Masoretic Text,[397] but those Dead Sea scroll copies aren't punctuated, so they cannot settle the issue. Unless an older, fully punctuated Hebrew manuscript (i.e., not a translation) is found that either omits this atnach or places it in a different spot, then the *atnach* of Daniel 9:25 cannot be excluded.

Why is this important? Traditionally, both sides of the atnach issue have followed one of two extremes. Asserting it requires Messiah to have arrived seven weeks after a decree issued, *or* excluding it prevents Daniel's seven and sixty-two weeks from being interrupted in any context.[398] Both views are vigorously defended, yet both have failed for centuries to produce a numerically precise, literal solution to Daniel 9:25.[399] This book presents an alternative path. If valid, the atnach simply indicates *where* a pause exists, without defining the separation,[400] as asserted already in 1869 by German theologian C. F. Keil:

> The Atnach does not always separate clauses, but frequently also shows only the point of rest within a clause [401] (Keil)

A.8.1 The First Year of Cyrus

The Bible dates the Edict of Cyrus to "the first year of Cyrus" (2 Chronicles 36:22; Ezra 1:1; 5:13; 6:3). Which BC year is this? Scripture, the Babylonian Chronicle, and other recovered tablets collectively reflect this sequence of events: [402]

1. October 12, 539 BC—Babylon fell to Persia.

2. Babylonian scribes immediately began dating tablets to the "accession year, Cyrus, **King of Babylon**." (e.g., BM56154, *Cyrus* 1)

3. October 29, 539 BC—Cyrus entered Babylon and appointed Ugbaru (Darius the Mede) to form a government. Babylonian scribes began dating tablets to "Cyrus, **King of Lands**" and not to "Cyrus, King of Babylon." (*Cyrus* 2, 4)

4. Daniel dated events to Darius the Mede (Daniel 9:1; 11:1) and not to Cyrus. Thus, we know Daniel didn't follow Babylonian scribal convention.

5. November 538 BC—Ugbaru died.

6. January 537 BC—Babylonian scribes resumed dating tablets to "Cyrus, **King of Babylon**." (*Cyrus* 22, 23)

7. March 12, 537 BC—Nisan 1 fell conspicuously early (figure 21).

Babylonian scribes applied the title "year one of Cyrus, *King of Babylon*, King of Lands" between January and March 537 BC. But the biblical date for his edict isn't from Babylonian scribes, but from Ezra, a Jewish scribe who followed Jewish convention (including Daniel) which differed from the Babylonian at times. This is one of those times. *How do we know?*

Daniel did not follow Babylonian scribal convention. Daniel recorded dates differently than Babylonian scribes did. Daniel dated events to Belshazzar before Babylon's fall, and then to Darius the Mede right after Babylon's fall (Daniel 7:1; 8:1; 9:1; 11:1). Daniel did not date to Nabonidus nor Cyrus, respectively. In contrast, Babylon's scribes dated tablets to Nabonidus before Babylon's fall, and then to Cyrus thereafter, and maintained a count of Cyrus' years, even despite a brief coregency of Cyrus and his son Cambyses. *Daniel dated differently.*

Babylonian scribal convention was also out of step with its own ideal function. Scribes were wrong-footed from the beginning, assuming Cyrus would immediately claim the title "King of Babylon" at conquest. This mistaken assumption is reflected in tablets from October 12 to 29 in 539 BC, dated to the "accession year, Cyrus **King of Babylon**."[403]

Then on October 29, 539 BC, Cyrus entered Babylon, lifted martial law, and promoted Ugbaru from military ruler to vassal king who appointed governors under him. At that point, scribes dropped the title "King of Babylon" from Cyrus, but continued dating documents to his imperial title, "Cyrus, King of Lands."[404]

There is no question that Cyrus was supreme ruler because Babylonian scribes dated events to him using his imperial title "King of Lands," and not "King of Babylon." Cyrus didn't hold the title "King of Babylon" for those fourteen months (neither did Ugbaru), until scribes resumed dating to "Cyrus, **King of Babylon**" in January of 537 BC.[405]

> Why is Darius the Mede identified *probably* as Ugbaru? See appendix A.2.1.

So *why didn't* scribes date to "Ugbaru, King of Babylon"? It's important to note that Daniel never used the title "King of Babylon" for Darius the Mede (take a look, it's not there) despite this being a common inference among scholars. DM held a different position.

The cuneiform record shows scribal convention forming right after Babylon's fall, and scribes sticking with it, dating to Cyrus by whatever title he held at the time and not interrupting his count of years. Any retroactive change to clay tablet documents would have been impractical. It was just easier to keep the count and move on, and we see they did that.

Daniel, like Nehemiah, was not a scribe but a court insider. We know he didn't follow Babylonian scribal convention because he dated some events to Darius, not to Cyrus.

> Darius was king *in* Babylon but not King *of* Babylon. Daniel referred to Darius as "Darius the Mede," "King Darius," "Darius, son of Ahasuerus, of Median descent," and "the king," but never, not once, as *"King of Babylon."* Daniel was a veteran state administrator who knew how to make proper references. Darius was Cyrus' vassal, whom Daniel called king, but wasn't *King of Babylon*.

Ugbaru (Darius the Mede) died in October 538 BC.[406] Three months later, Babylonian scribes added "King of Babylon" to Cyrus' title. We aren't told why, but it may have been due to Ugbaru's death, or to a different reason. What the cuneiform record makes certain is that the news that Cyrus finally took the title "King of Babylon" reached Babylon in January of 537 BC, and that Cyrus continued using that title until the end of his reign in 530 BC.

> Cyrus' son Cambyses held the title "King of Babylon" from May 538 BC until the end of that year. **Darius never held that title** but was instead a vassal king serving as Cyrus' agent and plausibly ruled Babylon alongside the much younger Cambyses until news of Ugbaru's death reached Cyrus, who then decided to take the title himself.

To Daniel, Cyrus started his first year as *King of Babylon* on Nisan 1 in 537 BC.[407] Nisan 1 that year fell freakishly early. Babylon skipped an expected intercalation (leap month). We aren't told why, but they might have wished to avoid delaying Cyrus' participation in the Nisan 1 *akitu* ceremony, marking his official reign as *King of Babylon*. Or there could be a different reason. What we do know is that Persian Nisan 1 would never fall so early ever again. Nisan 1 occurrences during Persian rule in Babylon are tallied in this chart.

Tally of Dates for Nisan 1 from the Fall of Babylon (539 BC) to the End of the Old Testament Era (c. 400 BC) Source: *PDBC*

Figure 21. Nisan 1 fell conspicuously early in 537 BC.

The orphan bar (12 March) **is from 537 BC**. It's a conspicuous outlier. 537 BC is missing an expected intercalation (i.e., added leap month).[408] There is almost certainly a reason for this. Plausibly, it could have been to avoid delaying the Nisan 1 *akitu* festival, which began Cyrus' legitimate first year bearing the official title "King of Babylon" and ended the year of Cambyses as official "King of Babylon." Nisan 1 would never again fall so early in the Persian period.

Daniel was not a scribe, so he was not bound to Babylonian scribal convention. Like Nehemiah ninety-one years later, Daniel was a Jewish court insider who counted the king's years per Judean method. To Daniel and all Jews thereafter, including Ezra, the first year of Cyrus began on **March 12 in 537 BC** (figure 13).

A.9.1 The Earliest Nativity Dating

The earliest known mention of the nativity year was written c. AD 180 by church father Irenaeus: **"our Lord was born about the forty-first year of the reign of Augustus."**[409]

This book does not ascribe scriptural authority to nonbiblical text. However, Irenaeus' authority as a historical source is profound. He was a direct disciple of Polycarp, who was a direct disciple of John the Apostle, who not only knew Jesus but also took his mother Mary into his household after Jesus' crucifixion (John 19:27). Mary was probably the last living eyewitness to the nativity and would have certainly recalled the correct year in terms familiar to her own Jewish culture. It's not something a mother forgets.

Because Irenaeus' remark is not part of any chronological argument, we have reason to believe it passed directly from John to Polycarp to Irenaeus. Thus, we can accept Irenaeus' "forty-first year" of Augustus as an authoritative *Jewish* reference to the nativity year. Later references' authorities are not as well established, and some may have simply paraphrased Irenaeus' date in terms familiar to other cultures' (e.g., Egyptian) dating systems.

Different scholars fit Augustus' *forty-first year* into different BC years by applying different dating methods and by equally weighting later, less authoritative sources.[410] But Judean dating method (appendices A.4.2 and D.1) used consistently throughout this book, places the *forty-first year* of Augustus between spring 5 BC and spring 4 BC. This harmonizes with a summer 5 BC nativity identified in chapter 9 and confirmed in chapter 10.

    A. Julius Caesar was murdered on March 15 of 44 BC. Caesar's will, opened before his dramatic funeral, named Augustus (Octavian) his heir. Augustus then began his ultimately successful rise to power as sole emperor.[411]

    B. Jews did not apply the accession year when they were in the land of Israel. Thus, Jews counted Augustus' first day to his "year one" (appendix A.4.2).

    C. Jews advanced the years of foreign kings (e.g., Augustus) from Nisan 1. In 44 BC, this fell on April 20,[412] about a month after his March accession. This means that by Judean counting, Augustus' first regnal year was about a month long and ended as his second year started on Nisan 1, which was April 20 of 44 BC.

Augustus' Years **per Judean Count**

From	BC	Year	BC	To	From	BC	Year	BC	To
Mar	44	1	44	Apr	Apr	24	22	23	Apr
Apr	44	2	43	Apr	Apr	23	23	22	Apr
Apr	43	3	42	Apr	Apr	22	24	21	Apr
Apr	42	4	41	Apr	Apr	21	25	20	Apr
Apr	41	5	40	Apr	Apr	20	26	19	Apr
Apr	40	6	39	Apr	Apr	19	27	18	Apr
Apr	39	7	38	Apr	Apr	18	28	17	Apr
Apr	38	8	37	Apr	Apr	17	29	16	Apr
Apr	37	9	36	Apr	Apr	16	30	15	Apr
Apr	36	10	35	Apr	Apr	15	31	14	Apr
Apr	35	11	34	Apr	Apr	14	32	13	Apr
Apr	34	12	33	Apr	Apr	13	33	12	Apr
Apr	33	13	32	Apr	Apr	12	34	11	Apr
Apr	32	14	31	Apr	Apr	11	35	10	Apr
Apr	31	15	30	Apr	Apr	10	36	9	Apr
Apr	30	16	29	Apr	Apr	9	37	8	Apr
Apr	29	17	28	Apr	Apr	8	38	7	Apr
Apr	28	18	27	Apr	Apr	7	39	6	Apr
Apr	27	19	26	Apr	Apr	6	40	5	Apr
Apr	26	20	25	Apr	Apr	5	41	4	Apr Nativity
Apr	25	21	24	Apr	Apr	4	42	3	Apr

Figure 22. Augustus' first forty-two regnal years per Judean dating method. April is proxy for Nisan 1. This harmonizes with the calculated August 12, 5 BC, nativity date.

Why source only Irenaeus? Other church fathers (i.a., Tertullian, Origen, Eusebius) also referenced different nativity years. Yet, attempting to reconcile all sources likely reduces, not increases, reliability for these reasons:

1. **Primacy**—Irenaeus provided the *first* known reference to the nativity year. Later references quite possibly sourced Irenaeus' date and then converted it into dates on other cultures' calendars (e.g., Greek, Syriac, Egyptian, etc.) with varying degrees of accuracy. We can't conclude this was so in every case, but was highly likely so in enough cases that inaccuracies appeared. Irenaeus was widely read in the ancient world.

2. **Authority**—Irenaeus was a disciple of Polycarp, who was a disciple of John the Apostle. John was not only a disciple of Jesus, but he also took Mary, mother of Jesus, into his household after the crucifixion (John 19:27). Irenaeus was in a position to know.

3. **Context**—Irenaeus mentioned this nativity year as an aside remark in a section having *nothing to do with chronology*. He was not trying to make a chronological argument. Some later sources did, to some degree. Again, not in every case, but surely in some. But in Irenaeus' case, there is no possibility of a tendentious argument, because it's not even an argument in the first place.

Thus, equally weighting additional references, as does, for example, Finegan, would reduce, not increase, reliability in identifying the nativity year.

A.9.2 John the Baptist Conceived after Pentecost

The three Hebrew pilgrimage festivals are Passover, Pentecost, and Tabernacles. After which festival was John the Baptist conceived?

Of the three, we may quickly exclude Tabernacles. Jesus, conceived six months after John, would have been born roughly fifteen months after John's *conception*. Fifteen months after Tabernacles (October) is squarely in winter (January). This chapter has shown the nativity did not occur in winter; thus John wasn't conceived after Tabernacles. This leaves Passover and Pentecost. Evidence favors Pentecost.

Scholars have often placed the nativity on a Hebrew holiday because other major events also occurred on holidays.

Jesus was conceived six months after John was conceived (Luke 1:36). If John were conceived after Passover (April), then Jesus would have been born about fifteen months later, in the Hebrew month *Tammuz* (July). The only Hebrew holidays in *Tammuz* are minor. A post-Passover conception for John lacks supporting evidence.

Evidence supports Pentecost. If John was conceived right after Pentecost (May/June), then Jesus would have been born about fifteen months later, in Hebrew months *Av* or *Elul* (August/September). This period does include one major Jewish holiday called **Tisha b'Av**.

Pentecost fell fifty days after the first weekly Sabbath after Passover.[413] In 6 BC, Pentecost fell on May 30, a Sunday.[414] Zechariah's priestly duties ended on the Sabbath after Pentecost, which was Saturday, June 5. Zechariah then went home to his wife Elizabeth and they conceived John. No intervening events are mentioned. Taken at face value, Scripture indicates John's conception *plausibly* on **June 5** in **6 BC**.[415]

A.10.1 Jeremiah's Prophecy of the Captivity

Chapter 10 asserts the seventy-year captivity of Jeremiah 29 ended on the date of Cyrus' edict. *Is this true?* Jeremiah foretold seventy years of captivity and desolation.

> For this is what the LORD says: 'When seventy years have been completed for Babylon, I will visit you and fulfill My good word to you, to bring you back to this place. (Jeremiah 29:10)

> This entire land will be a place of ruins and an object of horror, and these nations will serve the king of Babylon for seventy years. (Jeremiah 25:11)

Jeremiah 29 foretells Jews' captivity, and Jeremiah 25 foretells the land would lie in ruins. Both indicate a period of seventy years. The two periods of time—the *captivity* and the *desolation*—are often conflated. They partly overlap and are of equal lengths but are not identical. They start and end on different dates.[416]

The captivity began when the first Jewish captives were taken in 606 BC (chapter 2, appendix D.2). The desolation began when Jerusalem was destroyed in 587 BC (appendices A.13.1 and D.3). Our focus here is the **captivity**.

The captivity began when Daniel and others were forcibly removed to Babylon. It ended seventy prophetic years later with the Edict of Cyrus in 537 BC.[417] Chapter 10 places Cyrus' edict on July 22, 537 BC. If the captivity lasted seventy prophetic years (25,200 days), then we can calculate an imputed date of Daniel's capture:

Edict of Cyrus	JDN 1,525,487	July 22, 537 BC
Less 70 prophetic years	-25,200	days
Renders:	JDN 1,500,287	**July 25, 606 BC**

This falls in the correct year as shown in appendix D.2 (for JDN see appendix A.5.1).

A.11.1 The Chronology of Darius the Great

Zechariah used the accession year and advanced Darius at Nisan. *How can we know?*

Jews used the accession year when Judah was outside the land of Israel (appendix A.4.2). Ezra the scribe used the accession year (chapter 14) and dated the start of temple reconstruction to the second year of Darius.[418] Haggai dated this same event to the same year.[419] Therefore, Haggai also used the accession year. Haggai and Zechariah were contemporaries.[420] This indicates Zechariah also used the accession year.

Zechariah's prophecies, taken alone, do not show when he advanced Darius' years. But we know Haggai advanced Darius' years from Nisan because he dated one prophecy before Tishri and a later one after Tishri—to the *same* year of Darius.[421] This excludes a Tishri advance and indicates Nisan. Zechariah lived alongside Haggai. This indicates they both advanced Darius from Nisan.

Jews dated events using the same dating method concurrently (appendix D.1).

A.12.1 AD 8 Was Not Intercalated

In AD 8, the post-Adar new moon fell on February 25.[422] That year should have had a leap month added, all else being equal. History indicates however that all else was certainly not equal that year. The months leading into spring of AD 8 saw extreme famine in Judea.

In AD 7, Jews launched a rebellion against Rome. This was brutally crushed by the Roman military. Severe famine followed.[423] The Talmud writes that Jews didn't intercalate (add a leap month to) famine years.[424] Thus, Jews would not have intercalated AD 8. This puts Tishri 15 in AD 8 on September 3—extremely early in the solar year. The exact chronology is explained in greater depth in appendix C.12.

A.13.1 Jeremiah's Prophecy of the Desolation

Jeremiah 25:11 foretells, and 2 Chronicles 36:21 confirms, that the land of Judah would lie desolate for seventy years. This period is equal in length to the captivity and partly overlaps it.[425] The two periods—captivity and desolation—should not be conflated. *How can we know they're separate?* Scripture tells us so. Writing *after* Jews started rebuilding the temple but *before* Darius' decree, Zechariah wrote:

> Then the angel of the L ORD said, "L ORD of armies, how long
> will You take no pity on Jerusalem and the cities of Judah,
> with which You have been indignant for these seventy years?"
> (Zechariah 1:12)

These "seventy years" ended when a "measuring line will be stretched over Jerusalem" and "craftsmen" will "terrify" the "horns of the nations."[426] These seventy years ended when Darius' decree issued, and Jews no longer feared punishment for building, but suddenly their neighbors feared punishment for obstructing the work.

The desolation began when Babylon destroyed Jerusalem in 587 BC. Chapter 11 identified the date of Darius' decree as August 14, 518 BC. If the desolation lasted seventy prophetic years (25,200 days) as asserted, then we can calculate a date for Jerusalem's destruction:

Decree of Darius	JDN 1,532,449	**Aug 14, 518 BC**
Less 70 prophetic years	-25,200	**days**
Renders:	JDN 1,507,249	**Aug 16, 587 BC**

August 16, 587 BC, or Av 27, is the imputed date of Jerusalem's destruction. Although Babylon destroyed the temple on Av 9, they took longer to dismantle Jerusalem. That Jerusalem was destroyed in 587 BC, see appendix D.3. For JDN, see appendix A.5.1.

A.14.1 The Chronology of Artaxerxes Longimanus, per Ezra

Ezra dated Artaxerxes with the accession year and advanced his years each Tishri. Ezra was a Jewish scribe who followed Jewish scribal convention so other Jewish scribes could correctly understand his dates. So, what was Jewish scribal convention in 457 BC?

At some point shortly after Artaxerxes became king, Jewish scribes switched from a Nisan to a Tishri advance (appendix A.4.2). Evidence comes from papyri recovered from the Jewish community at Elephantine in Egypt. One recovered papyrus (AP6, January 464 BC) is dated to the "accession year" of Artaxerxes.[427] This shows Jewish scribes *at first* advanced the king's years at Nisan. If they had at first advanced at Tishri, then AP6 would have been dated to Artaxerxes' *first* year because scribes already knew he took the throne *before* Tishri of 465 BC. Evidence also shows Jewish scribes extended Artaxerxes' accession year past Nisan and started his first year in the next Tishri, according to this sequence:

1. Artaxerxes became king in August 465 BC.

2. At first, all scribes used the accession year and a Nisan advance.

3. Jews then decided to advance his years at Tishri, not Nisan.

4. Jewish scribes continued to date to his *accession year* after Nisan 1.

5. Jewish scribes dated to Artaxerxes' *first year* on Tishri 1, 464 BC.

Jewish scribes started Artaxerxes' first year on Tishri 1 in 464 BC, not 465 BC.[428] Ezra followed Jewish scribal convention. This puts Nisan in Artaxerxes' seventh year in 457 BC, as shown in the chart:

Artaxerxes' Years per Ezra

From	BC	YEAR	BC	To	
Aug	465	AY	465	Oct	
Oct	465	AY	464	Oct	*extended AY*
Oct	464	1	463	Oct	
Oct	463	2	462	Oct	
Oct	462	3	461	Oct	
Oct	461	4	460	Oct	
Oct	460	5	459	Oct	
Oct	459	6	458	Oct	
Oct	458	7	457	Oct	Nisan, 457 BC

Figure 23. Artaxerxes' years with the accession year extended to Tishri 1, 464 BC. Papyrus AP6 confirms the AY was extended (see below). October is proxy for Tishri 1.

Elephantine papyri confirm Jewish scribes advanced King Xerxes' years at Nisan and then advanced his son King Artaxerxes' years at Tishri.

> **Xerxes/Nisan:** Papyri AP5 and AP6 indicate Jews advanced Xerxes' years at Nisan. Although Horn and Wood present AP5 on a Tishri-based table in Xerxes' fourteenth year,[429] their text indicates Xerxes' fifteenth year. Fotheringham confirms AP5 to Xerxes' fifteenth.[430] This evidence confirms that Jews advanced Xerxes (the father) at Nisan, not Tishri.
>
> **Artaxerxes/Tishri:** Two papyri (Kraeling 3 and AP10) are dated to Artaxerxes' twenty-eighth year in *Elul* (Sep) and twenty-ninth year in *Kislev* (Dec), both in 437 BC. This shows a Tishri advance, as Tishri falls between Elul and Kislev, and the king's years advanced.[431] Ezra was a Jewish scribe and would have also followed this Jewish scribal convention.

Remarkably, Artaxerxes is the only "foreign" king that Jews advanced at Tishri, as they did for Judean kings. And there are other odd aspects of Artaxerxes' chronology.

First, for Artaxerxes, Jewish scribal convention is shifted one year from ideal. Jews counted the months after Tishri of 465 to his accession year, not to his first year as they normally should have. We know this because Elephantine papyrus AP6 (January 464 BC) is dated to Artaxerxes' "accession year," as noted above.[432] Second, AP6 is oddly dated to two kings: both Xerxes and Artaxerxes. This is highly unusual and possibly due to doubts that Artaxerxes would retain the throne, given the usurper Artabanus' authority at that time (chapter 4).

Further evidence is from cuneiform tablet LBAT 1419, which contains these entries:[433]

1. Eclipse observation astronomically fixed to June 5/6, 465 BC

2. "Month VI was intercalary" (announced in advance)

3. "Month V, [Av], the 14th[?], Xerxes—his son killed him." (August 465 BC)

This sequence shows why, after Xerxes' August death, both Jewish and Babylonian scribes began dating to Artaxerxes' accession year and intended to advance the new king's years from Nisan, as before. Then at some point before Nisan 1, *Jewish* scribes decided to advance Artaxerxes' years from Tishri instead, and thus extended his accession year to the next Tishri in 464 BC. Again, we aren't sure *why* Jews did this. We only know they did, because both the historical (AP6) and scriptural records reflect this.

Jewish scribes switched to Tishri after scribal convention was already set. Any retroactive change would have thrown contracts, deeds, loans, etc., into chaos. So, it was easier to extend the king's accession year rather than retroactively end it in the prior Tishri.[434] Their documents show they did exactly that.

By *Jewish* scribal convention, Artaxerxes' first year began on Tishri 1 (Oct) in 464 BC.[435] Thus, Jewish scribes counted Artaxerxes' years short by one relative to ideal.

A.14.2 Reconciling Ezra and Nehemiah

Ezra's dating of Artaxerxes doesn't align with Nehemiah's (see chapters 4 and 14). We cannot ignore the discrepancy. We must understand why they diverge. Remarkably, the difference is two years, not one. Figure 24 shows that Artaxerxes' year 7 to Ezra was Artaxerxes' year 9 to Nehemiah. Same year, different number. Why? Two reasons account for this:

Accession Year—One Year of Difference

Nehemiah used traditional nonaccession year dating (year one), and Ezra used accession year dating (year zero). Appendix A.4.2 shows how Jews abruptly adopted the accession year (year zero) in 587 BC when the Jewish people were removed from their land. When the center of Judaism moved back to Jerusalem in 457 BC, Jews resumed their traditional nonaccession (year one) dating. Ezra's decree issued right before that return and is dated with an accession year (year zero). Nehemiah's decree issued after that return and is dated with a nonaccession year (year one). This accounts for **one year** of the two-year difference.

Scribal Convention vs. Ideal—Another Year of Difference

The second year of difference is due to month of advance. Evidence shows Jewish scribal convention shifted by one year versus its own ideal function. This is most likely because Jews first intended to advance Artaxerxes' years at Nisan but later decided to advance them at Tishri instead. Scribal convention was already set when Jews switched to Tishri. This disrupted ideal scribal practice (appendix A.14.1). Ezra's count of Artaxerxes' years followed Jewish scribal convention, which lagged two years behind Nehemiah's traditional count. This accounts for the **second year** of the two-year difference.

That accounts for the two years of difference between Ezra's and Nehemiah's datings.

Artaxerxes' Regnal Years per

Ezra (AY), Nehemiah (NAY)

From		Year	Year		To
Aug	465	AY	1	465	Oct
Oct	465	AY	2	464	Oct
Oct	464	1	3	463	Oct
Oct	463	2	4	462	Oct
Oct	462	3	5	461	Oct
Oct	461	4	6	460	Oct
Oct	460	5	7	459	Oct
Oct	459	6	8	458	Oct
Oct	458	7	9	457	Oct
Oct	457	8	10	456	Oct
Oct	456	9	11	455	Oct
Oct	455	10	12	454	Oct
Oct	454	11	13	453	Oct
Oct	453	12	14	452	Oct
Oct	452	13	15	451	Oct
Oct	451	14	16	450	Oct
Oct	450	15	17	449	Oct
Oct	449	16	18	448	Oct
Oct	448	17	19	447	Oct
Oct	447	18	20	446	Oct

Figure 24. Artaxerxes' years, comparing the counts of Ezra and Nehemiah. Historical evidence indicates a two-year offset. October is proxy for Tishri 1.

A.15.1 Luke Dated Tiberius from AD 12

Luke began counting Tiberius' years either at his AD 12 co-regency accession or at Augustus' AD 14 death. This question splits scholarly opinion to this day.

Tiberius' contemporaries certainly dated his reign from Augustus' death in AD 14. Almost all documents and coins from Tiberius' reign were dated accordingly.[436] Moreover, Josephus wrote that Tiberius reigned 22½ years.[437] Counting back from his March AD 37 death places Tiberius' accession in AD 14. If Luke also dated Tiberius from the death of Augustus, then John the Baptist's ministry would have started in late AD 28 or 29.

The other view is that Luke dated Tiberius from January AD 12, when he became co-regent with Augustus—with equal authority outside Rome, including in Judea. This places the start of John's ministry in AD 25 or 26 (figure 16).

The key question is not how Josephus or other historians dated Tiberius, but rather how *Luke* dated Tiberius. Let's start by examining Luke's exact words:

> Now in the fifteenth year of the reign of Tiberius Caesar, when Pontius Pilate was governor of Judea, and Herod was tetrarch of Galilee and his brother Philip was tetrarch of the region of Ituraea and Trachonitis, and Lysanias was tetrarch of Abilene, in the high priesthood of Annas and Caiaphas, the word of God

came to John, the son of Zechariah, in the wilderness. And he came into all the region around the Jordan, preaching a baptism of repentance for the forgiveness of sins (Luke 3:1–3)

At first glance, it seems Luke made excessive effort to be precise. If Luke thought the dating method were obvious, then the other references to Herod, Lysanias, etc., would be redundant text, out of character for Luke. This suggests Luke knew the dating might not be obvious to us because he sought to resolve the ambiguity with those other references.

We know that people in Luke's time dated emperors' reigns from co-regency accession. Best evidence places Luke in or near the Roman Flavian period when Caesar Titus' years were dated from his accession as co-regent with his father Vespasian.[438] This does not prove Luke used co-regency dating, only that co-regency dating was used in Luke's day, even if not in Tiberius' day. So we can't dismiss co-regency dating simply because Tiberius' contemporaries didn't use it. This is *Luke's* date. Luke might have used it. *How can we know?* Scripture supports Luke's dating Tiberius from AD 12.

The Jews then said, "It took forty-six years to build this temple, and yet You will raise it up in three days?" (John 2:20)

To review chapter 9, temple construction began in Herod's eighteenth year (October 20 BC to October 19 BC).[439] Forty-six years later is October AD 27 to October AD 28. Because this verse was spoken during Passover, it was spoken in April of AD 28.[440]

This was the first recorded Passover of Jesus' ministry. This places Jesus' baptism before April AD 28 and indicates Luke dated Tiberius from his co-regency accession in AD 12.[441] Had Luke dated Tiberius from Augustus' AD 14 death, then Jesus could not have been baptized before Passover AD 28. Taking Scripture at face value brings us to this conclusion:

> If Luke counted the years of Tiberius according to that [co-regency] system, all his statements as to time in these early chapters are found to be consistent and accurate.[442] (Ramsay)

Thus, Luke dated Tiberius Caesar from his co-regency accession in January AD 12.

A.15.2 The Date of Jesus' Baptism

Scriptural accounts of Jesus' baptism are in Matthew 3:13–17; Mark 1:9–13; Luke 3:21–22. John's Gospel mentions the baptism but doesn't directly record it.

> Note that John 1:19-52 recounts events *after* Jesus' baptism. We know this because here, Jesus departed John the Baptist for Cana in Galilee, yet after his baptism, Jesus left "immediately" for the wilderness. There are many methods of synchronizing the Gospels. Many, but not all, harmonize with this thesis, but that's beyond our scope.

Jesus was baptized on Friday, April 18, AD 27. The Hebrew date is Nisan 21, the last day of the Festival of Unleavened Bread, an annual Sabbath falling right before the weekly Sabbath. Jesus departed for the wilderness, plausibly that Sunday (JDN 1,731,029), and stayed exactly forty days[443] until Friday, May 30, AD 27 (JDN 1,731,069), two days before attending Pentecost in Jerusalem on Sunday, June 1. This is an exact hand-in-glove fit.

> The Sabbath before his baptism—Saturday, April 12, AD 27 (JDN 1,731,021)—was the first weekly Sabbath after Passover, and fifty days before Pentecost (JDN 1,731,071), which was Sunday, June 1, AD 27.[444]

A.16.1 The Length of Jesus' Ministry

Does an AD 27 baptism fit an AD 31 crucifixion? The book of John indicates there were four Passovers during Jesus' ministry.

Passover 1	John 2:13	AD 28
Passover 2	implied	AD 29
Passover 3	John 6:4	AD 30
Passover 4	John 13:1	AD 31

The second Passover is deduced from Scripture. John 4:35 was spoken "four months" before the grain harvest. Thus, Jesus spoke these words in c. January[445] after the Passover of John 2:13 and before the major "feast" (Greek: *heorte*) of John 5:1. This *heorte* feast can only be a Passover or another (Pentecost or Tabernacles) falling after that Passover. Thus, there is a Passover, mentioned or not, *after* the one in John 2:13 and *before* the one in John 6:4.[446]

> The Gospels don't give a complete accounting of holidays during Jesus' ministry. There is much debate on this topic, and settling the issue is beyond this book's scope. The important point is the four identified Passovers support that Jesus' ministry lasted between three and four years. This fits this book's thesis. Confirming a fifth Passover would void the thesis.

A.17.1 Herod's Temple Function Disrupted

The function of Herod's Temple was disrupted at the time of Jesus' crucifixion according to both the Christian New Testament and the Jewish Talmud.

Upon Jesus' death, the temple veil "was torn in two from top to bottom" (Mark 15:38). The temple veil partitioned the temple's inner sanctuary (aka the holy of holies), where God's Spirit accepted sacrifice as atonement for sin (Leviticus 16). The inner sanctuary was closed off, set apart (Exodus 30:10; Hebrews 9:7). But when the veil was torn, the inner sanctuary was no longer set apart. Christian theology asserts that the Spirit of God left the temple at that point: "your House is left to you desolate" (Luke 13:35).

Intriguingly, a passage in the Jewish Talmud harmonizes with this view:

> During the forty years prior to the destruction of the Second Temple, the lot inscribed "for Hashem" [for God] did not come up in the Kohen Gadol's [High Priest's] right hand, nor did the tongue of red wool whiten, nor did the western lamp of the Temple Menorah remain lit. And the doors of the Sanctuary would open on their own[447] (Talmud)

This is evidence that temple function was disrupted at about the time of Jesus' crucifixion four decades before its AD 70 destruction. (Note that this book does not ascribe scriptural authority to the Talmud but cites it as a historical source.) The theology may be open for discussion, but the chronology is clear. The function of Herod's Temple was disrupted, if not terminated, from that time onward.

A.19.1 The Odds of Being Random

The odds that this solution to Daniel 9:25 could be due to blind luck alone are virtually nil. To truly grasp them, let's use the lottery as a familiar example. Imagine "Pat" wins a Powerball® jackpot on a single $2 ticket. You might congratulate Pat for being lucky, and maybe even hope for a party invite. So far, so good.

Then, on the very next day, Pat buys another single Powerball ticket and wins the next jackpot. Off-the-charts lucky? It's never happened before![448] Pat would surely get worldwide attention from journalists eager to interview the luckiest person ever. Pat might also gain a few quiet doubters, including the lottery board.

The next day, Pat buys another single $2 ticket and wins the very next jackpot—the third in a row. You might not feel so much like congratulating Pat. In fact, you—and the lottery board—might suspect foul play.

Even with no evidence of cheating, winning three times in a row is prohibitively improbable. The newspaper will call it a one-in-twenty-four-septillion chance. The lottery board would start an investigation before paying out and seek an injunction to prevent Pat from playing Powerball. And they'd surely get it—no competent judge would buy any "random luck" story at this point.

But the next day, Pat defiantly buys another single ticket and wins the next jackpot—the fourth in a row. Despite no direct evidence of cheating, Pat would likely sit in jail as the lottery board spent a fortune struggling to figure out how all of that just happened. Nobody would believe it was just down to luck.

> Odds of winning a Powerball jackpot on a single ticket are currently 1 in 292.2 million.[449] Winning four times straight on four tickets are 1 in 7 decillions. That's one chance in
>
> 7,000,000,000,000,000,000,000,000,000,000,000.
>
> The factors are: 292,201,338 x 292,201,338 x 292,201,338 x 292,201,338 = 7 x 10^{33}
> That's one chance in 7 with 33 zeros. There aren't that many grains of sand on earth.

Can we write Daniel's Seventy Weeks off to random luck? The probability is *even slimmer*. There are different ways to calculate the odds that Jesus' advents occurred as predicted simply due to chance. The simplest is to multiply the number of days of each fulfillment span together. This is conservative because it defines each maximum possible range as the span itself (the real possible ranges will be even larger, arguably double in each case), so the real odds will be even slimmer than our calculated probability of **1 in 10 undecillions.** That's one chance in 10^{37}, or written out, one chance in:

10,000,000,000,000,000,000,000,000,000,000,000,000.

Here are the factors, each a span of days, in order of appearance:

173,880 x 194,334 x 907,200 x 191,777 x 907,200 x 176,437 x 14,400 = 1 x 10^{37}.

That's one chance in 1 with 37 zeros. Note that the fulfillments for Jerusalem's AD 70 destruction and Jeremiah's prophecies are *excluded* here because history cannot confirm the precise dates. The pauses' confirmations are also excluded from this calculation. Including any of these would yield an even more extremely unlikely result.

Other methods may differ, but all will yield prohibitively slim odds—less than winning the Powerball jackpot four times in a row on four single tickets. Daniel 9:25 foretold the advents of Jesus. We cannot call it random.

A.19.2 This Points to Jesus and Nobody Else

To calculate the odds that someone other than Jesus had the exact same chronological fingerprint, we start with the total Jewish population at the time. Scholars estimate there were no more than one million Jews in ancient Palestine.[450] Let's conservatively assume there were 1.5 million, and that all were in the line of King David (most weren't).

A scholarly population-by-age study indicates people aged 30 to 34 accounted for eight percent of a natural Roman-era population.[451] This means that in AD 31, there were c. 120,000 Jews aged 30, 31, 32, 33, or 34. Roughly half (60,000) were men. One-fifth of these men (12,000) were born in 5 BC, as was Jesus. One in 365 were born August 12—a birthday cohort of 33. Put simply, roughly 33 Jewish men shared Jesus' exact birthday.

A boy born August 12 in 5 BC might well have first entered the temple at the feast of Tabernacles in AD 8, as did Jesus. So, we will conservatively not reduce the cohort here.

How many of the 33 were baptized on April 18, AD 27? As far as we know, only John was out baptizing at the time, not in a *mikvah* but in natural waters, conspicuously enough to draw the temple's attention. Assuming twelve hours of daylight, and a baptismal rate of one person per minute, John could have baptized 720 people that day. Conservatively assuming most were between ages 15 and 54, we can calculate the odds that someone other than Jesus, yet sharing his birthday, was also baptized that day.

Age cohorts from 15 to 54 accounted for 56 percent of the total population[452] or 840,000. The chance that any one of them shared Jesus' birthday is 33 divided by 840,000, which equals 0.0000393. Assuming John baptized 720 that day, the chance that one of those 33 were also baptized that day is 720 x 0.0000393 = 0.0283 or 3 percent. Not impossible—but not terribly likely either.

What are the odds that someone sharing Jesus' birth and baptismal dates also died on the same day Jesus was crucified?

Here, death is a conservative proxy for triumphal entry. Death (one per person) is far more likely than triumphal entry, and we have much better death rate data. This assumption is extremely conservative, by many orders of magnitude.

In that era, death rate was 0.11 (11 percent) from age 30 to 34.[453] Split evenly, chance of death in a single year was 0.022, and on any single day was 0.00006.[454] If chances that a person was both born and baptized on the right days are 0.0283, then chances they had Jesus' precise chronological fingerprint are conservatively 0.0000017, or one chance in 588,235.[455] We can confidently say that Daniel 9:25 points only to Jesus and to nobody else.

A.19.3 Christos Kyrios

The New Testament makes no explicit Daniel 9:25 argument for Jesus' messiahship. Because Daniel's prediction is purely chronological and points to Jesus' time, then we might expect to find a Daniel 9:25 argument in the Gospels, especially in Matthew, but we don't.

Daniel 12:4 and 9 state that Daniel's prophecies would remain "secret and sealed," meaning they wouldn't be fully understood until "the end of time," not *Messiah's* time. And people, even those around Jesus, indeed did not recognize the importance of that time (Luke 19:44). But it goes deeper than that.

In Luke 2:9–11, "an angel of the Lord" for whom the seal of Daniel 12 might not apply, announced the birth of "Christ the Lord." Luke's words in Greek, *Christos Kyrios*, bear a meaningful resemblance to the Hebrew *mashiach nagid* in Daniel 9:25.

> The angel's words to the shepherds were almost certainly relayed to Mary and Joseph in Hebrew or Aramaic. Luke almost certainly interviewed Mary directly (Luke 2:19, 51).

Christos means "anointed." It's the equivalent of "Messiah" (John 1:41) in English, and *mashiach* in the Hebrew of Daniel 9:25.

Kyrios means owner, master, Lord, or someone with absolute ownership rights. The title *Kyrios* is exceptionally strong, used even for God (Mark 11:9). The angel spoke of not just any Messiah but of one with extremely high authority. *Mashiach* appears thirty-nine times in the Old Testament, but only once is it combined directly with a title of worldly authority (*nagid*) to form a composite title like *Christos Kyrios*—only once in the entire Hebrew Scripture. That's in Daniel 9:25, which foretells the advent of *mashiach nagid*, "Messiah the Prince."

> *Nagid* appears forty-four times in the Old Testament as leader, ruler, king, or prince (appendix 1.3.1). There are places where *mashiach* appears as the object of an authority (e.g., "The Lord's anointed" in 1 Samuel 26:23), but there is no other with *nagid* or any title of worldly authority (e.g., *melek, nasi, adon, shalit*) to form a compound title except in Daniel 9:25.[456] In short, the *only* such Gospel reference matches the *only* such Old Testament reference, *precisely when* it was foretold to happen.

The seal remained intact. The Gospel writers didn't see a connection between Jesus and Daniel 9:25. Yet, that connection was verbally proclaimed precisely when, where (Micah 5:2), and from whom we might have expected it. In short, we can't say we weren't told.

A.19.4 Cumulative Probability and Confirmation

This solution was achieved by interpreting Scripture and the historical record. How can we be confident in the result? After all, such a process isn't foolproof. The historical record is not always accurate or complete. There are many ways to interpret Scripture, but not all of them are valid. This book's author is human, and humans can make mistakes. Moreover, some of these steps were assumptions. On its own, this process wouldn't give a correct conclusion if any one of its steps were incorrect.

> For example, a three-step process, where each step has a 90 percent chance of success, has a cumulative 73 percent chance of success, because:
>
> $$(0.9)^3 = 0.9 \times 0.9 \times 0.9 = 0.73 = 73\%.$$

Can we have confidence in this book's solution to Daniel 9:25 when its individual steps aren't 100 percent certain? Actually, we can. *How so?* Let's demonstrate by familiar example.

You may be old enough to remember when people dialed telephone numbers from memory, one digit at a time. To call your friend, you had to remember a seven-digit sequence and dial it correctly. If you were 99 percent sure to remember and dial each digit accurately, you would have a 93 percent chance of dialing correctly $[(.99)^7 = 0.932]$. How can we go from 93 percent to virtually 100 percent confidence of success (or failure)?

The 93 percent odds resolve to 100 or 0 percent when the phone is answered. If your friend answers, then you know each digit was dialed correctly. You have a 100 percent confirmation. If this seems glaringly obvious to you, it should.

Importantly, and please pay careful attention right here, this confirmation is valid *no matter the number of steps or their probabilities*. This part might not be so glaringly obvious.

Sticking with the telephone example, maybe your friend lives in another country so you must dial fifteen digits, not seven. Maybe you hadn't called this friend in over a year and weren't sure of the number. Perhaps it was dark, you couldn't see the keypad, and you had bandages on your fingers. Suppose your chance of dialing each digit correctly is no longer 99 percent, but 90 percent. That drops the odds of dialing correctly to 21 percent $[(0.90)^{15}=0.21]$ when the call goes out. Not terribly likely.

But if your friend answers, you can still be 100 percent certain that each digit was dialed correctly. If you get a wrong number, you know you didn't. Either way, you get confirmation, *no matter the number of steps or the probabilities of each*.

Whether we dial with a high or low probability of success, the confirmation still gives certainty of either success or failure. It is valid no matter the number of steps, the probability of each step, or the cumulative probability of the entire process. [end of example]

In this book's solution, the number, validity, or probability of any or all steps, including its assumptions, are all moot points once there is a confirmation.

For Daniel 9:25, few would have predicted our finding a precise solution that fits all related scriptural, historical, and physical evidence, given the number of steps and the unknown (but less than certain) probabilities of each. After all, this verse has eluded people for centuries. But we did find that solution. We know this because we have *confirmation*.

What counts as confirmation here exactly? The short answer is **everything**. The standard of **everything** is both scientific and scriptural.

Scientific method favors ideas that best explain all related evidence over other ideas that do not. Examples include germ theory, general relativity, and plate tectonics. These were accepted only after they were shown to best explain all known evidence. In other words, **everything**.

The standard of **everything** is also scriptural. It comes directly from Jesus:

> Now He said to them, "These are My words which I spoke to you while I was still with you, that all the things that are written about Me in the Law of Moses and the Prophets and the Psalms must be fulfilled." (Luke 24:44)

Note "all the things," from the Greek *panta*, also translated *"everything"* (NIV), refers to everything written about Jesus in the *entire* Old Testament (Torah, Prophets, and Writings). This solution reconciles the directly related chronological statements of both Old and New Testaments with each other, with the historical record, and with astronomical and physical evidence. It shows prophecies from Daniel and Ezekiel to be fulfilled precisely to the day. It places four key advents of Jesus on biblical Hebrew holidays. And remarkably, it reconciles Bible passages that have stumped and divided people for centuries, such as Daniel 1:1, Ezekiel 4, and Jeremiah 52:29.

Most importantly, this solution identifies the promised Messiah by finding the dates of his key advents, as Daniel intended. It does so by using a *uniform method* of chronology and taking Scripture at *face value*. It never changed dating methods and never tortured scriptural, historical, or physical evidence—not even once. The evidence is *objectively verifiable*.

This is a confirmation. We know this prophecy is accurately fulfilled because **everything** fits. **Everything** is a high standard—maybe the highest *possible* standard—one given by Jesus himself. When we see that **everything** fits, we can be confident we have found Truth.

A.20.1 Evidence to the Contrary

So, what about evidence to the contrary? Although atheists often admit to having no proof of God's nonexistence, they also assert that atheism doesn't require proof, not even evidence, because atheism allegedly only rejects the idea that God exists yet isn't a positive assertion he doesn't.[457] In this way, atheists shun any burden of proof to place it only on believers.[458] But this view could only be valid if there were indeed no evidence of God. *But there is evidence of God.* This book presents direct evidence of God, and it's neither the first nor the only such evidence. To be blunt, the proverbial shoe is on the other foot. Evidence of equal validity—not just empty dismissal—is required to address it.[459]

> Objections, like assertions, must also be based on evidence, also "beyond a reasonable doubt." To doubt only one but never the other—like Kierkegaard's "false doubt" that "doubts everything except itself"—is fallacy.[460] Lack of supporting evidence can render the anti-theist position as, by definition, *presuppositional*.

This is simply how we humans have always evaluated ideas. This book has demonstrated, using traditional Aristotelian logic, the existence of a supernatural entity who is God of the Bible. Rejecting the conclusion requires equal or greater evidence to the contrary. If no such contrary evidence can be found, then the thesis conclusion stands.

American economist and Nobel Laureate Milton Friedman explained how that works:

> Factual evidence can never "prove" a hypothesis; it can only fail to disprove it, which is what we generally mean when we say, somewhat inexactly, that the hypothesis has been "confirmed" by experience.[461] (Friedman)

At this point, a claim that there is no evidence for God is not persuasive. There is such evidence, and this book has presented yet more.[462]

A.20.2 The Future

A legitimate question remains: *Can this solution to Daniel 9:25 inform the dating of future prophetic events?* The short answer is yes. But note three points straightaway.

First, this book examines the past and avoids addressing the future. There is a practical reason for this. This book confirms its results using both scriptural and physical evidence and the historical record. Obviously, the future can't be evaluated in quite the same way. This doesn't mean it can't be investigated at all, only that we must approach the future very differently than we approach the past. This requires a different book, even a different *type* of book.

> Are we in, or entering "the last days" or "the time of the end"? This question, though intriguing, is beyond our present scope.[463]

Second, Daniel 9:25 is now shown to be true in a robust, literal, and astoundingly precise sense. Now consider the other three verses of Daniel's Seventy Weeks. There is every reason to believe those words are just as exactingly chosen and precisely true to an extent that also far exceeds traditional expectations.[464]

Third, any prophetic date we could reasonably calculate is surely **not** the date of Jesus' return. He told us directly:

> **But about that day and hour no one knows, not even the angels of heaven, nor the Son, but the Father alone. (Matthew 24:36)**

It's hard to make Jesus' words any clearer than they already are. We simply won't know the date of his return, and we won't finesse ourselves into a position to know. We might be able to calculate dates of *other* foretold events that *also* await fulfillment, but no supportable calculation will reveal the day and hour of Jesus' return. We only know that he *will* return, at an hour we *don't* expect (1 Thessalonians 5:2). The best advice is from Jesus himself:[465]

Be Ready.

This Government has been informed that a Jewish state has been proclaimed in Palestine, and recognition has been requested by the *provisional* Government thereof.

The United States recognizes the provisional government as the de facto authority of the new ~~Jewish~~ *State of* ~~state.~~ *Israel.*

Harry Truman

Approved,
May 14, 1948.

6:11

US recognition of Israel dated May 14, 1948, at 6:11 p.m. Washington time, which was 12:11 a.m. on May 15 in Jerusalem. Israel was reborn ten minutes prior. The handwritten edits were made personally by President Truman upon signing.

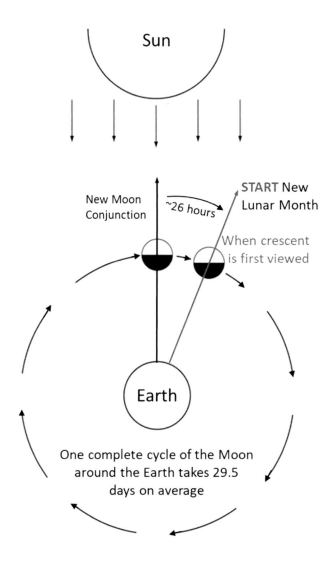

Figure 25. Lunar cycle diagram. Each lunar month is one complete cycle of the moon around the earth. Each lunar month begins when the thin lunar crescent is first visible after sunset, at least twenty-six hours (at Jerusalem's latitude 31°N) after a new moon conjunction, when the moon passes directly between the earth and sun. *Not to scale.*

APPENDIX B
THE CALENDAR

> This appendix presents the Hebrew calendar used in the biblical era. The biblical Hebrew calendar is different from the modern Hebrew calendar used today.

In the biblical era, the Hebrew calendar functioned differently than it does today.

> The history of the Jewish calendar may be divided into three periods. [...] The first rested purely on the observation of the sun and the moon, the second on observation and reckoning, the **third entirely on reckoning.**[466]
> (*Jewish Encyclopedia*, bolding and color added)

The second period (observation and reckoning) is our focus. This was the calendar observed during the time of Jesus' earthly ministry. The **third period**, from c. AD 359 onward, is the **modern Hebrew calendar observed today**, which cannot be applied to the biblical era.[467] This appendix presents the Hebrew calendar as it was observed from the Babylonian exile to after Jesus' time on earth.[468]

> Then God said, "Let there be lights in the expanse of the heavens to separate the day from the night, and they shall serve as signs and for seasons, and for days and years (Genesis 1:14)

Almost all ancient cultures worldwide used the moon as a calendar. It was perfect for the job. Everybody could see it, nobody could tamper with it, and its movement was regular. Many ancient cultures, including the Hebrew culture, used the moon to track the months of the year and the days of each month. To them, it wasn't complicated at all.

A Lunar Month Is One Orbit of the Moon around the Earth

The Hebrew calendar's basic unit is the lunar month. Each lunar month is exactly one lunar cycle—put simply, one trip of the moon around the earth. It takes 29 ½ days on average for the moon to make one of these trips.[469] When the moon passes directly between the earth and sun, that alignment is called the *lunar conjunction*, or commonly, the *new moon* (figure 25).

We can't see a new moon because when it moves exactly between us and the sun, it reflects sunlight directly away from us. Only when the moon moves far enough into its new cycle, about a day after the new moon conjunction, does the moon begin to appear to us as a thin crescent.

The only time of day we can see a brand new crescent moon is right after sunset, during those few minutes when the sun has just dipped below the horizon, and the lagging crescent moon still hangs above it in the darkening western sky.

Observing the new crescent moon right after sunset was highly important to Hebrews who saw it as a direct sign from God marking the start of a new month, and sometimes of a new year.[470] So, how did this work during the time of Jesus' earthly ministry?

This starts a new lunar month

New lunar crescent in the western sky right after sunset. Its appearance marks the first day of a new Hebrew month. Hebrew days begin and end at nightfall.

The New Month

Each Hebrew month began when the moon's thin crescent was first visible right after sunset,[471] after the new moon conjunction.

For Jews in the biblical era, it was a high honor to report a new crescent moon sighting to the temple. It was so important, that Sabbath travel restrictions were lifted for anyone reporting a crescent sighting.[472] When the temple accepted sightings from two or three witnesses, they declared that evening to be the start of a new month, known in Hebrew as *rosh chodesh* (literally, "head of month").

The lunar cycle is 29½ days long on average, so the crescent was seen in the evening after the 29th or 30th day of the prior Hebrew month.[473] Thus, that evening started the first day of a new month. This is why Hebrew days start at sundown, and Hebrew months were either twenty-nine or thirty days long, set not by fixed schedule but instead by ***directly observing the moon***.

Occasionally, clouds could obscure a visible crescent. However, if the previous month was already thirty days long, then the new month would begin anyway, sighting or no sighting, because Hebrew months could not, by rule, exceed thirty days.[474] Any error due to cloud cover would have been corrected with the next month's moon sighting, or the next.

Twelve lunar months have 354 days—that's 11¼ days less than a solar year. To keep holidays from drifting ever earlier out of season, Hebrews applied special rules to determine when to start the month of *Nisan*. This governed the length of the Hebrew year.

This starts the month of Nisan

Barley in *aviv*, meaning the grain is "in the ear" (Exodus 9:31). This was a key sign of spring in the biblical era. The month of Nisan could begin with a crescent sighting after the barley reached that stage of maturity, typically in March or April.

The New Year

Hebrews called the month Nisan (March/April) the first month,[475] even though their civil year began with the seventh month *Tishri*. Nisan 1 was declared only when the crescent moon appeared **after natural springtime had arrived**. But what happened if the twelfth month *Adar* ended but there was no sign of spring?

Hebrew Months

1.	**Nisan**	**(Mar/Apr)**	7. **Tishri**	**(Sep/Oct)**
2.	Iyyar	(Apr/May)	8. Heshvan	(Oct/Nov)
3.	Sivan	(May/Jun)	9. Kislev	(Nov/Dec)
4.	Tammuz	(Jun/Jul)	10. Tevet	(Dec/Jan)
5.	Av	(Jul/Aug)	11. Shevat	(Jan/Feb)
6.	Elul	(Aug/Sep)	12. Adar	(Feb/Mar)
	There are many spelling variants		*13. Adar II*	*(Feb/Mar)*

Figure 5. (From chapter 4) Biblical Hebrew months. *Adar II* is a leap month added once every two or three years to keep the 354-day lunar year from drifting out of solar season.

Intercalation

If natural spring had still not arrived when the twelfth month Adar ended, then an extra month called *Adar II* was inserted after Adar and before Nisan, creating a leap year of thirteen lunar months (c. 384 days). Thus, the Hebrew month Nisan began not on a fixed schedule but at the first crescent moon sighting after natural spring had visibly arrived.

> Biblical reference post-Exodus to "the first month" indicates Nisan. Yet, the Hebrew civil year started in the autumn, on Tishri 1. Its timing was governed by the start of the prior Nisan.[476] Hebrew civil years are numbered sequentially. For example, Hebrew year 5784 starts in the autumn of 2023 AD and ends in the autumn of 2024 AD.

Scholars call adding a leap month "intercalation." This was necessary because the normal 354-day lunar year and its holidays would have otherwise drifted out of solar season. Hebrews added the leap month, Adar II, after the month Adar and before Nisan. Only a full lunar month was ever added—never more, never less.[477] Unlike modern leap years that have one extra day every four years, Hebrew leap years were one extra month every two or three years, and in unpredictable sequence in the era of our study.

> Before AD 359, Hebrews didn't determine months and leap months by any fixed schedule. Thus, **Hebrew dates before AD 359 can't be converted on the internet**. This is because internet converters are based on the algorithmic modern (Hillel II) Hebrew calendar. No date referenced anywhere in the Bible can be converted on the internet.

In Jesus' time, springtime was defined by three criteria: the maturity of the barley, the maturity of the fruit trees, and the equinox.[478] Famine years were not intercalated.[479]

By rule, Hebrews required Tabernacles (Sukkot) to fall *after* the autumn equinox.[480] This required Nisan 1 to fall *after* March 17 (Julian) in the time of Jesus, and *after* March 20 in the time of Ezra (appendix A.5.2). Nisan 1 would fall no earlier than these dates, except in a year with famine.

Who Managed the Calendar?

In the time of Jesus, the calendar was governed by the temple's *beit din*, a subgroup of the Sanhedrin, who calculated the equinox, received reports of new moons and springtime, and managed the Hebrew calendar from the temple for all Jews.

> Jesus often criticized temple priests, but notably not for calendar management.

How Did They Notify the People?

At one point, Jews used signal fires to announce the new month (*rosh chodesh*) to the nation. Those signals were relayed from the Temple Mount via a chain of high points, outward to distant Jews even as far as Babylon. But the temple stopped using signal fires after Samaritans (Cutheans) lit false signal fires to interfere. Jews then used messengers instead.

Originally, they would light a relay of torches, to spread the word of when Rosh Chodesh [new month] had been declared. When the Cutheans [Samaritans] disrupted the process, [the Sages] instituted that messengers should go forth to spread the word.[481] (Talmud)

Those messengers, heralding the new month, could travel only so far before the new month's holidays began. Jews living outside the messengers' range could not be sure on exactly which day a holiday fell, though they knew it had to be on one of two possible days. Thus, Jews outside the messengers' effective range celebrated major holidays on not one but two days, a tradition that continues even now.

According to Rambam [Maimonides], whether Yom Tov Sheni [double holiday] is observed in a specific place does not depend upon its proximity to Jerusalem. Rather, it depends upon how many days of Yom Tov were celebrated there during the period when messengers spread the word about the sanctification of the month. Areas which celebrated only one day because the messengers reached them before Sukkot, even in the Diaspora, continue to celebrate one day. Areas where the messengers did not reach, even within Eretz Yisrael, continue to celebrate two days.[482] (Melamed)

Appendix B Main Points

- The Hebrew calendar during the time of Jesus was governed by reckoning (equinox) and observation of the moon and natural springtime.

- Unlike today, Hebrew intercalation (leap years) in the biblical era were discretionary, not fixed.

- Internet calendar converters are not valid for Hebrew dates in the biblical era.

Intercalation was regulated annually by the judgment of the Sanhedrin, not by a fixed cycle, in the time of Our Lord.[483] (Fotheringham)

Fortunately, we have what we need to reconstruct the biblical Hebrew calendar in the era of our study. Modern astronomers can calculate the exact times of each new moon conjunction going back thousands of years. This enables us to identify the most probable start date for any Hebrew month in the biblical era. Any month of interest must be investigated separately, on a case-by-case basis. Appendix C presents this study's key date calculations in detail.

And don't be intimidated. Although many modern cultures are thoroughly unfamiliar with the lunar calendar, its function is basic and knowable. It's not rocket science. It was used by almost every ancient culture on earth, literate or not, in similar fashion—they all used the moon as a calendar.

After all, it was perfect for the job (Genesis 1:14).

Then God said, "Let there be lights in the expanse of the heavens to separate the day from the night, and they shall serve as signs and for seasons, and for days and years (Genesis 1:14)

APPENDIX C
KEY DATES

> This appendix converts this solution's key dates between the Julian and Hebrew calendars. You should expect to see this type of evidence in any biblical chronology.

Converting biblical Hebrew dates requires careful attention. Never let anyone (self included) tell you biblical Hebrew date X is Julian date Y without showing evidence.

In the biblical era, each Hebrew month began with the sighting of the lunar crescent after sunset (appendix B). Finding any biblical Hebrew date requires knowing when that month's crescent moon was first visible. There are three common methods for this. Two are valid, and one is not. We must first address the one that isn't because it's used too often.

1. Not Valid—The modern Hebrew calendar and internet date converters

The modern Hebrew (Hillel II) calendar was adopted in c. AD 359, long after the biblical era. It is fully automatic. It replaced observation of the moon and natural springtime with pure calculation (appendix B) and assigned a fixed number of days to each month. Most importantly, it has a fixed schedule of leap years. The advantage was that it allowed uniformity going forward, so Jews could maintain their calendar after being dispersed abroad—often far from Judea. But it was not the same calendar used during the biblical era. Adopting the modern calendar in AD 359 may have been the Sanhedrin's last official decision before disbanding (though that is difficult to verify).

The modern Hebrew calendar can't be used for dates before AD 359. This excludes it for the entire biblical era. The modern Hebrew calendar is the algorithmic basis for internet calendar converter programs, so those are invalid for all biblical dates.

Using the internet for biblical dates is probably the *single most common mistake* in biblical chronology. Whenever you see statements like, "In year X, Passover fell on a Friday," you should ask for evidence. It has become too easy to just type a date into a web page and simply accept what pops out. That leads to errors. That method is not valid for any date found anywhere in the Bible and isn't used anywhere in this book.

2. Valid—Modern astronomical calculation

Modern astronomy can calculate the movements of the moon and planets with astounding precision. These calculations, known as the "ephemerides" (rhymes with *Wheaties*®)[484] serve many uses. One such use is finding when each new crescent moon will be visible. Even today, cultures that still observe a lunar calendar (e.g., Islamic) use the ephemerides to predict when the crescent moon should first be visible. This method is fully reliable for calculations in the *modern* era.

But we must be cautious applying the ephemerides to the *ancient* era. Of course, the farther into the past we calculate, the larger our margin of error grows, and the reliability of our result shrinks. For crescent visibility (*not eclipses*), going back two thousand years *might* exceed our tolerance for error—or it might not—there's just no good way to tell. *Why not?*

The ephemerides describe all aspects of lunar motion that influence crescent visibility on earth. Many such aspects are confirmed by historical observation, but some aren't. This reduces the ephemerides' reliability for the ancient era. If even one aspect is off, it might produce a false result, especially in a borderline case.

> "Reliability" is a relative term, raising the question: "Reliability for what purpose and to what tolerance?" Our purpose is *ancient* crescent sightings *precise to the day*.[485]

The ephemerides are certainly reliable for calculating the times of ancient eclipses. We are certain of ancient lunar conjunction times and other eclipse-related aspects because the ephemerides' eclipse calculations are *calibrated by ancient eclipse records*. If we were only concerned with eclipses and conjunction times, then the ephemerides would be perfectly suitable for the biblical era.

But we are not focused on eclipses. We are concerned with lunar crescent visibility. There are some aspects of lunar motion that influence crescent visibility but not eclipses. Some of those aspects lack direct historical confirmation, thus cannot be calibrated.[486]

In short, it's not that we believe the ephemerides' crescent calculations for that era are wrong, it's just that we can't be sure they're right. We can't directly confirm their precision for lunar crescent visibility in the ancient era. So, the ephemerides will serve as a secondary check when our primary method (next section) gives a borderline result. Fortunately, one method is valid *and* reliable, and it comes to us directly from the era of our study.

3. Valid—The Babylonian method

Ancient Babylonian astronomers left us a clear rule: *a crescent should be visible after sunset, at least twenty-four hours after a new moon conjunction*.[487] "Twenty-four hours" is almost certainly an approximation. If not precisely twenty-four hours, then we understand it as something close to it. Fortunately, modern astronomy verifies this.

A modern study of lunar crescent visibility finds that at latitude 30°N, it takes on average twenty-five hours after conjunction for a crescent to be visible after sunset. The study also finds that the observer's latitude influences this time threshold.[488] Since Jerusalem sits at 31°N, we adjust this threshold slightly to assert that a **twenty-five-hour crescent will probably not be visible, but a twenty-six-hour crescent probably will be visible**. This gives us a clear cutoff in harmony with the Babylonian rule. This Babylonian method has two advantages.

First, it's reliable. It's based on conjunction times calibrated by ancient eclipse observations and known with virtual certainty to within minutes. This method does not rely on aspects of lunar motion which aren't confirmed by the historical record.[489]

Second, this method is from the biblical era, from Babylonian astronomers who declared lunar months by observing the lunar crescent essentially as Hebrews did.[490] They are authorities on this topic, especially for their own time, which happens to be the era of our study. To put it bluntly: they were there, and we were not.

Although the Babylonian method lacks the ephemerides' precision and is certainly not the method of choice for predicting sightings in the *modern* era, its reliability and authority make it best suited to calculate lunar crescent visibility in the *ancient* era. But for accuracy, we will use both methods—the Babylonian method as our primary method, and the ephemerides as a secondary backup in borderline cases.

JS Brown   February 12, 2020

Dear Mr. Brown,

Below are the correct lunar conjunction times corresponding to each of the requested
lunations. Note that all dates are on the Julian Calendar. Note also that time is given as
Universal Time (UT).

Lunation Date	Conjunction (UT)
5 August, 518 BCE	10:25
25 March, 457 BCE	05:16
3 August, 5 BCE	02:31
19 August, 8 CE	13:22
26 March, 27 CE	17:59
10 April, 31 CE	11:36

These dates and times are calculated directly from the JPL's definitive DE431 ephemeris and
agree very closely with those given by Dr. Fred Espenak.

Sincerely,
Dr. Geza Gyuk
Senior Associate
Kavli Institute for Cosmological Physics

William Eckhardt Research Center (ERC) - Suite 499, 5640 South Ellis Avenue, Chicago, IL 60637

Figure 26. Key lunation dates and times. Note that the astronomer Dr. Gyuk was
presented with a list of lunations and requested to calculate their dates and times without
any knowledge of this book's context or thesis. You can verify these conjunctions online.
Two online sources are:
http://astropixels.com/ephemeris/phasescat/phasescat.html (Espenak),
http:// www.astro.com/swisseph/swepha_e.htm.
Scholarly sources should agree to within an hour or so in this era.

Key Lunations

Ch.	Year	Ast.Yr	Day	Conjunction Time				Viewed on:	
				UT	+ ΔT	+ Geo	= TT	*Day	hours
5	AD 31	0031	10-Apr	11:36	2:50	2:20	16:46	Apr 12	49
9	5 BC	-0004	3-Aug	02:31	2:55	2:20	7:46	Aug 4	36
11	518 BC	-0517	5-Aug	10:25	4:50	2:20	17:35	Aug 6	26
12	AD 8	0008	19-Aug	13:22	2:55	2:20	18:37	Aug 20	**
14	457 BC	-0456	25-Mar	05:16	4:30	2:55†	12:41	Mar 26	30
15	AD 27	0027	26-Mar	17:59	2:50	2:20	23:09	Mar 28	43

*Evening on this date starts the first day of a Hebrew month.
Note that Jerusalem twilight falls later in August than March.
**By Talmudic rule, Tishri 1 always followed Elul 29 in this era.
†Note the 457 BC sighting was in Babylon, not Jerusalem.

Figure 27. Lunar Crescent Visibility Table used to identify key dates in this book. Note that this table finds the first day of the relevant Hebrew month, which in turn identifies the target date. The columns are defined in the following text.

Converting Hebrew Dates

Astronomers record the year 1 BC as 0000 (zero), 2 BC is –0001, 3 BC is –0002, and so forth. Thus, to astronomers, 457 BC is –0456 and 446 BC is –0445. AD years are intuitive, for example, AD 1 is 0001, AD 27 is 0027, and so on.

Delta-T: In the twentieth century, scientists confirmed that the earth's rotation is slowing extremely slightly. The amount of slowing, called "delta-T" (ΔT), can be referenced online.[491] Because new moon conjunction times are typically recorded in Universal Time (UT), we must add delta-T to calculate Terrestrial Time (TT), the time to an actual observer standing at the Prime Meridian (Greenwich) on the indicated date.[492]

$$UT + \Delta T = TT$$

Geo location: We add time to TT to adjust for location (e.g., Jerusalem is 2:20 ahead of Greenwich) to pinpoint the actual local conjunction time in Jerusalem (or Babylon, +2:55). Anyone familiar with modern time zones should quickly understand.

Hebrew days start and end at sundown. This requires care in counting forward from the first of a month. *Charting is required.* Mistakes almost always creep in when charts are omitted or contain gaps.

Jewish Nisan 1 is calculated to fall normally between **March 17** and **April 19** in the New Testament era and between **March 20** and **April 22** in the Old Testament era from Cyrus to Nehemiah, except in famine years (appendix A.5.2).

The first date conversion (C.5) is presented in greater detail to serve as an illustrating example.

C.5* April 22, AD 31, Is Nisan 10

> This first conversion is presented in greater detail to serve as an illustrating example. References below are explained on the facing page.

Step 1: Define the task. The key question is: in AD 31, on which Julian date was Nisan 10?

Step 2: Find the Nisan moon. In AD 31, the only new moon falling in the normal window for Nisan, between March 17 and April 19 (appendix A.5.2), occurred on April 10.

Step 3: Find the relevant Hebrew month. In this conversion, Nisan is the relevant month.

Step 4: Find the conjunction time (UT) then adjust for delta-T (ΔT) and geolocation. The April 10 conjunction occurred at 11:36 UT (figure 26). Correcting for delta-T (add 2 hours 55 minutes for AD 31) and Jerusalem's location (add 2 hours 20 minutes) produces a total adjustment to UT of five hours and ten minutes.[493] Thus, the Nisan new moon conjoined on **April 10 at 16:46** (4:46 p.m.) local Jerusalem time (figure 27).

Step 5: Find when the crescent was visible. At sunset April 11, the moon was twenty-five hours old and likely not visible (section 3 to this appendix). On April 12, the moon was forty-nine hours old and visible. Thus, Nisan likely started on the evening of April 12.

Step 6: Chart the days. Nisan 10 fell on **Sunday, April 22,** in **AD 31**. On that day, Jesus made his triumphal entry into Jerusalem. Never skip charting, and never leave gaps.

Step 7: Look up the JDN. The JDN (appendix A.5.1) for April 22, AD 31, is 1,732,492.

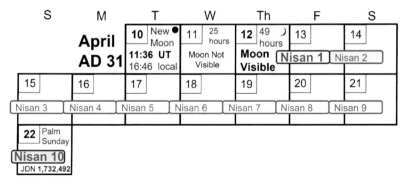

Figure 28. Nisan 10 (daytime) in AD 31 fell on April 22. This is the date of Jesus' triumphal entry into Jerusalem, calculated in chapter 5.

This can be verified by referencing (figure 26, and online[494]) this new moon:

Year: **0031**   Date: **Apr 10**   Time (UT): **11:36**

Once verified, it's apparent that Nisan 10 in AD 31 fell on Sunday, **April 22.**

---

* The number of the appendix locators refers to the corresponding chapter number.

C.9   August 12, 5 BC, Is the Ninth of Av (Tisha b'Av)

This is the nativity date. The key question is, did Tisha b'Av (Av 9) in 5 BC fall on August 12?

In 5 BC, only the April 6 new moon falls inside the normal range for Nisan 1. Av is the fifth Hebrew month. Its new moon conjunction fell on August 3 at 02:31 UT (figure 26). Correcting for delta-T and Jerusalem's location produces a total adjustment to UT of five hours and fifteen minutes.[495] Therefore, the Av new moon conjoined on **August 3** at **07:46** Jerusalem time (figure 27).

At sunset on August 3, the new moon was twelve hours old and certainly not visible. The next evening, August 4, the moon was thirty-six hours old and certainly visible. So, Av 1 in 5 BC began the evening of August 4, and Av 9 started on the evening of **Saturday, August 12**. The JDN is 1,719,821.

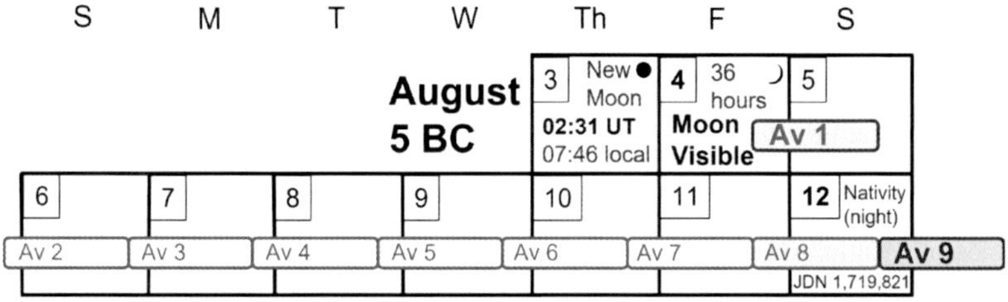

Figure 29. Tisha b'Av (Av 9) started on August 12 in 5 BC. This is the calculated nativity date.

This can be verified by referencing (figure 26, and online[496]) this new moon:

Year: −0004   Date: **Aug 03**   Time (UT): **02:31**

Once verified, it's apparent that Av 9 began on August 12 in 5 BC. Note that in astronomical style, −0004 is 5 BC.

C.11   August 14, 518 BC, Is the Ninth of Av (Tisha b'Av)

This is the issue date of Darius' decree. The key question is, which date is Av 9 in 518 BC?

In 518 BC, only the April 9 conjunction falls within the normal range for Nisan 1. Av is the fifth new moon which occurred on August 5 at 10:25 UT (figure 26). Correcting for delta-T and Jerusalem's location yields a total adjustment to UT of seven hours and ten minutes.[497] Thus, the Av new moon conjoined on **August 5** at **17:35** Jerusalem time (figure 27).

At sunset on August 6, the moon was twenty-six hours old and probably visible. So, Av 1 in 518 BC began the evening of August 6, and Av 9 began the evening of August 14. The decree of Darius issued on **August 14, 518 BC**. The JDN is 1,532,449.

This can be verified by referencing (figure 26, and online) this new moon:[498]

Year: −0517   Date: **Aug 05**   Time (UT): **10:25**

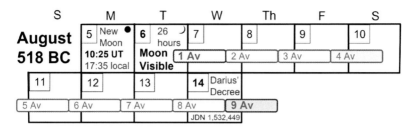

Figure 30. Tisha b'Av started on August 14 in 518 BC.

Once verified, it's apparent that Av 9 likely began on August 14 in 518 BC. Note that astronomers write 518 BC as −0517. Note also, this is a borderline result. The ephemerides predict the crescent was visible August 7. Note also that this is the earliest of our lunations, and the ephemerides' prediction is also borderline, so it should not override the Babylonian method's result.

C.12 September 3, AD 8, Is Tishri 15

This is the imputed date of Jesus' first temple entry. The key question is, which Hebrew date is this?

AD 8 was likely not intercalated (appendix A.12.1) due to famine, so the Nisan moon fell extremely early, on February 25. Tishri is the seventh month. Its conjunction occurred on August 19 at 13:22 UT (figure 26). Correcting for delta-T and Jerusalem's location produces an adjustment to UT of five hours and fifteen minutes.[499] Thus, the Tishri new moon conjoined on **August 19** at **18:37** Jerusalem time (figure 27). This was close to sunset, the start of the Hebrew date Elul 29. By Talmudic rule, the next evening must be Tishri 1, observation or not.

The Talmud (Beitzah 6a) records: "From the days of Ezra the prophet and onward, we never found Elul to be full."[500] In other words, Hebrews did not add a thirtieth day to the month of Elul since the time of Ezra, who lived before Jesus. Thus, this rule is applicable in AD 8, and requires Tishri 1 to immediately follow Elul 29, regardless of observation.

August / September in AD 8

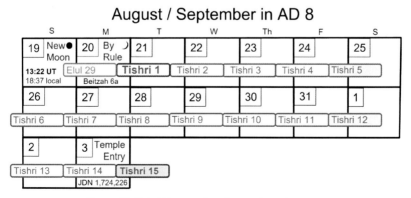

Figure 31. Tishri 15 started on September 3 in AD 8.

This date falls extremely early in the solar year, and therefore must be investigated. Spring of AD 8 fell in the second year after a sabbatical year. (Zuckerman places the prior sabbatical year from Tishri AD 5 to Tishri AD 6.) The Talmud writes that Jews did not intercalate (add a leap month to) the sabbatical year (AD 5/6) nor to the first year *after* a sabbatical year (AD 6/7). So, AD 7/8 (i.e., spring of AD 8) should have been intercalated, if it had no famine. But there *was a famine.* Josephus judged it "severe." The Talmud also writes that famine years were not intercalated. So, by this Talmudic rule, AD 8 was not intercalated. Thus, the Nisan moon conjoined early, on February 25, and Tishri 1 in AD 8 began August 20. This places Tishri 15 on the evening of **September 3**, JDN 1,724,226. This can be verified by referencing (figure 26, and online) this new moon conjunction:[501]

Year: 0008   Date: **Aug 19**   Time (UT): **13:22**

It's certain that Tishri 15 began on September 3 in AD 8. Note that if we ignore the Talmudic rule and follow the Babylonian method, we would have a borderline result predicting sighting on August 21. Yet, the ephemerides predict sighting on August 20, in agreement with the Talmudic rule, and is not borderline. In any case, our best evidence places September 3 of AD 8 on Tishri 15, and the JDN is 1,724,226.

C.14   March 27, 457 BC, Is Nisan 1

This is the issue date of Artaxerxes' decree to Ezra. The key question is, when was Nisan 1 in 457 BC?

Note that this date is from Babylon. Parker and Dubberstein, authoritative for Babylon, place Nisan 1 daytime on March 27.[502]

The Nisan new moon conjoined March 25 at 05:16 UT (figure 26). Correcting for delta-T and Babylon's location requires adjusting UT seven hours and twenty-five minutes.[503] Thus, the Nisan new moon conjoined on **March 25** at **12:41** Babylon time (figure 27).

At sunset on March 26, the moon was thirty hours old and visible. Thus, Nisan 1, the start of Ezra's journey (we safely assume they started travel in daylight, not darkness), is **March 27** in **457 BC**. The JDN is 1,554,590.

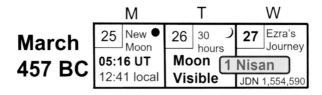

Figure 32. Nisan 1 (daytime) fell on March 27 in 457 BC.

This can be verified by referencing (figure 26, and online[504]) this new moon:

Year: −0456   Date: **Mar 25**   Time (UT): **05:16**

Once verified, it's apparent that Nisan 1 (day) fell on March 27, 457 BC. This is confirmed by both *PDBC* and the ephemerides. Note that astronomers write 457 BC as −0456.

This event occurred in Babylon, not Judah. This date for Nisan 1 also matches Parker & Dubberstein (*PDBC*), authoritative for Babylon. March 27, 457 BC, is a Wednesday, when travel was lawful.

C.15 April 18, AD 27, Is Nisan 21

This is the calculated date of Jesus' baptism. The key question is, on what Hebrew date did April 18, AD 27, fall?

In AD 27, the only conjunction in the range for Nisan 1 occurred on March 26 at 17:59 UT (figure 26). Correcting for delta-T and Jerusalem's location yields a total adjustment to UT of five hours and ten minutes.[505] Therefore, this new moon conjoined on **March 26** at **23:09** Jerusalem time (figure 27).

At sunset on March 27, the new moon was nineteen hours old and not visible. The next evening, March 28, the moon was forty-three hours old and certainly visible. Nisan 1 in AD 27 began on the evening of March 28.

Charting reveals that April 18 (daytime) is **Nisan 21**. The JDN is 1,731,027.

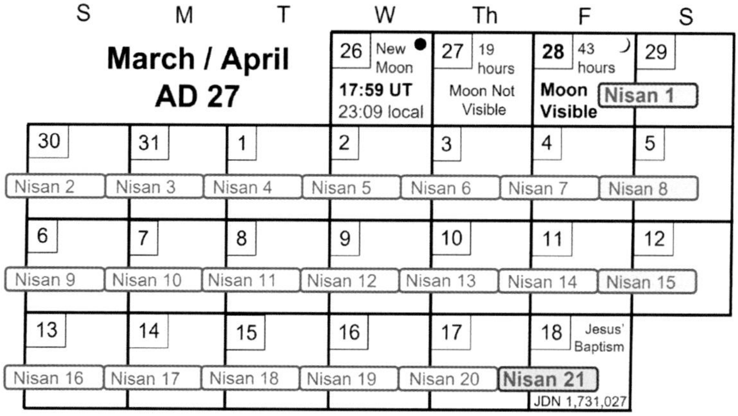

Figure 33. April 18, AD 27, fell on Nisan 21 (daytime).

This can be verified by referencing (figure 26, and online[506]) this new moon:

Year: **0027** Date: **Mar 26** Time (UT): **17:59**

Once verified, it's apparent that Jesus was baptized on Nisan 21—an annual Sabbath, the seventh day of the Feast of Unleavened Bread (Leviticus 23:8). The modern ephemerides give a borderline result of visibility on March 27, but this is highly unlikely given the crescent's extremely young age (19 hours) on that evening.

Remember the former things long past,
For I am God, and there is no other;
I am God, and there is no one like Me,
Declaring the end from the beginning,
And from ancient times things which have not been done,
Saying, 'My plan will be established,
And I will accomplish all My good pleasure'
(Isaiah 46:9–10)

Therefore I declared them to you long ago,
Before they took place I proclaimed them to you,
So that you would not say, 'My idol has done them,
And my carved image and my cast metal image have commanded them.'
You have heard; look at all this.
And you, will you not declare it?
I proclaim to you new things from this time,
Hidden things which you have not known.
(Isaiah 48:5–6)

APPENDIX D

AN ABSOLUTE CHRONOLOGY

> This appendix presents an absolute chronology of key biblical events in and around the reign of Nebuchadnezzar II, king of Babylon (605–562 BC).

Chronology, aka the "backbone of history," can be rock-solid evidence, sorting the possible from the impossible—but only if it's *correct*. Here we identify the years of Daniel's capture and of Jerusalem's destruction. The dates calculated in appendices A.10.1 and A.13.1 must be confirmed before we can claim **everything** fits. First, how can we know these BC years at all? In a word: *eclipses*—that ancients recorded, and moderns have calculated.

D.1 Establishing a Framework of BC Years

The Bible gives a *relative* chronology. It dates events to kings' years (e.g., "third year of the reign of Jehoiakim" in Daniel 1:1). This alone doesn't tell us the BC year. For that, we need an *absolute* chronology, meaning one that places biblical events in specific BC years. An absolute chronology requires fixed anchor points of BC years that are certain.

We have fixed anchor points thanks to Babylonian astronomers who dated eclipses to the years of kings' reigns, often in the format: "Nebuchadnezzar year 4, month 1, [day] 13." [507] Modern astronomy can calculate the times of these ancient eclipses to within minutes. This allows historians to calibrate the Babylonian calendar with the familiar Julian calendar. [508] We know this example eclipse happened in 601 BC. *How?* Two sources are particularly useful: (1) Ptolemy's Canon and (2) the Babylonian tablet VAT 4956.

1. Greek astronomer Ptolemy's (c. AD 100–170) master work *Almagest* includes many dated astronomical observations and a list of kings and the lengths of their reigns. This list, called "**Ptolemy's Canon**," gives an unbroken chronology over nine centuries, from Babylonian King Nabonassar in 747 BC to Roman Emperor Antoninus (d. AD 161). [509] Scholars consider Ptolemy's Canon valid for several reasons. It stands in accord with other ancient sources [510] and observations, from an eclipse in 721 BC down to Ptolemy's own observations. Modern astronomy confirms Ptolemy's Canon, and its recorded years of Babylonian king Nebuchadnezzar. [511]

2. Cuneiform astronomy tablet **VAT 4956** records many astronomical observations during Nebuchadnezzar's thirty-seventh year. Modern astronomy places these observations with certainty between spring 568 BC and spring 567 BC, [512] in harmony with Ptolemy's Canon. With Nebuchadnezzar's thirty-seventh year identified, we can know the BC years of events, including Babylon's 539 BC fall to Persia (chapter 2). [513]

Other recovered tablets confirm VAT 4956 and Ptolemy's Canon (see key to figure 34). [514] Even if we ignored Ptolemy's Canon or VAT 4956, many other sources sufficiently confirm this era's absolute chronology and identify with high confidence the exact BC years of Nebuchadnezzar's reign.

Allegations of error in recording, copying, or observation methods (esp. VAT 4956) are not persuasive. Such allegations would require hundreds of errors to conspire to produce a false yet synchronized dating. Multiple errors by different observers at different times would have produced chaos and contradiction, yet the historical astronomical record reflects internal consistency.

The Years of Nebuchadnezzar, Astronomically Fixed

A	B	C	D	A	B	C	D	A	B	C	D	A	B	C	D	A	B	C	D
609	JFM	16		599	JFM	5	3	589	JFM	15		579	JFM	25		569	JFM	35	
BC	AMJ	17			AMJ	6			AMJ	16			AMJ	26			AMJ	36	
	JAS	17			JAS	6			JAS	16			JAS	26			JAS	36	
	OND	17			OND	6			OND	16			OND	26			OND	36	
608	JFM	17		598	JFM	6		588	JFM	16	6	578	JFM	26		568	JFM	36	
	AMJ	18			AMJ	7			AMJ	17			AMJ	27			AMJ	37	12
	JAS	18			JAS	7			JAS	17			JAS	27			JAS	37	12
	OND	18			OND	7			OND	17			OND	27			OND	37	12
607	JFM	18		597	JFM	7	4	587	JFM	17	7	577	JFM	27		567	JFM	37	12
	AMJ	19			AMJ	8			AMJ	18			AMJ	28	9		AMJ	38	
	JAS	19			JAS	8			JAS	18			JAS	28			JAS	38	
	OND	19			OND	8			OND	18			OND	28			OND	38	
606	JFM	19		596	JFM	8		586	JFM	18		576	JFM	28		566	JFM	38	
	AMJ	20			AMJ	9			AMJ	19			AMJ	29			AMJ	39	
	JAS	20			JAS	9			JAS	19			JAS	29			JAS	39	
	OND	20			OND	9			OND	19			OND	29			OND	39	
605	JFM	20		595	JFM	9		585	JFM	19		575	JFM	29		565	JFM	39	
	AMJ	21	1		AMJ	10			AMJ	20			AMJ	30			AMJ	40	
	JAS	AY			JAS	10			JAS	20			JAS	30			JAS	40	
	OND	AY			OND	10			OND	20			OND	30			OND	40	
604	JFM	AY		594	JFM	10		584	JFM	20		574	JFM	30		564	JFM	40	
	AMJ	1			AMJ	11			AMJ	21			AMJ	31			AMJ	41	
	JAS	1			JAS	11			JAS	21			JAS	31			JAS	41	
	OND	1			OND	11			OND	21			OND	31			OND	41	
603	JFM	1		593	JFM	11		583	JFM	21		573	JFM	31		563	JFM	41	
	AMJ	2			AMJ	12			AMJ	22			AMJ	32	10		AMJ	42	
	JAS	2			JAS	12			JAS	22			JAS	32	11		JAS	42	13
	OND	2			OND	12			OND	22			OND	32			OND	42	
602	JFM	2		592	JFM	12		582	JFM	22		572	JFM	32		562	JFM	42	14
	AMJ	3			AMJ	13			AMJ	23			AMJ	33			AMJ	43	
	JAS	3			JAS	13			JAS	23			JAS	33			JAS	43	
	OND	3			OND	13			OND	23			OND	33			OND	AY	15
601	JFM	3		591	JFM	13	5	581	JFM	23		571	JFM	33		561	JFM	AY	
	AMJ	4	2		AMJ	14			AMJ	24			AMJ	34		Key:			
	JAS	4			JAS	14			JAS	24			JAS	34		A	BC year		
	OND	4			OND	14			OND	24			OND	34		B	months		
600	JFM	4		590	JFM	14		580	JFM	24		570	JFM	34		C	king's year		
	AMJ	5			AMJ	15			AMJ	25			AMJ	35		D	reference		
	JAS	5			JAS	15			JAS	25	8		JAS	35		eclipse			
	OND	5			OND	15			OND	25			OND	35		key event			

Figure 34. Astronomically fixing **Nebuchadnezzar's** years, between the reigns of his father Nabopolassar and his son Evil-merodach. Column B shows the initials of each Julian month. April and October are proxy for Nisan and Tishri, respectively. Column C shows the Babylonian count of each king's regnal years. Column D records events (see key to this figure).

#s	From Column D	BC Year	Date	Source	Reference	Ref. page
1	Battle of Carchemish	605	Summer	BM 21946	Jeremiah 46:2	
2	eclipse	601	Apr 10	LBAT 1420	Stephenson (2008)	164
3	eclipse	599	Feb 19	LBAT 1420	Stephenson (2008)	165
4	Jehoiachin captured	597	Mar 17	BM 21946	2 Kings 24:12	
5	eclipse	591	Mar 22	LBAT 1420	Stephenson (2008)	196
6	eclipse	588	Jan 18	LBAT 1420	Stephenson (2008)	196
7	eclipse	587	Jan 7	LBAT 1420	Stephenson (2008)	165
8	eclipse	580	Aug 14	LBAT 1420	Stephenson (2008)	165
9	eclipse	577	Jun 13	LBAT 1420	Stephenson (2008)	197
10	eclipse	573	Apr 1	LBAT 1420	Stephenson (2008)	166
11	eclipse	573	Sep 25	LBAT 1419	Stephenson (2008)	197
12	many observations	568-7	Apr-Apr	VAT 4956	Neuffer (1979)	43
13	eclipse	563	Sep 5	LBAT 1421	Stephenson (2008)	197
14	eclipse	562	Mar 2	LBAT 1421	Stephenson (2008)	152
15	Evil-merodach accession	562	October	BM 35603	2 Kings 25:27; Jer 52:31	

Key to **figure 34**

But what about the exact dates of biblical events? Pinpointing biblical dates requires two more steps:

- Find the exact dates of key events referenced in *both* the Bible and Babylonian sources, for example items 1, 4, and 15 above.

- Determine the exact dates of biblical events relative to the key events identified in step 1.

Scholars have a firm understanding of the Babylonian calendar and scribal convention. Babylonians recorded the day a new king took the throne to the new king's *accession year* (year zero). A king's *first year* started on the next Nisan 1 (Mar/Apr), and his *second year* started on the following Nisan 1, and so on.[515]

> Nebuchadnezzar's *accession* year started September 7, 605 BC. His *first* year started on the next Nisan 1, which was April 2 of 604 BC. He died in early October of 562 BC. His son Evil-merodach then began his *accession* year.

Key Anchor Point Events

Figure 34 lists three key events dated in both the Bible and Babylonian Chronicle. These are numbered 1, 4, and 15 in figure 34, column D.

#1. Carchemish—605 BC: The Babylonian Chronicle places this major battle in the summer of 605 BC. Jeremiah 46:2 places Carchemish in Judean King Jehoiakim's fourth year. Neither source records the month and day, but the year 605 BC is astronomically fixed.[516]

#4. King Jehoiachin's capture—March 16, 597 BC: The Babylonian Chronicle places King Jehoiachin's (a son of Jehoiakim) capture on Adar 2 (March 16) in 597 BC. Second Kings 24:10–12 places this event in Nebuchadnezzar's eighth year (appendix A.4.2).

#15. Evil-merodach's accession—October, 562 BC: Evil-merodach took the throne in October 562 BC.[517] Second Kings 25:27 and Jeremiah 52:31 refer to Evil-merodach's accession year,[518] which ended April 6 of 561 BC. In his accession year, Evil-merodach released Jehoiachin from prison on April 2 in 561 BC.[519] With the dates of these three key events (figure 34) identified, we can find the exact dates of other biblical events.

Absolute Dates of Biblical Events

The books of Ezekiel, Daniel, Jeremiah, 2 Kings, and 2 Chronicles each date events in this era. Finding exact dates requires knowing the dating method they applied. A key question is whether different Jewish Bible writers used the same or different dating methods at the same time. An assumption currently pervades that Jewish sources used different dating methods concurrently. This book finds that Jewish sources used the same method concurrently.[520] In other words, all Jewish sources applied the same dating method *at any given time*, and whenever the method changed, *all* Jewish sources reflected that change. The following defines this uniform method and presents evidence for it.

> Many scholars follow the chronology of American scholar Dr. Edwin Thiele's 1983 book, *The Mysterious Numbers of the Hebrew Kings*. Thiele reconciled the reigns of Judean and Israelite kings in the divided kingdom era (c. 930-721 BC). Thiele's work was excellent but not perfect—notably his extrapolating divided kingdom dating methods into the era of our study (post-Josiah), centuries after the era of Thiele's primary focus.

Two key concerns are (1) whether Jews applied the accession year (AY) or nonaccession year (NAY), and (2) if they advanced kings' years at Nisan or Tishri (chapter 4, appendix A.4.2). These points are vital for placing biblical events in their correct BC years.

Judean dating method appears to be concurrently universal. That method, used uniformly throughout this book, is summarized as follows:

A. **Accession date** is obtained from the historical record.

B. **First regnal day** (all kings) was counted to:
   1. first year (NAY, year one) when Jews were in the land, or
   2. accession year (AY, year zero) when Judah was outside the land (587 to 457 BC).

C. **Month of advance** (when to count up to the king's next year):
   1. Tishri 1 for Judean kings (and for Artaxerxes Longimanus[521]), or
   2. Nisan 1 for foreign kings[522] (except Artaxerxes Longimanus).

As will be shown, the above dating method reconciles all dated biblical events in the era of our study (post-Josiah). It does not require different sources to use different methods concurrently, nor any scriptural text to be amended or ignored. In other words, it brings all related scriptural statements regarding time into harmony.

A careful examination reveals that *all* Jews used NAY (nonaccession year, year one) dating before their removal from Judah in 587 BC and then used AY (accession year, year zero) dating in Babylon until their return in 457 BC (appendix A.4.2). Jews advanced Judean kings in Tishri and foreign kings in Nisan. How can we know *for sure*?

Same or Different?

Some scholars assume that different biblical sources used different dating methods concurrently. For example, Thiele required Daniel to advance at Tishri yet Jeremiah at Nisan *for the same king at the same time*.[523] Unfortunately, that assumption—that Jews used different methods *at the same time*—pervades the literature. But that is highly unlikely when you consider not only the real-world implications but also the full body of evidence.

Daniel, Ezekiel, Jeremiah, and the authors of Kings and Chronicles each intended their recorded dates to be correctly understood. That's the whole point of recording a date.

> The Bible has c. 100 unique events dated to a king's year. None explains its method (e.g., month of advance, etc.). Historical evidence indicates uniform dating methods. The fifth century BC Elephantine papyri show Jewish scribes dating civil events identically as Ezra, also a scribe, dated scriptural events.[524] Jewish sources used uniform dating at the same time. When methods changed (and they did), they changed for everyone.

But what does Scripture say? The Bible never hints of different sources using different methods *concurrently*. Moreover, the Talmud interprets much Old Testament chronology yet also never mentions different sources applying different methods concurrently. Granted, this is argument from silence, but we should really expect to see something here if there were indeed something here. In fact, the Talmud often states that "Jews reckoned" (collectively), implying one uniform dating method was used by all biblical sources at any given time.

A study by American chronologist Rodger Young[525] examined evidence from Ezekiel, Jeremiah, and 2 Kings separately. It did not force any assumption of uniform dating method. Instead, it methodically isolated the methods used by each source. These all harmonize[526] with the method identified in this book (facing page). In other words, different Bible writers applied the same dating method at the same time. That method always differentiated between Judean and foreign kings. When it changed, it changed for all.

Advance in Tishri or Nisan?

Jews advanced Judean kings' years at Tishri. The Torah scroll was found (2 Kings 22:3) and then Passover celebrated (2 Kings 23:23), both in King Josiah's eighteenth year. We know Josiah's years advance at Tishri because the many intervening events could not have fit between Nisan 1 and 14. Only a Tishri advance works for Josiah, a Judean king.

Jews advanced Nebuchadnezzar at Nisan. Jehoiachin was taken captive in Adar of Nebuchadnezzar's seventh Babylonian (AY) year[527] and in his eighth Jewish (NAY) year (2 Kings 24:10–12). This date is astronomically fixed to March 16, 597 BC. Only a Nisan advance for Nebuchadnezzar fits the biblical reference. If Jews advanced Nebuchadnezzar in Tishri, then the 2 Kings date would fall too early. It must be Nisan for that foreign king.

The Talmud directly states that Jews advanced Cyrus, a foreign king, and the kings of Israel (also foreign to the Southern Kingdom of Judah) at Nisan.[528]

Accession Year or Not?

Jews used the nonaccession year (NAY, year one) for all kings in the decades prior to 587 BC. Jehoiakim became king shortly after Tishri 1 in 609 BC.[529]

> Jehoiakim's years are shown by Jeremiah 25:3, which states that from Josiah's thirteenth year to Jehoiakim's fourth year is 23 years, inclusive. Also, we know Jehoiakim's fourth year is the astronomically fixed Carchemish year (Jeremiah 46:2) of 605 BC. Therefore, his first year began in Tishri (see below) of 609 BC, regardless of AY/NAY.

How can we know Jews used the nonaccession year for his reign? The below chart shows the possible *Jewish* reckonings of:

- **Jehoiakim** (Tishri), where T1 = Tishri with a nonaccession year and T0 = Tishri with an accession year.
- **Babylonian kings** (Nabopolassar/Nebuchadnezzar's years, Nisan) where N1 = Nisan with a nonaccession year and N0 = Nisan with an accession year:

Jewish Count of Kings' Years

		Jehoiakim			Nab/Nzzr	
		T1	**T0**		**N1**	**N0**
609	OND	1	0	*Jehoiakim*	17	16 *Nabopolassar*
608	JFM	1	0		17	16
BC	AMJ	1	0		18	17
	JAS	1	0		18	17
	OND	2	1		18	17
607	JFM	2	1		18	17
BC	AMJ	2	1		19	18
	JAS	2	1		19	18
	OND	3	2		19	18
606	JFM	3	2		19	18
BC	AMJ	3	2		20	19
	JAS	3	2	Dan 1:1	20	19
	OND	4	3		20	19
605	JFM	4	3		20	19
BC	AMJ	4	3	Jer 46:2	21	20 **Carchemish**
	JAS	4	3	Jer 25:1	1	0 *Nebuchadnezzar*
	OND	5	4		1	0

Figure 35. Possible Judean dating methods, showing Jews did not use the accession year during this period. The abbreviations (JFM, AMJ, etc.) are of calendar months. April and October are proxy for Nisan and Tishri, respectively.

Given the astronomically fixed anchor point of Carchemish (605 BC), Judean dating method can be isolated in three steps:

1. Carchemish occurred in summer of 605 BC. Nebuchadnezzar became king on September 7, 605 BC,[530] after Carchemish. That date is astronomically fixed.

2. Jeremiah 46:2 places Carchemish in Jehoiakim's *fourth* year. **This excludes T0.** (Jews must have used the nonaccession year, T1, for Jehoiakim.)

3. In Jeremiah 25:1, "the fourth year of Jehoiakim" overlaps the "first year of Nebuchadnezzar," meaning at some point before October of 605 BC, because Jews advanced Jehoiakim's year from fourth to fifth on Tishri 1. This excludes T0 and N0. Jews applied the nonaccession year to both Nebuchadnezzar *and* Jehoiakim. This aligns with traditional Jewish practice (appendix A.4.2).

Moreover, Jeremiah applied the nonaccession year to Nebuchadnezzar also for events up to and including the fall of Jerusalem and then switched to an accession year when Judah was removed from its land (appendix A.4.2).

In conclusion, this method reconciles all related scriptural statements regarding time and enables us to find the correct dates of key biblical events.

D.2   Daniel's Capture and Captivity's Start (606 BC)

> **In the third year of the reign of Jehoiakim king of Judah, Nebuchadnezzar king of Babylon came to Jerusalem and besieged it. (Daniel 1:1)**

This occurred in 606 BC, a year before the battle of Carchemish.[531] *How do we know?* Note that Jeremiah 46:2 places Carchemish in the "fourth year of Jehoiakim":

> **To Egypt, concerning the army of Pharaoh Neco king of Egypt, which was by the river Euphrates at Carchemish, which Nebuchadnezzar king of Babylon defeated in the fourth year of Jehoiakim the son of Josiah, king of Judah (Jeremiah 46:2)**

The battle of Carchemish occurred in summer 605 BC—the year is astronomically fixed[532] which overlapped the fourth year of Jehoiakim. Daniel 1:1 occurs in the *third* year of Jehoiakim, in 606 BC (figure 35) *before* Carchemish. This face-value approach will prove valid. Yet, current scholarly consensus puts Daniel 1:1 in 605 BC, *after* Carchemish.

The 605 BC consensus is dominant. There are three major reasons. One is that Daniel 1:1 uses the full title "Nebuchadnezzar king of Babylon." The assumption is that Daniel would have used that title only if Nebuchadnezzar were already senior king of Babylon *at that time*. A second reason is the assumption that the events of Daniel 1:1 were among those predicted by Jeremiah 25 and 36, given in the "fourth year of Jehoiakim." A third reason is that the Babylonian Chronicle records Nebuchadnezzar in the "Hatti-land" in 605 BC after Carchemish, but not in 606 BC.[533] To Babylonians, Hatti-land covered a large area from Turkey to Egypt, and included Jerusalem. Under closer scrutiny, those reasons aren't persuasive. All three can be addressed.

First, Daniel's using Nebuchadnezzar's full title doesn't indicate he was already senior king at the time. Daniel also wrote "Belshazzar king of Babylon" (Daniel 7:1) for someone who *never* became senior king of Babylon (his father was still king at Babylon's fall). We moderns would call Belshazzar a crown prince. Nebuchadnezzar was also crown prince before his father's death. We don't fully understand Babylonian regal protocol, but Daniel certainly did, and he wrote "king of Babylon" for both. We know Belshazzar was never senior king, so we can't conclude Nebuchadnezzar was senior king at the time of Daniel 1:1 either.

> Daniel wrote "Nebuchadnezzar" twenty-nine times yet used his full title "king of Babylon" only once, right here at its earliest mention. Daniel wrote Belshazzar's name eight times and used the full title "king of Babylon" also only once—also at its earliest mention (in time). Daniel simply used full reference at first mention and then abbreviated references, a common literary practice used even today (also in this book).

Jeremiah 46:2 also uses Nebuchadnezzar's full title when dating an event (Carchemish) that we know occurred *before* he became senior king. Thus, Daniel's using Nebuchadnezzar's full title is not persuasive evidence for his being already senior king in Daniel 1:1.[534]

The second reason, the assumption that Jeremiah 25 and 36, given in Jehoiakim's fourth year, must have foretold also Nebuchadnezzar's first siege of Jerusalem is simply unsound. Both chapters foretell that Babylon will "destroy this land" which "will be a place of ruins." This describes Jerusalem's 587 BC destruction but not the events of Daniel 1:1. In fact, it doesn't even describe Nebuchadnezzar's second siege of Jerusalem in 597 BC either. Insisting that it must have predicted all of Babylon's actions against Judah, including the events of Daniel 1, is simply not supported.[535]

To the third reason, the Babylonian Chronicle regularly noted the king's movements. It placed Nebuchadnezzar in the Hatti-land during seven of his first eight years. Only once, in year 7, does it mention Jerusalem. Nebuchadnezzar being in the Hatti-land in 605 BC, the year he took the throne, isn't particularly meaningful. He was there—somewhere—almost every year. This isn't evidence against his being in Jerusalem in 605 BC, only that the Babylonian Chronicle doesn't indicate that he was.

The chronicle mentions Nebuchadnezzar's whereabouts in 607 BC, but not in 606 BC. This isn't odd, as the Babylonian chronicle duly reported his father's movements as senior king. The chronicle doesn't say where Nebuchadnezzar was or wasn't in 606 BC.

History places Nebuchadnezzar in Judah *before* Carchemish, his having been sent by his still-living father, King Nabopolassar:

> **Nabolassar** [sic] who was king of Babylon, […] sent his son Nebuchadnezzar against Egypt, and **against our land**, with a great army[536] (Josephus, bolding added)

Josephus wrote that Nebuchadnezzar did not "take" Judah *after* Carchemish:

> So the king of Babylon passed over Euphrates, and took all Syria, as far as Pelusium, **excepting Judea**.[537] (Josephus, bolding added)

Nebuchadnezzar was in Judah *before* Carchemish, and Josephus claims he did not "take" Judah right *after* Carchemish. Daniel 1:1 describes him subjugating (but not destroying) Jerusalem. Of course, Josephus doesn't hold scriptural authority, but he does convey ancient understanding of these events. In short, the historical record places Nebuchadnezzar in Judah *before* Carchemish and not immediately *after* Carchemish. This evidence supports the 606 BC thesis and opposes the 605 BC consensus view.

Arguments for 605 BC are not persuasive.[538] At face value, both scriptural and historical evidence place Daniel 1:1 in 606 BC. And we have yet further scriptural evidence which places Daniel 1:1 in 606 BC, and excludes 605 BC.

Daniel's Education

Scripture presents this sequence of events:

1. In captivity, Daniel began three years of education.[539]

2. Daniel was examined after "the days which the king had specified."[540]

3. Daniel passed the exam and was hired into the king's personal service.[541]

4. In his **second year**, Nebuchadnezzar had a dream that Daniel interpreted.[542]

5. Nebuchadnezzar immediately promoted Daniel "ruler over the entire province of Babylon, and chief prefect over all the wise men of Babylon."[543]

Obviously, 3 occurred before 5 because Daniel's passing his exams and being hired into the king's service would be absurd if he were already head over "all the wise men of Babylon" and provincial governor. Thus, Daniel *had to have been in captivity for three years before Nebuchadnezzar's second year ended.*

Daniel's Months of Education—Two Scenarios

606	JAS	3		**606 BC**	
BC	OND	6			
605	JFM	9			
BC	AMJ	12			
	JAS	15		Carchemish	
	OND	18	3	**605 BC**	
604	JFM	21	6	End Nzzr. AY	
BC	AMJ	24	9		
	JAS	27	12		
	OND	30	15		
603	JFM	33	18	End Nzzr. 1	
BC	AMJ	36	21		
	JAS	39	24		
	OND	42	27		
602	JFM	45	30	End Nzzr. 2	
BC	AMJ				
If taken captive 606 BC					
If taken captive 605 BC					

Figure 36. Maximum possible months of Daniel's education per this book's 606 BC thesis (yellow) and modern 605 BC consensus (gray). Even the most permissible set of assumptions doesn't allow three years of education before Nebuchadnezzar's dream if Daniel were taken in 605 BC. Note: JFM, AMJ, etc., are quarters of calendar months. April 1 is proxy for Nisan 1. "Nzzr" is Nebuchadnezzar. "Carchemish" refers to the battle of Carchemish, the date of which is astronomically fixed to the summer of 605 BC. The numbers are months elapsing since Jerusalem's siege, the earliest point at which Daniel could have started his education. Altering dating assumptions (e.g., using NAY) would further reduce this time window, making the modern consensus (605) view even more untenable.

If Daniel were taken captive in 605 BC, he could not have completed three years of education. Even the most permissive possible assumptions would allow at most only thirty months before Nebuchadnezzar's second year ended. If Daniel was taken captive in 606 BC, the same assumptions would allow forty-five months, easily enough time to complete those three years of education. Put simply, 45 is more than 36, and 30 is less than 36. Thus, 606 BC fits and 605 BC does not. Daniel 1:1 occurred in 606 BC.

The 605 BC consensus view, despite its current popularity, lacks both scriptural and historical support.

The 606 BC thesis fits both Scripture and the historical record. Thus, Daniel's captivity falls *before* Carchemish and harmonizes with the date calculated in appendix A.10.1.

> Josephus (*AJ* 10.9.7) dated Nebuchadnezzar's dream to "two years after the destruction of Egypt" (at Charchemish). Given that Daniel had completed *three* years of Babylonian education by the time of Nebuchadnezzar's dream, this also shows that Jews (in AD 94) held that Daniel's captivity began well *before* Carchemish, not after.

Appendix A.10.1 calculated the start date of Daniel's captivity as July 25, 606 BC, by following a completely independent line of scriptural evidence.

D.3   Jerusalem's Destruction (587 BC)

A	B	C	D	E	F	G	H
599	JFM	5	6				
	AMJ	6	7				
	JAS	6	7				
	OND	6	7				
598	JFM	6	7				
	AMJ	7	8				
	JAS	7	8				
	OND	7	8				
597	JFM	7	8	1	1		1
	AMJ	8	9	1	1		
	JAS	8	9	1	1		
	OND	8	9	2	2		
596	JFM	8	9	2	2		
	AMJ	9	10	2	2		
	JAS	9	10	2	2		
	OND	9	10	3	3		
595	JFM	9	10	3	3		
	AMJ	10	11	3	3		
	JAS	10	11	3	3		
	OND	10	11	4	4		
594	JFM	10	11	4	4		
	AMJ	11	12	4	4		
	JAS	11	12	4	4		
	OND	11	12	5	5		
593	JFM	11	12	5	5		
	AMJ	12	13	5	5		
	JAS	12	13	5	5		
	OND	12	13	6	6		
592	JFM	12	13	6	6		
	AMJ	13	14	6	6		
	JAS	13	14	6	6		
	OND	13	14	7	7		
591	JFM	13	14	7	7		
	AMJ	14	15	7	7		
	JAS	14	15	7	7		
	OND	14	15	8	8		
590	JFM	14	15	8	8		
	AMJ	15	16	8	8		
	JAS	15	16	8	8		
	OND	15	16	9	9		

A	B	C	D	E	F	G	H
589	JFM	15	16	9	9		
	AMJ	16	17	9	9		
	JAS	16	17	9	9		
	OND	16	17	10	10		
588	JFM	16	17	10	10		
	AMJ	17	18	10	10		
	JAS	17	18	10	10		
	OND	17	18	11	11		
587	JFM	17	18	11	11		
	AMJ	18	19	11	11		
	JAS	18	19	11	11		2
	OND	18	18	12		1	3
586	JFM	18		12		1	4
	AMJ	19		12		1	
	JAS	19		12		1	
	OND	19		13		2	
585	JFM	19		13		2	
	AMJ	20		13		2	
	JAS	20		13		2	
	OND	20		14		3	
584	JFM	20		14		3	
	AMJ	21		14		3	
	JAS	21		14		3	
	OND	21		15		4	
583	JFM	21		15		4	
	AMJ	22		15		4	
	JAS	22		15		4	
	OND	22		16		5	
582	JFM	22		16		5	
	AMJ	23		16		5	
	JAS	23		16		5	
	OND	23		17		6	
581	JFM	23		17		6	
	AMJ	24		17		6	
	JAS	24		17		6	
	OND	24		18		7	
580	JFM	24		18		7	
	AMJ	25		18		7	
	JAS	25		18		7	
	OND	25		19		8	

A	B	C	D	E	F	G	H
579	JFM	25		19		8	
	AMJ	26		19		8	
	JAS	26		19		8	
	OND	26		20		9	
578	JFM	26		20		9	
	AMJ	27		20		9	
	JAS	27		20		9	
	OND	27		21		10	
577	JFM	27		21		10	
	AMJ	28		21		10	
	JAS	28		21		10	
	OND	28		22		11	
576	JFM	28		22		11	
	AMJ	29		22		11	
	JAS	29		22		11	
	OND	29		23		12	
575	JFM	29		23		12	
	AMJ	30		23		12	
	JAS	30		23		12	
	OND	30		24		13	
574	JFM	30		24		13	
	AMJ	31		24		13	
	JAS	31		24		13	
	OND	31		25		14	5
573	JFM	31		25			
	AMJ	32		25			
	JAS	32		25			
	OND	32		26			
572	JFM	32		26			
	AMJ	33		26			
	JAS	33		26			
	OND	33		27			
571	JFM	33		27			
	AMJ	34		27			
	JAS	34		27			
	OND	34		28			
570	JFM	34		28			
	AMJ	35		28			
	JAS	35		28			
	OND	35		29			

A	B	C	D	E	F	G	H
569	JFM	35		29			
	AMJ	36		29			
	JAS	36		29			
	OND	36		30			
568	JFM	36		30			
	AMJ	37		30			
	JAS	37		30			
	OND	37		31			
567	JFM	37		31			
	AMJ	38		31			
	JAS	38		31			
	OND	38		32			
566	JFM	38		32			
	AMJ	39		32			
	JAS	39		32			
	OND	39		33			
565	JFM	39		33			
	AMJ	40		33			
	JAS	40		33			
	OND	40		34			
564	JFM	40		34			
	AMJ	41		34			
	JAS	41		34			
	OND	41		35			
563	JFM	41		35			
	AMJ	42		35			
	JAS	42		35			
	OND	42		36			
562	JFM	42		36			
	AMJ	43		36			
	JAS	43		36			
	OND	AY		37			6
561	JFM	AY		37			7

▎Nebuchadnezzar
▎Evil-Merodach

The dates of events
1 and 6 are fixed
astronomically.

Figure 37. Quarterly year counts from Jehoiachin's capture to Evil-merodach's accession (Key on next page). Note column D in late 587 BC, where Jews adopted the accession year making Nebuchadnezzar's nineteenth year suddenly his eighteenth (not a typo, see appendix A.4.2).

Columns in Figure 37

A BC Year
B Months
C Babylonian count (AY) of Nebuchadnezzar's years   Nisan advance
D Judean count (NAY) of Nebuchadnezzar's years   Nisan advance
E Jehoiachin's exile years   Tishri advance
F Zedekiah's years   Tishri advance
G Years *"after"* Jerusalem's destruction   Tishri advance
H References to Events

References (column H)

1	Jehoiachin taken captive	2 Kings 24:12
2	**Jerusalem Destroyed - 587 BC**	see text
3	Captives taken in Nebuchadnezzar's 18th year	Jeremiah 52:29
4	Ezekiel Informed	Ezekiel 33:21
5	Exile 25 = 14 years post destruction	Ezekiel 40:1
6	Death of Nebuchadnezzar	PDBC p12
7	Exile 37 - Jehoiachin freed Adar 27	2 Kings 25:27

Key to **figure 37**

The Bible dates Jerusalem's destruction to the "eleventh year of King Zedekiah." [544] Modern consensus splits evenly between 586 and 587 BC. Unfortunately, the Babylonian Chronicle section which recounts this time period is not yet recovered. Fortunately, Scripture provides more than enough evidence to identify the year.

Most helpfully, Ezekiel dates several events to the years of King Jehoiachin's (Jeconiah) exile and captivity that began on March 16 (2 Adar) in 597 BC. This date is an astronomically fixed anchor point, referenced in both the Bible and the Babylonian Chronicle.

Nebuchadnezzar died in October 562 BC.[545] His son Evil-merodach then began his accession year. This date is also an astronomically fixed anchor point. Scripture places this accession year in the thirty-seventh year of Jehoiachin's exile (2 Kings 25:27). This harmonizes (figure 37) and provides a **reliable measuring rod marked by each year of Jehoiachin's exile** (purple numbers) **between two astronomically fixed dates**.

> Note the eleven years of Zedekiah (column F) are identical to the first eleven years of Jehoiachin's exile (column E). The years of exile and years after Jerusalem's destruction are not kings' years and thus do not include accession years.

In Ezekiel 33:21, reports of Jerusalem's destruction reached Ezekiel in the month of Tevet in the "twelfth year of our exile," which is January of 586 BC. So, the destruction had to have fallen *before* January 586 BC. This excludes the summer of 586 BC and allows the summer of 587 BC. (Remember, BC years count down as time passes.)

Ezekiel 40:1 equates the "fourteenth year after the city was taken" with the twenty-fifth year of exile, which started October of 574 BC. The count of years is noted in figure 37, column G (green numbers). This verse excludes 586 BC and indicates 587 BC.

> The word "after" in Ezekiel 40:1 indicates an antedated count, meaning the first year "after" the destruction would have started in October (Tishri) of 587 BC and then followed sequentially, as depicted on figure 37, column G.

Thus, given the fixed anchor points of Jehoiachin's 597 BC exile and Nebuchadnezzar's 562 BC death, Scripture places the destruction of Jerusalem in 587 BC.

Does 587 BC Fit Other Scriptural Evidence?

Direct, scriptural references to the year of Jerusalem's destruction include:

- 2 Kings 25:2, "eleventh year of King Zedekiah"—column F

- 2 Kings 25:8, "nineteenth year of King Nebuchadnezzar"—column D

- Jeremiah 1:3, "eleventh year of Zedekiah"—column F

- Jeremiah 39:2, "eleventh year of Zedekiah"—column F

- Jeremiah 52:12, "nineteenth year of King Nebuchadnezzar"—column D

- Jeremiah 52:29, "eighteenth year of Nebuchadnezzar"—column D

Each of the above passages place the destruction of Jerusalem in 587 BC, as figure 37 presents. This year is identified by applying the Judean dating system used consistently throughout this book and taking scriptural text at face value, without alteration or omission.

> The interesting twist in Jeremiah 52:29, when Jews abruptly adopted the Babylonian accession year at the very same time Judah was removed from the land of Israel, as detailed in appendix A.4.2. This thesis solution accounts for this anomaly.

Does 587 BC Fit Historical Evidence?

Historical evidence is scant. The relevant section of the Babylonian Chronicle remains unrecovered. However, this passage from the Talmud is helpful:

> When the Temple was destroyed for the first time, that day was the afternoon [Heb. *erev*, alt. evening] of Tisha b'Av [9th of Av], it was the day after the sabbath, it was the year after *sheviis* [sabbatical year].[546] (Talmud)

If we read *erev* as "evening," then the above can fit 587 BC. According to the lunar tables, Av 9 in 587 BC fell on Saturday, July 29 daytime. Had Hebrews not observed the Av crescent moon, e.g., due to clouds (appendix B), then Av 9 would have fallen on Sunday, July 30, the "day after the sabbath" which fits the above passage perfectly.

In contrast, in 588 and 586 BC, Av 9 fell on Tuesday and Thursday, respectively and could not have fallen right after a Sabbath, regardless of crescent sightings.[547] Of course, Talmudic evidence does not hold scriptural authority, and there can be alternate readings of this text, but only 587 BC can fit—588 and 586 BC cannot.

> The seven-day cycle of weekdays has remained unchanged (appendix E.2).

Wacholder's rota of sabbatical years allows 587 BC as a year after a sabbatical year. Zuckermann's rota allows 588 BC.[548] No rota accepted by scholars allows 586 BC.

Historical evidence for Jerusalem's destruction in 587 BC is supportive. Scriptural evidence for Jerusalem's destruction in 587 BC is conclusive.

APPENDIX E

ATTESTATIONS

E.1   Mathematics Audit

Dr. Greg Michalski, PhD Professor of Mathematics, reviewed all mathematical statements of this book, including the appendices and endnotes, and found them correct.

POST OFFICE BOX 8093	DEPARTMENT OF MATHEMATICAL SCIENCES
STATESBORO, GEORGIA 30460-8093	
TELEPHONE: (912) 478-5390	

August 10, 2023

To Whom It May Concern:

I have reviewed the mathematical statements made in "Three Proofs of God" by James Brown. I attest that they are all correct.

Greg Michalski, Ph.D.
Senior Lecturer of Mathematics
Georgia Southern University
65 Georgia Ave. Room 3008
P.O. Box 8093, Statesboro GA 30460

E.2   The Days of the Week Cycle Is Unchanged

The United States Naval Observatory attests that there is no known evidence of any disruption to the seven-day cycle of the week (i.e., Sunday, Monday, Tuesday, etc.).

N. N. Ob. 24

in sent connect and the words
of the little out
supplementary naval collaboration
washington, D. C.

REFER TO No.

EN23/H5(14)(1)

NAVY DEPARTMENT

U. S. NAVAL OBSERVATORY

WASHINGTON, D. C.

12 March   1932

Inclosures. 2.

Dear Sir:

Your letter of 25 February, 1932, containing questions on the continuity of the weekly cycle is at hand.

As to Question (1) - I can only state that in connection with the proposed simplification of the calendar, we have had occasion to investigate the results of the works of specialists in chronology and we have never found one of them that has ever had the slightest doubt about the continuity of the weekly cycle since long before the Christian era.

As to Question, (2) - There has been no change in our calendar in past centuries that has affected in any way the cycle of the week.

As to Question (3) - The answer is implied in the answer given to question (1).

Through the courtesy of the Superintendent, Captain Hellweg, I am inclosing an article on Calendar Reform, published by Admiral Upham, that might be of interest to you.

I am also returning your very interesting debate with Mr. Eastman. It was very considerate of you, for which, I thank you.

Sincerely yours,

James Robertson,
Director American Ephemeris.

ENDNOTES

1. "Natural law" is used here in its scientific sense (i.e., the natural and often predictable regularities observed in our universe).

2. Humans simply can't truly know the future. If we could, then Wall Street would function very differently, weather forecasts would always be right, and there would be no insurance industry. Although in theory, information may travel faster than light, no credible theory allows it to travel backwards in time, even a nanosecond, much less over centuries. Violating time's directionality could also require revising our concept of entropy, specifically, the second law of thermodynamics. A violation of this well-established law would provide a secure warrant to claim that natural law was indeed broken.

3. A timing constraint is required because if given infinite time, any prediction could eventually become true, and thus could never be disproven.

4. Daniel 8:7–8, 20–21; 11:2–4; Edward J. Young, *The Prophecy of Daniel: A Commentary* (Grand Rapids: Wm. B. Eerdmans Publishing Co., 1972), 24.

5. Young, E., *Daniel,* 25; On Daniel's composition date, Miller notes "there is little middle ground on the issue." Stephen B. Miller, *The New American Commentary: Daniel, An Exegetical and Theological Exposition of Holy Scripture*, vol. 18 (Nashville: B&H Publishing Group, 1994), 22–23, 36.

6. "Jews did not doubt the canonicity of Daniel." James VanderKam and Peter Flint, *The Meaning of the Dead Sea Scrolls: Their Significance for Understanding the Bible, Judaism, Jesus, and Christianity* (New York: HarperSanFransisco, 2002), 137 (Fragment 4Q114 / 4QDan^c); Young, E., *Daniel*, 25; First century Jews certainly had canonical Scripture. Josephus affirmed that Jews had "twenty-two books, which contain the records of all the past times; which are justly believed to be divine. [. . .] No one has been so bold as either to add anything to them, to take anything from them, or to make any change." Flavius Josephus, *The New Complete Works of Josephus*, trans. William Whiston (Grand Rapids: Kregel Publications, 1999), 939–940 (*AA* 1.8); Josephus, in AD 94, noted Daniel as "among the sacred writings." *Josephus,* 351 (*AJ* 10.10.4).

7. Daniel 9:26.

8. "The eschatological Anointed One, the Messiah. Within the canon of the OT [Old Testament] there are only two unambiguous references to this figure, both in Dan 9 (25,26)." Willem VanGemeren, *The New International Dictionary of Old Testament Theology and Exegesis*, 5 vols. (Grand Rapids: Zondervan, 1997), 2:1126. There are other messianic references in the OT, but none which specify the timing of his advents (arrivals).

9. Matthew 24:15. See also appendix A.3.1.

10. Oliver B. Greene, *Daniel: Verse by Verse Study* (Greenville, SC: The Gospel Hour, Inc., 2011), 359; H. A. Ironside, *Daniel* (Grand Rapids: Kregel Publications, 2005), 86; Desmond Ford, *In the Heart of Daniel: An Exposition of Daniel 9:24–27* (Lincoln, NE: iUniverse, 2007), x; James Montgomery Boice, *Daniel: An Expositional Commentary* (Grand Rapids: Baker Books, 2006), 99.

11. Francis S. Collins, *The Language of God: A Scientist Presents Evidence for Belief* (New York: Simon and Schuster, 2006), 78.

12. Isaac Newton, *Observations upon the Prophecies of Daniel and the Apocalypse*

of St. John (London: J. Darby and T. Browne, 1733), 15.

13. Newton deemed Christianity to be "founded upon his [Daniel's] Prophecy concerning the Messiah." Newton, I., *Observations*, 25; Ford, *Heart of Daniel*, xi.

14. Baldwin named Daniel 9 "one of the most difficult passages in the OT, and the interpretations which have been offered are almost legion." Joyce G. Baldwin, *Daniel: An Introduction and Commentary* (Downers Grove, IL: InterVarsity Press, 2009), 182; Young, E., *Daniel*, 191; Montgomery voiced a collective frustration, labeling Daniel 9 not only a "most vexed passage," but also the "dismal Swamp of O.T. criticism," and that [centuries of failed attempts] "would seem to preclude any use of the 70 Weeks for the determination of a definite prophetic chronology." James A. Montgomery, *A Critical and Exegetical Commentary on the Book of Daniel* (Edinburgh: T. & T. Clark, 1927), 377, 400–401. Daniel 12:4 and 9 directly indicate otherwise.

15. Daniel 12:4, 9. The Hebrew for "these words" is *haddebarim*, a plural of *dabar*, also used in Daniel 9:25.

16. Note, math is *not* numerology, just as astronomy is not astrology. The math in this book is limited to *arithmetic* (i.e., add, subtract, multiply, divide).

17. Commonly attributed to Carl Sagan.

18. Daniel 1:1–6. These events were foretold in Isaiah 39:7.

19. Per Anderson, the captivity "began in the third year of Jehoiakim, i.e., B.C. 606." Robert Anderson, *The Coming Prince* (Grand Rapids: Kregel Classics, 1957), 55n3; Per Keil, "606 BC begins the seventy years' Babylonian bondage" C. F. Keil, F. Delitzsch, *Commentary on the Old Testament*, trans. J. Martin, M. G. Easton (Peabody, Mass.: Hendrickson Publishers, 2001), 8:229. Per Henry, "from this first captivity, most interpreters think the seventy years are to be dated." Matthew Henry, *Matthew Henry's Commentary on the Whole Bible* (Peabody, Mass.: Hendrickson Publishers, 1991), 4:798.

20. Edwin R. Thiele, *The Mysterious Numbers of the Hebrew Kings* (Grand Rapids: Kregel Academic, 1994), 184; Siegfried H. Horn, "The Babylonian Chronicle and the Ancient Calendar of the Kingdom of Judah," *Andrews University Seminary Studies* 5, no. 1 (1967), 20.

21. Daniel 1:7; 2:1. Daniel was given the Babylonian name *Belteshazzar*. Note the many similarities in the lives of Daniel and Joseph (Genesis 37–50).

22. Daniel 2:12–13. Note, Daniel had already entered the king's service at this point.

23. Daniel 2:48. Interpreting this profound dream is beyond our present scope.

24. Daniel 1:19–21; Richard Parker and Waldo Dubberstein, *Babylonian Chronology: 626 B.C.–A.D. 75 (PDBC)* (Eugene, OR: Wipf and Stock Publishers, 2007), 12.

25. Pierre Briant, *From Cyrus to Alexander: A History of the Persian Empire*, trans. Peter T. Daniels (Winona Lake, IN: Eisenbrauns, 2002), 41; Parker and Dubberstein, *PDBC*, 14; William H. Shea, "Nabonidus, Belshazzar, and the Book of Daniel," *Andrews University Seminary Studies* 20, no. 2 (1982), 146. See also appendix D.1.

26. Xenophon recorded that Babylonians "laughed at his [Cyrus'] preparations, knowing they had supplies to last them more than twenty years." Xenophon, *The Education of Cyrus (Cyropaedia)*, ed. F. M. Stawell, trans. H. G. Dakyns (London: J. M. Dent & Sons, 1910), 237 (7.5.13); Briant, *Cyrus to Alexander*, 42.

27. Daniel 5:1–6. "His hip joints loosened and his knees began knocking together."

28. Albright asserted that the Babylonian Chronicle is "generally recognized as the

most objective and historically reliable annals that have come down to us from the ancient Orient." William F. Albright, "The Nebuchadnezzar and Neriglissar Chronicles," *Bulletin of the American Schools of Oriental Research*, no. 143 (1956), 28. Note that here, "Babylonian Chronicle" refers collectively to many recovered tablets (Nabonassar Chronicle, Nabonidus Chronicle, etc.).

29. Andrew R. Burn, *Persia and the Greeks: The Defense of the West* (London: Minerva Press, 1968), 55. Gutium was a region in Media.
30. Herodotus, *The Histories of Herodotus*, ed. E. H. Blakeney, trans. George Rawlinson, 2 vols (London: J. M. Dent & Sons, 1964), v.1.97 (1.191).
31. Xenophon, *Cyropaedia*, 238 (7.5.20).
32. Xenophon recorded some violence. "Some were struck down and slain" but the invaders "covered the cry with their shouts, as though they were revelers themselves. And thus, making their way by the quickest route, they soon found themselves before the king's palace." Xenophon, *Cyropaedia*, 239 (7.5.26). King Belshazzar was executed that night.
33. Herodotus, *Histories*, 1:97 (1.191); Shea noted that many Babylonians saw Cyrus "as deliverer from the disliked Nabonidus and his son Belshazzar." William H. Shea, "The Search for Darius the Mede (Concluded)," *Journal of the Adventist Theological Society* 12, no. 1 (2001), 99.
34. Briant, *Cyrus to Alexander*, 42; Shea, "The Search for Darius," 98.
35. Burn, *Persia and the Greeks*, 56.
36. Shea concluded that "the close correspondence of these materials has led to the identification of Ugbaru as the king of Babylon during that brief period." William H. Shea, "An Unrecognized Vassal King of Babylon in the Early Achaemenid Period: Part 3," *Andrews University Seminary Studies* 10, no. 1 (1972), 117; And "when these details are compared, they make a good case for identifying Darius the Mede as Ugbaru." William H. Shea, "Nabonidus Chronicle: New Readings and the Identity of Darius the Mede," *Journal of the Adventist Theological Society* 7, no. 1 (1996), 14. See also appendix A.2.1.
37. Daniel 6:2. Daniel's appointment was another kingly duty.
38. Daniel 9:2; Jeremiah 25:1-11; Peter J. Gentry, "Daniel's Seventy Weeks and the New Exodus," *Southern Baptist Journal of Theology* 14, no. 1 (2010), 29.
39. Leviticus 26:18 (i.e., multiplied by seven).
40. Daniel 9:3-19.
41. Daniel 9:20-23.
42. Lange asserted, "know therefore and understand [. . .] directs the notice of both the hearer and the reader to the importance of the disclosures now to be made, and to the duty of subjecting them to serious and thoughtful consideration." Johann P. Lange, *A Commentary on the Holy Scriptures: Critical, Doctrinal, and Homiletical*, trans. Philip Schaff (Grand Rapids: Zondervan, 1978), Daniel, 196. Some interpret Daniel's numbers symbolically. Although "seven" has symbolic meaning, "sixty-two" is plainly unsymbolic.
43. Matthew 24:15; Mark 13:14. Both include "let the reader understand" in the Greek text. Note that Greek did not have parentheses in that era.
44. Gerald Sigal, *The 70 Weeks of Daniel: (9:24-27)* (Bloomington, IN: Xlibris LLC, 2013), 32; Ironside, *Daniel*, 90.
45. Walvoord noted "at least four decrees concerning the rebuilding of Jerusalem recorded in Scripture." John F. Walvoord, *Daniel: The Key to Prophetic*

Revelation (Chicago: Moody Press, 1989), 225. The four are from Cyrus, from Darius, from Artaxerxes to Ezra, and from Artaxerxes to Nehemiah.

46. Harold W. Hoehner, *Chronological Aspects of the Life of Christ* (Grand Rapids: Zondervan, 1977), 117; Talmud, *Talmud Bavli* (Babylonian Talmud), *Schottenstein Edition* (ArtScroll), 73 vols. (Rahway, NJ: Mesorah Publications, Ltd., 2021), vol. 47, 40a.1n3, and Mishnah Sanhedrin 5:1. These passages translate *shabua* ("week") as a seven-year (*shemitah*) cycle, and as a septennial (seven-year period), "a month, a year, a septennial." *Talmud*, vol. 43, "Bava Metzia," 111a.2. Note, this book does not ascribe scriptural authority to the Talmud but cites it as a reliable source of Jewish history and culture.

47. According to Young, "this view [weeks of days] is almost universally rejected." Young, E., *Daniel*, 196.

48. Leviticus 25:8, 10. Jewish scholar Zuckermann stated, "the period of Jubilee consists of 49 years." Benedict Zuckermann, *A Treatise on the Sabbatical Cycle and the Jubilee*, trans. A. Löwy (New York: Hermon Press, 1974), 7, 20. Jubilees and weeks of years are also referenced in the Dead Sea Scrolls (Damascus Document): "As for the exact determination of their times to which Israel turns a blind eye, behold it is strictly defined in the *Book of the Divisions of the Times into their Jubilees and Weeks*." Geza Vermes, *The Complete Dead Sea Scrolls in English*, trans. Geza Vermes (London: Penguin Books, 2011), 139.

49. Daniel 10:2–3. *Yamim* is a plural of *yom*, Hebrew for *day*; Gentry noted, "Daniel 10:2–3 are the only instances of the phrase 'week of days' in the OT, a phrase required by the context in proximity to chapter 9 where the word has a different sense." Gentry, "Daniel's Seventy Weeks," 33.

50. Per Tanner, "the early church fathers, along with Jewish scholars, interpreted each 'week' as a period of seven years and applied this quite literally." J. Paul Tanner, "Is Daniel's Seventy Weeks Prophecy Messianic? Parts 1 & 2," *Bibliotheca Sacra* 166:662–63 (April–September 2009), 198; First quoted R. Yose on Daniel 9, "seventy weeks of years." Mitchell First, *Jewish History in Conflict: A Study of the Major Discrepancy between Rabbinic and Conventional Chronology* (Jerusalem: Jason Aronson Inc., 1997), 154; Zuckermann even used the weeks of Daniel 9:25–27 as an example: "it is obvious that the [Hebrew] people were acquainted with the septennial [seven-year] cycles," tacitly asserting Daniel's weeks as weeks of years. Zuckermann, *A Treatise*, 38–39.

51. Daniel 8:14. Some interpret this as 1,150 days (evenings and mornings separately). Either way, it can't fit a week of days, yet it fits a week of years.

52. Hoehner asserted that "shabua in Daniel 9:24–27 [. . .] refers to units of seven years." Hoehner, *Chronological Aspects*, 117; Walvoord noted that "scholarship, however, agrees that time unit should be considered years." Walvoord, *Daniel*, 218; Jewish author Sigal also asserted that Daniel's seventy weeks "are to be understood as seventy 'weeks of years,' (i.e., as a period of 490 years)." Sigal, *The 70 Weeks*, 11. Note, the quotation marks around "years" are intentional.

53. Anderson, *Coming Prince*, 74–78; Hoehner, *Chronological Aspects*, 135. True, this 360-day period isn't a solar or Hebrew year, but is indeed the period that Daniel indicates, no matter what we call it.

54. Daniel 7:25; 12:7; Revelation 11:2–3; 12:6, 14; 13:5.

55. Three and a half solar years are 1,278 days, not 1,260 days as in Revelation 11:3.

56. Exodus 12:41 is precedent for counting long time spans to the precise day.

57. Anderson, *Coming Prince*, 127–128.
58. Lloyd applied a *"Chaldee* Year [. . .] of *three hundred and sixty Days to the Year."* Benjamin Marshall, *Three Letters in Farther Vindication of the Late Bishop Lloyd's Hypothesis of Daniel's Prophecy of the Seventy Weeks* (London: James and John Knapton, 1728), 117. Note, the pagination is disrupted, the reference is to the *second* page 117; Lange referred to "Chaldee years of 360 days." Lange, *Commentary*, Daniel 209(7). Lloyd *and* Lange predate Anderson.
59. Hoehner, *Chronological Aspects*, 138.
60. Newton, I., *Observations*, 131.
61. George Montagu, *The Times of Daniel: Chronological and Prophetical* (London: James Darling, 1845), 423–433; Montgomery, *Daniel*, 390–401; Lange, *Commentary*, Daniel 205–213. These summarize many proposed solutions.
62. Matthew 24:15; Mark 13:14. For example, in Matthew 12:39–40, Jesus referenced the sign of Jonah but explained its meaning. In Matthew 24, he urged us to read and understand Daniel 9, without giving its explanation.
63. Gentry also deemed this prophecy "recursive" in a different yet not completely unrelated sense. Gentry, "Daniel's Seventy Weeks," 36.
64. Some (e.g., E. Young) allegorize Daniel's "seven and sixty-two" noting that "seven" is richly symbolic yet omitting that "sixty-two" is plainly unsymbolic.
65. Of course, there may be more than only one face-value reading. Many commentaries remark that no literal solution to Daniel 9:25 has kept a consensus. Yet ironically, many still enforce the same assumptions that have failed for centuries. This book departs from two such assumptions to discover a new and valid solution.
66. Imagine a friend hands you a paper with some numbers on it, claiming they are the combination code to a locked safe. The best way to know if your friend's claim is true or not is of course to see if the code opens the safe—in other words, to start by assuming the code *might* be valid. This logic isn't circular (i.e., proving validity by assuming validity) because if the code is valid, it must *open the safe*. That's the best way to know. Similarly, we take Scripture *at face value* in order to test its validity. It must produce a solution ("open the safe"). If valid, then a solution might be found. Thus, the logic is not circular.
67. Nehemiah 2:1–8.
68. Mark 11:7–11.
69. Nehemiah 2:1–8; Anderson, *Coming Prince*, 63; Hoehner, *Chronological Aspects*, 127.
70. Lange asserted that Nehemiah's time "was clearly that of Artaxerxes I. (Longimanus)." Lange, *Commentary*, Ezra 74, Nehemiah 3; Per Anderson, "So thorough is the unanimity with which the Artaxerxes of Nehemiah is now admitted to be Longimanus, that it is no longer necessary to offer proof of it." Anderson, *Coming Prince*, 251. Anderson then listed several proofs; Ian Foley, *The Time Is Near: Volume 1—A Reference Commentary on the Visions of Daniel* (Bloomington, IN: Balboa Press, 2014), 199; Neuffer described how views evolved as archaeological evidence appeared. Julia Neuffer, "The Accession of Artaxerxes I," *Andrews University Seminary Studies* 6, no. 1 (1968), 60.
71. Neuffer, "Accession of Artaxerxes," 64; Parker and Dubberstein, *PDBC*, 17.
72. Lloyd Llewellyn-Jones and James Robson, *Ctesias' History of Persia: Tales of the Orient* (New York: Routledge, 2012), 185.

73. Parker and Dubberstein, *PDBC*, 17; Neuffer, "Accession of Artaxerxes," 63–65; H.F. Clinton, *Fasti Hellenici* (Cambridge: Cambridge University Press, 2013), 40; According to Greek historian Ctesias, Artabanus "reigned for seven months." Briant, *Cyrus to Alexander*, 564, 566; Ctesias' account is found also in Llewellyn-Jones and Robson, *Ctesias' History*, 187.
74. Hermann Hunger, *Astronomical Diaries and Related Texts from Babylonia* (Vienna: Publishing House of the Austrian Academy of Sciences, 2001), 21 (credit also to Abraham Saks); See also British Museum (BM 32234). Although scholars were aware of LBAT 1419 by the 1950s, formal translation wasn't published until 2001. The eclipse used to time the event is in F. Richard Stephenson, *Historical Eclipses and Earth's Rotation* (New York: Cambridge University Press, 1997), 153; Note, this date from LBAT 1419 harmonizes with the Greek histories (Clinton, *Fasti Hellenici*) cited by Anderson.
75. Thiele noted that to understand ancient dates, "a primary requisite is that the chronological procedure of that nation be understood." Thiele, *Numbers*, 43.
76. Lange noted, "That Nehemiah is the author of the book, all agree. Much of it is written in the first person, and claims thus to be the writing of Nehemiah himself." Lange, *Commentary*, Nehemiah 2.
77. Thiele, *Numbers*, 43.
78. Thiele, *Numbers*, 43. Thiele showed which nations used which systems (71n8); Siegfried H. Horn and Lynn H. Wood, *The Chronology of Ezra 7* (Calhoun, GA: TEACH Services, Inc., 2006), 120.
79. Thiele, *Numbers*, 43–44. This (AY or NAY) is *always* important.
80. In fact, Thiele claimed several changes of method. Thiele, *Numbers*, 105.
81. Thiele, *Numbers*, 44; The Bible lacks any evidence of anniversary advance (e.g., as do English monarchs). Keil, *Commentary*, 9:526n1. The ancients counted years not for the sake of their kings but for the practical purpose of referencing calendar years for the sake of a functioning society.
82. Hoehner, *Chronological Aspects*, 127; *Talmud*, vol. 18, "Rosh Hashanah," 3b.1. Both sources reach the same conclusion for the same reasons. Note, this book does not ascribe scriptural authority to the Talmud but cites it as a reliable source of Jewish history and culture, just as it cites Josephus, Tacitus, etc.
83. Nehemiah 2:1–8.
84. Nehemiah 2:7–9.
85. Anderson asserted that because the date isn't given, the first of Nisan is implied. Anderson, *Coming Prince*, 122; Hoehner correctly noted a lack of scriptural support for Anderson's assertion but ultimately followed it. Hoehner, *Chronological Aspects*, 138. Scripture simply doesn't disclose the exact date.
86. Parker and Dubberstein, *PDBC*, 26, 32. Dates are daytime of the first day of a lunar month. Note, *PDBC* is authoritative for Persia and Babylon in this era.
87. Seidelmann noted, "the codified [modern] Hebrew calendar as we know it today is generally considered to date from A.M. 4119 (+359) [AD 359], though the exact date is uncertain." P. Kenneth Seidelmann, ed., *Explanatory Supplement to the Astronomical Almanac* (Sausalito, CA: University Science Books, 2006), 588; The *Jewish Encyclopedia* asserts, "Later Jewish writers agree that the calendar was fixed by Hillel II in [. . .] 359 C.E." *Jewish Encyclopedia*, Isidore Singer, managing editor (New York: Funk And Wagnalls Company, 1916) "Calendar, History of," 3:500; English astronomer

Fotheringham asserted that "intercalation was regulated annually by the judgment of the Sanhedrin, not by a fixed cycle, in the time of Our Lord." Fotheringham, "Date of the Crucifixion," 156. The modern Hebrew calendar wasn't observed during the biblical era and can't be used to calculate biblical dates. This remains an extremely common error, one that we will avoid.

88. Exodus 12:3; 1 Corinthians 5:7.

89. Luke 19:44.

90. Exodus 23:12; Deuteronomy 5:14 both directly mention *donkey*; Luke 19:35–39.

91. Seidelmann, *Explanatory Supplement*, 55. JDN makes calendar math easier.

92. NASA, "Julian Day and Civil Date Calculator," https://core2.gsfc.nasa.gov/time/julian.html; See also United States Naval Observatory, "Julian Date Converter," https://aa.usno.navy.mil/data/JulianDate; See also Espenak, "Astropixels Calendar Date Converter," http://www.astropixels.com/ephemeris/calendarconverter.html. Note that current language AI models (2023) are not yet capable of reliable JDN calculations.

93. NASA, "Julian Day"; Espenak, "Converter." See also appendix A.5.1.

94. Hoehner, *Chronological Aspects*, 98; Gentry, "Daniel's Seventy Weeks," 37.

95. Church father Julius Africanus in c. AD 221 placed Jesus' resurrection in AD 31. In fragment 16.3, he wrote the "second year of the 202nd Olympiad," which started August 16, AD 30, and ended August 16, AD 31. Nisan (Mar/Apr) of that period fell in AD 31. Bickerman, *Chronology of the Ancient World* (Ithaca, New York: Cornell University Press, 1980), 120. This isn't conclusive. Other church fathers identified different years so we can't select any single year from them alone. The point is that Africanus is a credible source and attested AD 31.

96. Seidelmann, *Explanatory Supplement*, 588. The point is the modern Hebrew calendar, the basis for internet calendar converters, was adopted *after* the biblical era and isn't reliable for biblical dates. Using internet date converters is today probably the *single most common error* in biblical chronology.

97. Jesus referred to the entire Old Testament. "Psalms" (writings) is part of the *Tanakh*, the Hebrew abbreviation of *Torah* (law), *Nevi'im* (prophets), and *Ketuvim* (writings). Note that this does not require that *all* prophecy have a literal, mathematical fulfillment, only that all points to Jesus.

98. Mark 1:15; Luke 19:44. Both refer to "time."

99. Luke 2:46.

100. See also Haggai 2:7–9, often interpreted as messianic.

101. Rashi, on Genesis 49:10 noted, "until Shiloh comes: [refers to] King Messiah, to whom the kingdom belongs." Chabad.org, "Complete Jewish Bible With Rashi Commentary," translated by The Judaica Press, https://www.chabad.org/library/bible_cdo/aid/8165/showrashi/true. *Targum Onkelos* (authoritative Aramaic translation of the Hebrew Scriptures) also interprets *shiloh* here as "King Messiah"; H. Freedman, *Midrash Rabbah: Deuteronomy, Lamentations* (London: Soncino Press, 1939), 137n6.

102. The Talmud's plays on words (e.g., *shila/shiloh,* et al.) use actual messianic prophecies. *Talmud*, vol. 49, "Sanhedrin," 98b.3.

103. Arthur W. Pink, *Gleanings in Genesis* (Chicago: Moody Press, 1922), 324. See Esther 4:11; 5:2 in which the king used his scepter to spare Esther's life.

104. The Talmud reads, "in this verse, Jacob promises Judah that the kings of the Jewish people will emerge exclusively from his tribe, until the advent of the

105. Ezra 1:8 (i.e., *nasi* or "exilarch"). That prince wasn't always of Judah. During the Hasmonean period, Judean kings were not of Judah, breaking Torah law.
106. Josephus, 736 (*Wars* 2.8.1). Note that King Herod condemned many to death.
107. John 18:31 speaking to Pilate: "The Jews said to him, 'We are not permitted to put anyone to death.'" Still, Jews would later stone Stephen (Acts 7).
108. Judean regency and capital punishment rights span the era, but with caveats. For example, the Hasmonean kings (c. 140–37 BC) were of the tribe of Benjamin, not Judah. Also, Jews continued to execute murderers until c. AD 30, when the Sanhedrin vacated the temple's "chamber of hewn stone" and were thus no longer authorized (Deuteronomy 17:10) to issue a death sentence. *Talmud,* vol. 52, "Avodah Zarah," 8b.4. However, in Genesis, Jacob spoke of *two* entities, not one. In AD 6, Judah lost *both* regency *and* legal authority *concurrently.* Jacob referenced both, so AD 6 is indicated.
109. Hoehner, *Chronological Aspects*, 131. Hoehner noted Daniel 9:24 isn't yet fulfilled to *Israel and Jerusalem.* Thus, the seventy weeks aren't complete.
110. Greene, *Daniel*, 393. The earliest assertion of this pause is by Clement of Alexandria in c. AD 200.
111. Gentry, "Daniel's Seventy Weeks," 30 (and many others).
112. Newton, I., *Observations*, 137.
113. Per Hengstenberg, "seven and the sixty-two weeks are not a mere arbitrary dividing into two of one whole period." Keil, *Commentary*, 9:729.
114. Sigal asserts the *atnach* "requires a break between the seven weeks and the sixty-two weeks." Sigal, *The 70 Weeks*, 32; R. Shalomim Halahawi, *The Way: The Prophetic Messianic Voice to the Path of the Edenic Kingdom Redemption* (Morrisville, NC: Lulu, 2007), 224.
115. VanderKam, *Dead Sea Scrolls*, 87.
116. Feinberg quoted Allen MacRae, who identified "an interval after the first as well as the second division of the seventy weeks." John S. and Paul D. Feinberg, *Tradition and Testament: Essays in Honor of Charles Lee Feinberg* (Chicago: Moody Press, 1981), 210.
117. Greene, *Daniel*, 389. This is currently a minority, yet biblically supported view.
118. McComiskey asserts, "the significance of the division of the sixty-nine weeks into seven and sixty-two is left undefined." Thomas E. McComiskey, "The Seventy 'Weeks' of Daniel Against the Background of Ancient Near Eastern Literature," *Westminster Theological Journal* 47, no. 1 (1985), 25.
119. Walvoord, *Daniel*, 225; Hoehner, *Chronological Aspects*, 121–124.
120. Ezra 6:14 links those three kings' decrees with God's command for *building.* There is one word (*dabar*) from God, yet Daniel's starting point is instead when that word actually issued (*min motsa dabar*) as Ezra 6:14 tells us, via these three Persian kings (i.e., God's word issued more than once). Second, consider that the language of Ezra 6:14 is Aramaic, not Hebrew, when directly comparing it with any Hebrew text (e.g., Daniel 9:25).
121. This section of Ezra is in Aramaic, not Hebrew.
122. Young warned, "It is not justifiable to distinguish too sharply between the building of the city and the building of the temple." Young, E., *Daniel*, 203; Gentry concurred, "Rebuilding the city and rebuilding the temple were one and the same thing to the Jewish people (cf. Isaiah 44:28)." Gentry, "Daniel's

Seventy Weeks," 35; Intriguingly, Scripture directly equates the city with the temple. In Ezra 4:21, the king forbade rebuilding the *city* (not "temple"), and in v. 24, we read that construction of the *temple* (not the "city") was halted as a result. Of course, there may be any number of interpretations, but taken in full context, this one—equating Jerusalem with the temple—cannot be excluded.

123. 2 Chronicles 36:22–23; Ezra 1:2–4.
124. One biblical standard of a true prophet is that all must come true. If any prophecy fails, then he is a false prophet (Deuteronomy 18:22). Anyone unsure of Isaiah's validity as a prophet is invited to read Isaiah 53:2–6, noting that this text appears on the Great Isaiah Scroll (1QIsa[a]) carbon dated to before 100 BC. VanderKam, *Dead Sea Scrolls*, 31.
125. Nehemiah 2:3–5. This is not the Artaxerxes of Ezra 4, who *halted* construction.
126. The language supports this. The word for command in Ezra 6:14 is the Aramaic *taim* (tav-ayin-mem) used also (with different vowel pointing) for the decrees issued from Cyrus, Darius, and Artaxerxes to Ezra (Ezra 6:3, 12; 7:13). Because these are in Aramaic and Daniel 9:25 is in Hebrew, we can't consider it conclusive, but the language does associate the decrees issued by those three earthly kings with Daniel's *dabar* via the divine command in Ezra 6:14.
127. This cannot be verified and is not a claim of primacy, but rather that no such approach has yet been discovered in published sources.
128. Ezra 1:1–4; 6:1–12; 7:12–25; Nehemiah 2:4–8.
129. Young concluded that [the decree of Cyrus] "is thus to be regarded as the *terminus a quo* [starting point] of the 70 sevens." Young, E., *Daniel*, 203.
130. Haggai 2:7–9; Malachi 3:1. There is no year zero between 1 BC and AD 1.
131. 2 Chronicles 36:19–21; Jeremiah 29:10.
132. 2 Chronicles 36:22–23; Ezra 1:1–4.
133. Ezra 5:13.
134. Cyrus' son Cambyses briefly held the title "King of Babylon" from c. May to December of 538 BC, at which time Cyrus took the title for himself. William H. Shea, "Darius the Mede in His Persian-Babylonian Setting," *Andrews University Seminary Studies* 29, no. 3 (1991), 237n7. Contra Shea, this does not disqualify Ugbaru as Daniel never referred to Darius the Mede as "King of Babylon." DM held local authority as Cyrus' agent in Babylon, but not supreme authority.
135. Daniel 9:1; 11:1. Shea, "Vassal King," 114, 117.
136. *Talmud*, vol. 18, "Rosh Hashanah," 3b.1.
137. Parker and Dubberstein, *PDBC*, 29.
138. Why did Nisan 1 fall exceptionally early in 537 BC? See appendix A.8.1.
139. Bruce D. Forbes, "Christmas Was Not Always Like This: A Brief History," *Word & World* 27, no. 4 (2007), 401–402. Specifically, *Saturnalia* and *Sol Invictus*.
140. Archibald T. Robertson, *A Harmony of the Gospels for Students of the Life of Christ* (New York: HarperCollins Publishers, 1922), 262.
141. *Josephus*, 522 (*AJ* 15.11.1); *Jewish Encyclopedia* "Temple of Herod," 12:85. The sanctuary was finished in eighteen months, but the outbuildings were under construction for eighty years, so we know this was spoken in AD 28 (i.e., 46 years after construction start). October is proxy for the Hebrew month *Tishri*.
142. There is no year between 1 BC and AD 1, so the calculation is 19 + 28 − 1 = 46.
143. *Josephus*, 565 (*AJ* 17.6.4).
144. Josephus put Herod's death "thirty-four years since he had caused Antigonus

to be killed," *Josephus*, 566n3 (*AJ* 17.6.4), and "thirty-seven years since he had been made king." *Josephus*, 726 (*Wars* 1.33.8). This indicates 4 BC. Yet, his death after a different eclipse in 1 BC is advocated by some. It's beyond our scope to resolve the 4 BC vs. 1 BC eclipse, as Herod's death any time after 5 BC fits this book's thesis. Herod's death *before* 5 BC would void it.

145. William M. Ramsay, *Was Christ Born at Bethlehem? A Study on the Credibility of St. Luke* (London: Hodder and Stoughton, 1898), 194.

146. A bit of hearsay has misled people for ages. Some expositors claim that lambs around Bethlehem were out all night during winter. This is cited to the *Talmud*, vol. 12:20a.2, "Mishnah Shekalim," 7:4. The reference, however, does not support the claim. It instead describes a radius around Jerusalem "in any direction" in which stray lambs found before Passover may be used as Passover sacrifices. The text says nothing about mangers, priests being shepherds, or lambs being out at night in winter. The claim seems to originate in Edersheim's 1883 book, *The Life and Times of Jesus the Messiah* (London: Longmans, Green and Co., 1883), 1:186, and has spread since. Sadly, much hearsay exists, and readers should check that references support the claims. Hold this book to the same standard. Nothing is *too good to check* (Acts 17:11).

147. Luke 2:4–5.

148. Luke 2:1. The KJV translates Luke's *apographesthai* (registered) as *taxed*; Meyer asserted the word is "regarded as the direct registration into the tax-lists." H. A. W. Meyer, *Critical and Exegetical Hand-Book to the Gospels of Mark and Luke*, trans. R. E. Wallis and W. P. Dickson (New York: Funk & Wagnalls, 1884), 264. Note that Roman census and taxation were not like today's.

149. *Talmud*, vol. 47, "Sanhedrin," 11a.3n35.

150. Exodus 23:14–17; Deuteronomy 16:16.

151. Even though Bethlehem is near Jerusalem, the census enrollment covered a much wider area. This excludes enrollment on or near the major feast days.

152. William F. Albright, "The Gezer Calendar," *Bulletin of the American Schools of Oriental Research*, 92 (December 1943), 23, 25. Barley harvest is April to May, followed by the wheat harvest in May to June, then threshing.

153. Zuckermann, *A Treatise*, 61. Zuckermann provided a table of sabbatical years. Wacholder also listed the year 5 BC as non-sabbatical.

154. Robertson asserted "a narrow limit for this notable occurrence, B.C. 6 or 5." Robertson, *Harmony of the Gospels*, 262; Hoehner concurred, "5 B.C. or early 4 B.C. best satisfies all the evidence." Hoehner, *Chronological Aspects*, 25.

155. Luke 1:24–38.

156. Luke 1:5.

157. Luke 1:23–24.

158. 1 Chronicles 28:13. *Abijah* was originally the eighth of the twenty-four orders. Evidence suggests the orders' service sequence may have been rearranged after the Babylonian captivity. *Talmud*, vol. 67, "Arachin," 12b4.

159. 2 Chronicles 23:8; David "ordained that one course should minister to God eight days, from sabbath to sabbath." *Josephus*, 263 (*AJ* 7.14.7).

160. 1 Chronicles 24:10; Luke 1:5.

161. Exodus 23:14–17; Deuteronomy 16:16.

162. *Talmud*, vol. 16, "Succah" 55b2n15 .

163. Luke 1:26–38.

164. Elizabeth's sixth month indeed covers November, 6 BC, exactly. She was thought barren, so we can't assume normal (pre)conception dynamics.
165. Keith Moore, "How accurate are 'due dates'?," *BBC News*, February 3, 2015, http://www.bbc.com/news/magazine-31046144.
166. Due date is 266 days from conception (not LMP). Marion H. Hall, "Definitions Used in Relation to Gestational Age," *Paediatric and Perinatal Epidemiology* 4, no. 2 (1990), 123.
167. Bethlehem was a small village. We may assume that most families, especially Joseph's, would have willingly sheltered his heavily pregnant fiancée in more suitable quarters, unless of course Sabbath restricted everyone's mobility.
168. If it were different, we would have had a very different Nativity story.
169. Exodus 12:3 related to the very first Passover.
170. Exodus 12:6.
171. Leviticus 23:11.
172. Acts 2:1–4.
173. *Talmud*, vol. 19, "Taanis," 29a. *Pogroms* are violent riots, usually against Jews.
174. Lewin calculated an August nativity following the same general reasoning of this book. Thomas Lewin, *Fasti Sacri or a Key to the Chronology of the New Testament* (London: Longmans, Green, and Co., 1865), 115.
175. *Chabad.org*, "The Legalities of Destruction," http://www.chabad.org/parshah/article_cdo/aid/52753/jewish/The-Legalities-of-Destruction.htm.
176. Tzvi Ben Gedalyahu, "Today Marks Ninth of Av Fast Day - Birthday of the Messiah," *Arutz Sheva*, August 10, 2008, http://www.israelnationalnews.com/News/News.aspx/127128#.Vv17J3rOear.
177. Howard Schwartz, *Tree of Souls: The Mythology of Judaism* (New York: Oxford University Press, 2007), 484; H. Freedman, *Midrash Rabbah*, 137n5.
178. Scripture shows the two atonement periods as *sequential* and not overlapping because Ezekiel first lies on his left side, and then afterward on his right. Precedent for this day-year principle appears in Numbers 14:34.
179. Tomasino asserts the Essenes "understood Ezekiel's 390 years to begin with the Babylonian Exile, they began their chronology at this point, interpreting Dan. 9:24–27's decree in light of Ezek. 4:5." Anthony J. Tomasino, "Oracles of Insurrection: The Prophetic Catalyst of the Great Revolt," *Journal of Jewish Studies* 59, no. 1 (2008), 98.
180. Exodus 12:41. Gentry, "Daniel's Seventy Weeks," 32.
181. Jeremiah 29:10.
182. In Daniel 9, Jeremiah's seventy years are *speculatively* multiplied by seven to render seventy weeks of years. Also, *very speculatively*: compare "iron pan" cover (Ezekiel 4:3) and "sky like iron" (Leviticus 26:19); also 2 Chronicles 36:21, the land kept Sabbath "until seventy years were complete," with Leviticus 26:34–35, "the land will rest and restore its Sabbaths." This isn't proof but does show connections to Leviticus 26, part of the *Torah* (Law of Moses).
183. Evans noted that in continental Europe, "the day following October 4, 1582, was called October 15. That is, ten days were omitted. However, there was no break in the sequence of the days of the week." James Evans, *The History and Practice of Ancient Astronomy* (New York: Oxford University Press, 1998), 168. *Why round here to the tenths of days?* Unlike the other time spans, this one covers the transition from Julian to Gregorian calendars. This transition fell

between leap years, so the leap year contribution should be noted for both the Julian and Gregorian segments. This also applies to the math on page 75.

184. *Eretz Israel* = the land of Israel. The promise of return appears also in Deuteronomy 30:1–5; Jeremiah 16:15; Ezekiel 39:28; Micah 2:12, and others.

185. "Declaration of Establishment of State of Israel," Israel Ministry of Foreign Affairs, https://www.gov.il/en/Departments/General/declaration-of-establishment-state-of-israel. Those objecting that modern Israel cannot fulfill OT prophecy because it is a secular, nonobservant state are reminded that historical Israel was chronically nonobservant.

186. Hall asserted that due date is 266 days after conception (not LMP). Hall, "Gestational Age," 123.

187. See also Luke 1:20—Gabriel's words to John's father Zechariah would *"be fulfilled at their proper time."* Again here, Scripture interprets itself.

188. Why not 180 days? "Sixth month" (Luke 1:36) is the time between John's conception and Gabriel's visiting Mary, not between John's and Jesus' births.

189. This was the Saturday after the UN's Thanksgiving recess.

190. Isaiah 40:3; Luke 1:76; John 1:23.

191. Ezra 4:1–6.

192. Ezra 4:11–24. Bardiya (aka Smerdis, Gaumata) is the Artaxerxes of Ezra 4. The king forbade building *the city* (v. 21), and then *temple* construction was halted (v. 24). It's a subtle distinction, but that is indeed in the text.

193. Haggai 1:15. *Darius, Xerxes,* and *Artaxerxes* are recurring throne names in Persia's Achaemenid Dynasty. First, *Jewish History*, 162n5.

194. Ezra 5:3–5; Haggai 1:13–15. Tattenai was governor of Transeuphrates, a large region that included Judah. Zerubbabel was Judah's governor (Haggai 2:21).

195. Ezra 6:1–3. Xenophon, *Cyropaedia*, 290 (8.6.22). The decree was on a scroll, not a cylinder. Note, the Cyrus Cylinder (BM90920) doesn't bear this decree.

196. Ezra 6:13.

197. Haggai 1:15. Ezra advanced Darius' years in Nisan. See also appendix A.11.1.

198. Ezra 7:9. Ezra took four months to travel this distance in the other direction.

199. Parker and Dubberstein, *PDBC*, 15; L. King, R. Thompson, and E. Budge, *The Sculptures and Inscription of Darius the Great on the Rock of Behistûn in Persia* (London: British Museum, 1907), 10–13nXIII; First, *Jewish History*, 161n1.

200. Poole deduced "because none but he [Cambyses] and Smerdis [Bardiya] were between Cyrus and this Darius." Matthew Poole, *A Commentary on the Holy Bible* (Mclean, VA: MacDonald Publishing Company, 1990), 1:873 (to Ezra 4:6).

201. First, *Jewish History*, 162n5.

202. Malachi 3:1; Haggai 2:7. Oddly, Matthew didn't mention his infancy presentation as fulfilling prophecy, thus his entry at an age of responsibility is the key one.

203. Luke 2:41–50.

204. *Talmud*, vol. 72, 45b.1, "Mishnah Niddah," 5:6.

205. Luke 2:46. Again, this has nothing to do with any *bar mitzvah*.

206. *Pirkei Avos,* ed. Rabbi Menachem Davis, (Rahway, NJ: Mesorah Publications, Ltd., 2020), 81–82 (aka *Mishnah Pirkei Avot*).

207. Haggai 2:7; Malachi 3:1; Luke 2:42.

208. Jeremiah 25:11. Second Chronicles 36:19–21 gives this sequence: (1) Temple and Jerusalem destroyed, (2) desolation until seventy [prophetic] years were complete. For confirmation of the 587 BC date, see appendix D.3. The captivity

started earlier, when Jews (incl. Daniel) were taken captive, and released seventy prophetic years later by Cyrus in 537 BC. We know the periods aren't identical because Zechariah 1:12 dates to after Cyrus but before the end of the desolation. The two seventy-year periods partially overlap but aren't identical.

209. Leviticus 26:18.
210. Evans noted, "the day following October 4, 1582, was called October 15. That is, ten days were omitted. However, there was no break in the sequence of the days of the week: this sequence has therefore continued uninterrupted since its inception." Evans, *Ancient Astronomy*, 168.
211. Jerusalem was taken in battle almost always from the north, the only side without natural defense. We know of two exceptions—one when King David captured it (c. 1000 BC), and the other in 1967. (Note, General Allenby's 1917 entrance occurred after the city had peacefully surrendered.)
212. *Talmud*, vol. 72, 45b.1, "Mishnah Niddah," 5:6.
213. Eric Hammel, *Six Days in June: How Israel Won the 1967 Arab-Israeli War* (New York: Maxwell Macmillan International, 2010), 25; Tom Segev, *1967: Israel, the War, and the Year that Transformed the Middle East*, trans. Jessica Cohen (New York: Metropolitan Books, 2007), 210.
214. According to Israeli historian Tom Segev, "this was the largest battle in the north since the War of Independence." Segev, *1967*, 210.
215. William F. Albright, *The Biblical Period from Abraham to Ezra* (New York: Harper & Row, Publishers, 1963), 87.
216. Ezra 4:5–6; Albright, *Abraham to Ezra*, 87; Josephus notes, "they did not please the neighboring nations, who all of them bore an ill-will to them." *Josephus,* 365 (*AJ* 11.4.1).
217. Ezra 9:1–2; Haggai 2:16–17.
218. Ezra 7:5–6. Note the decree text in Ezra 7:12–25 is originally in Aramaic.
219. Ezra 7:9.
220. Parker and Dubberstein, *PDBC*, 32 (authoritative for Babylon).
221. Leading thousands to break Sabbath is unthinkably out of character for Ezra.
222. Ezra 7:28.
223. *Talmud*, vol. 15, "Succah," 20a.3.
224. The Talmud records Jews' changing dating methods: "From the days of Ezra the prophet and onward we never found Elul to be full." *Talmud*, vol. 17, "Beitzah," 6a.1. Jews no longer added a thirtieth day to Elul, as Babylonians did. Significantly, this calendrical change occurred in the "days of Ezra." Also, the Elephantine Papyri indicate, "The Jewish Calendar showed some variations from that of the Babylonians" and "Jews after the exile did not adopt the Babylonian calendar part and parcel." Horn and Wood, *Ezra 7*, 83, 83n25.
225. Mark 1:9–11.
226. Luke 3:1–3. *The fifteenth year of Tiberius Caesar* refers to the year "the word of God came to John," and not to Jesus' baptism as is so often assumed. Jesus could have been baptized in that year or a later year, but not before.
227. Per Wm. Ramsay, "authority equal to that of Augustus in all the provinces and armies of the empire was granted to Tiberius [. . .] on 16th January, A.D. 12," and "the fifteenth year [of Tiberius coincides] with A.D. 25–6." Ramsay, W., *Christ Born at Bethlehem*, 200–201.
228. Tacitus wrote, "it was announced, in one and the same breath, that Augustus

was dead, and that Tiberius was in possession of the government." G. G. Ramsay, *The Annals of Tacitus: Books 1–6, An English Translation* (New York: E. P. Dutton & Company, 1904), 11 (*Annals* 1.5.6).
229. Matthew 3:16–17; Mark 1:9; Luke 3:21.
230. Leviticus 23:8.
231. Luke 3:23.
232. Counting age is culture-specific. For example (until very recently) Koreans were considered age one at birth. Other Asian cultures had similar age count systems which differed from ours. By writing "about," Luke speaks to all.
233. Leviticus 12:2–4. Seven days unclean plus thirty-three days waiting.
234. Luke 2:22–23.
235. Matthew 4:1–2.
236. Acts 1:3.
237. Ezekiel 4:6. As for God's forty-year generational patience, see Psalm 95:9–11.
238. Numbers 29:1. "High Sabbath" should not be confused with *Shabbat Hagadol*.
239. *Josephus*, 907 (*Wars* 6.10.1). Josephus referenced Greek months (e.g., Greek *Gorpeius* instead of its equivalent Hebrew month *Elul*).
240. *Josephus*, 906 (*Wars* 6.9.2).
241. *Josephus*, 909 (*Wars* 7.1.1).
242. Cassius Dio, *Roman History: Books 61–70*, ed. Herbert B. Foster, trans. Earnest Cary, vol. 8, LCL (Cambridge, MA: Harvard University Press, 1925), 271 (65.7.2).
243. ...despite its perfectly suiting this book's thesis to have done so.
244. The eyewitness Josephus recorded, "it was in Gessius Florus's time that the nation began to grow mad with this distemper, who was our procurator, and who occasioned the Jews to go wild with it by the abuse of his authority, and to make them revolt from the Romans." *Josephus*, 587 (*AJ* 18.1.6).
245. *Josephus*, 759 (*Wars* 2.17.5).
246. *Josephus*, 759 (*Wars* 2.17.6).
247. *Josephus*, 760 (*Wars* 2.17.7).
248. *Josephus*, 760 (*Wars* 2.17.8).
249. *Josephus*, 760 (*Wars* 2.17.8).
250. *Josephus*, 760–761 (*Wars* 2.17.9).
251. *Josephus*, 761 (*Wars* 2.17.10).
252. *Josephus*, 761 (*Wars* 2.18.1).
253. *Josephus*, 761 (*Wars* 2.17.10).
254. Proverbs 25:2. Here, "matter" is from the Hebrew *dabar,* as in Daniel 9:25.
255. Ezra was preceded by Zerubbabel, yet the center of Judaism remained in Babylon until Ezra arrived in Jerusalem. See also Zechariah 1:12 and chapter 14.
256. 1 Kings 6:38.
257. 2 Samuel 7:2.
258. 1 Chronicles 22:7–8. David had shed too much blood.
259. 1 Chronicles 28:11–19.
260. 1 Chronicles 21:18; 22:14–19.
261. 1 Chronicles 22:1–6; 29:19. "the temple for which I have made provision."
262. The wording over "My people Israel," also in 2 Samuel 5:2, identifies the time as David's accession after Ishbosheth's death, two years after Saul's death.
263. 2 Samuel 2:4.
264. 2 Samuel 2:10.

265. 2 Samuel 4:7–8.
266. 2 Samuel 5:1–3.
267. David's forty years start at Saul's death. First Kings 2:11 and 1 Chronicles 29:27 record seven years in Hebron and thirty-three in Jerusalem. Those seven years in Hebron are in *both* 2 Samuel 2:11 and 5:5 (i.e., counted from Saul's death).
268. 1 Kings 6:38.
269. Malachi 3:1.
270. This *doesn't* mean construction had ended, but that it had been ongoing for forty-six years at that point and was still ongoing.
271. Joshua 14:7.
272. Deuteronomy 2:14.
273. Numbers 21:12–13; Deuteronomy 2:18.
274. Deuteronomy 3:12, 16. There are many different definitions of "the Land."
275. Joshua 11:18.
276. Joshua 11:23.
277. Joshua 14:10, 15.
278. Briant, *Cyrus to Alexander*, 566; Horn and Wood, *Ezra 7,* 166; Clinton *Fasti Hellenici*, 40; Egyptian historian Manetho listed seven months of Artabanus.
279. Briant wrote that the usurper Artabanus "reigned for seven months." Briant, *Cyrus to Alexander*, 566; Lloyd Llewellyn-Jones and James Robson, *Ctesias' History of Persia: Tales of the Orient* (New York: Routledge, 2012), 187.
280. The final chapter also confirms the pause lengths in solar, not prophetic, years.
281. Intriguingly, Daniel doesn't mention the Edict of Cyrus, yet he certainly witnessed it and may have even played a role in it. (Daniel 10:1 dates to the third year of Cyrus, two years after the edict.) This remarkable lack of mention raises extremely interesting speculation, beyond our scope.
282. In our only departure from arithmetic, the results are easy to grasp visually.
283. For you gearheads: $r^2 = 0.9945$ and $p = 0.0028$. In simple linear regression, correlation this tight is strong evidence for a relationship between (x) decree years and (y) pause lengths. Coincidence can't be excluded, but is too improbable to assert. Note that x and y bear identical units (solar years).
284. For those unfamiliar with correlation, note two points: (1) You have surely heard the true phrase "correlation is not causation." Yet this chapter's claim is to a connection, not causation. No causation is asserted. (2) Correlation (r^2) near but below 100 percent is evidence for, not against, a valid connection and suggests there might be yet more to consider (e.g., yet another covariate).
285. Exodus 12:3. Also known as the first *Shabbat Hagadol*.
286. The math: $(354/14)^4 = 408{,}791$. There is no single definitive count of major holidays, however the Jewish Federation of St. Louis lists fourteen (https://www.jfedstl.org/news-events/upcoming-events/jewish-holiday-list/). This result conservatively assumes non-intercalated Hebrew years of 354 days.
287. The exception is Pentecost, which (Leviticus 23:16) must fall on a Sunday (the day after a weekly Sabbath). Colossians 2:16–17. Paul wrote this *after* Jesus.
288. Mark 1:10; Luke 3:22.
289. The English "completion" misses the mark, but the Hebrew *shalam* (root of *shalom*), meaning "to complete, make safe, finish, restore," fits perfectly.
290. Ironside, *Daniel*, 86.
291. Acts 17:11; 1 John 4:1–3. Examine the Scriptures to "see whether these things

were so." Nothing is ever *too good to check.*

292. Apologies to Arlo Guthrie's "Alice's Restaurant."
293. Messiah of Daniel 9:26 is "cut off," as is the servant in Isaiah 53 which also describes Jesus Christ to the exclusion of everyone else in history.
294. The Gospels are the first four books of the New Testament. They are four separate narratives of Jesus' life and teachings.
295. VanderKam, *Dead Sea Scrolls*, 137.
296. The Melchizedek Scroll reads, "the Anointed one of the spirit, concerning whom Daniel said, Until an anointed one, a prince (Dan. ix, 25)." Vermes, *The Complete Dead Sea Scrolls*, 533; Tomasino wrote, "the conclusion that 11QMelch is built on the chronological framework of Daniel 9:24–27 is inescapable." Tomasino, "Oracles," 99; Steudel noted, "when 11QMelchisedek was composed, about the end of the second century BC, the Book of Daniel belonged to the 'canon' of the Essenes." Annette Steudel, "'The End of the Days' in the Texts from Qumran (1)," *Revue de Qumran* 16, no. 2 (1993), 234.
297. Roger T. Beckwith, "Daniel 9 and the Date of Messiah's coming in Essene, Hellenistic, Pharisaic, Zealot and Early Christian Computation," *Revue de Qumran* 10, no. 4 (December 1981), 525.
298. Luke 10:23–24.
299. Tomasino noted messianic "expectations were percolating in the Jewish consciousness in the first century." Tomasino, "Oracles," 94; Tacitus recorded that Jews "alluded to the present as the very time when [. . .] from Judea would go forth men destined to rule the world." Cornelius Tacitus, *Tacitus: The Histories*, trans. Kenneth Wellesley (New York: Penguin Books, 1982), 279 (*Histories* 5.13); Suetonius concurred: "A firm persuasion had long prevailed through all the East, that it was fated for the empire of the world, at that time, to devolve on some who should go forth from Judaea." Suetonius, *The Twelve Caesars*, ed. T. Forrester, trans. Alexander Thomson (Oxford: Benediction Classics, 2014), 284 (*Vespasian* 4); Josephus noted an "ambiguous oracle that [. . .] 'about that time, one from their country should become governor of the habitable earth.'" *Josephus*, 899 (*Wars* 6.5.4); Beckwith noted that *ambiguous oracle* "was surely Daniel 9." Beckwith, "Daniel 9," 532.
300. Tanner noted that "not until rather late—with Irenaeus about A.D. 180—is the first substantial discussion of Daniel's seventy-weeks prophecy recorded." Tanner, "Daniel's Seventy Weeks," 198; Montgomery noted the Seventy Weeks "is not made use of at all in Justin Martyr's Apologies." Montgomery, *Daniel*, 398. Here, Montgomery referred to Justin Martyr's *Dialogue with Trypho* (c. AD 160), which quotes Daniel often, yet does not mention Daniel 9:25.
301. "Words" in Daniel 12:4, 9 are the Hebrew *haddebarim*, a plural of *dabar*.
302. Other known solutions usually fail on calendrics but also for not following all aspects of Daniel 9:25 (especially dividing the seven and sixty-two weeks). This doesn't disclaim partial or less-precise versions of this solution—those may be valid, but are incomplete.
303. Put simply, it's an objective case no matter how hard to follow, no matter who makes it, who hears it, or what they already believe. *Avoid those fallacies* (e.g., *ad verecundiam, ad populum, ad hominem, personal incredulity,* etc.).
304. Demonstrating God's existence by reason alone is sometimes referred to as "Natural Theology." For examples of attempted disproofs, see Victor J.

Stenger, *God: The Failed Hypothesis—How Science Shows That God Does Not Exist* (Amherst, NY: Prometheus Books, 2008), 31-33.

305. Some forms of logic, such as syllogistic (term) logic can be irrefutable but in impractically limited contexts.

306. Including here, *QED.*

307. Meaning to the exclusion of alternate rational explanations.

308. Not *all* mathematical truths can be proven (Gödel, 1931), but irrefutable mathematical proofs certainly do exist. Excluding them requires excluding reason itself, which is by definition *irrational.*

309. Yet another two reasons: 3. We can't assume to fully know any natural system's "initial conditions." 4. Increasing a measurement's precision for one aspect can reduce precision for related aspects (Heisenberg, 1927).

310. Some forms of logic (e.g., a priori definitions, term logic) may be irrefutable but have extremely limited (if any) practical application and are closely related to mathematics, even arguably identical.

311. Noah Webster, *Webster's Revised Unabridged Dictionary of the English Language* (Springfield, MA: G. & C. Merriam Company, 1913). This definition is chosen for its succinct clarity. Other scholarly (outside the dictionary) definitions are often more obtuse yet convey the same meaning. Note again that "proof" and "truth" are different concepts. Proof is subjective, but truth is objective. Truth is true *whether we believe it or not, even if we exist or not.*

312. Paraphrasing Bertrand Russell. There is, of course, no evidence for this.

313. Also *experiential* evidence. For example, the claim "I own a fire-breathing dragon" absent evidence, can be rejected simply because nobody has seen a real one before. Yet, Jonas Salk's 1952 claim of an effective vaccine against polio had also never been seen before. Of course, the rational response was to evaluate Salk's evidence *on its merits*, not previous experience nor expectations. Similarly, this book claims a viable solution to Daniel's Seventy Weeks and presents evidence in support. The rational response is to evaluate that evidence on its merits and not on previous experience nor expectations.

314. Blaise Pascal, *Thoughts* [Pensées], ed. Charles W. Eliot, trans. W. F. Trotter, vol. 48, passage 710 (New York: PF Collier & Son, 1910), 240. The wording "infinite weight" is consensus English translation of Pascal's French *"force divine."* Note, this is passage 709 in some editions.

315. Of course, we can apply natural law to calculate predictions (e.g., each return of Halley's comet), but the issue here is foretelling the specific dates of *human* affairs (even unique affairs) by *revelation*, not calculation or pattern.

316. "Preternatural," something that doesn't *seem* natural, describes our *perception* of a thing, and not the thing independent of the perceiver (Kant's *das Ding an sich*). *Preternatural* isn't an alternative, despite its similar name. What we perceive as preternatural is ultimately either natural or supernatural.

317. This *modus ponens* argument can also be written as *modus tollens*: **1.** If there is no supernatural entity, then there is no true prediction. **2.** It is not the case that there is no true prediction (Daniel 9:25 provides one). **3.** Thus, it is not the case that there is no supernatural entity. **4.** Therefore, a supernatural entity exists. In symbols, if **p** = there is a *supernatural entity,* and, **q** = there is a *true prediction,* as defined herein. Then: **1.** $\neg p \rightarrow \neg q$ (premise); **2.** $\neg \neg q$ (double negation; **3.** $\therefore \neg \neg p$ (*modus tollens*, 1, 2); **4.** $\therefore p$ (double negation, 3).

318. Jeremiah 25:8; 29:10; Ezekiel 3:27; 4:13; Daniel 9:23; Micah 3:5. Remarkably, these prophets *refer to each other by name*: Ezekiel to Daniel (Ezekiel 14:14, 20), Daniel to Jeremiah (Daniel 9:2), and Jeremiah to Micah (Jeremiah 26:18). One biblical standard of a true prophet is that all must be true. If any prophecy fails, then he is a false prophet (Deuteronomy 18:22). Thus, a true prophet makes *true predictions*; this requires a supernatural predictor. Each of these prophets claimed their source to be the Abrahamic God of the Bible.

319. "On the testimony of two or three witnesses every matter shall be confirmed" (2 Corinthians 13:1) referencing Deuteronomy 19:15.

320. Mario Livio, *The Golden Ratio: The Story of Phi, the World's Most Astonishing Number* (New York: Broadway Books, 2003), 115.

321. Livio, *Golden Ratio*, 9, 109, 112; H. Ulmer, C. Kelleher, and M. Dunser, "George Clooney, the Cauliflower, the Cardiologist, and Phi, the Golden Ratio," *British Medical Journal* (December 11, 2009), BMJ 2009;339:b4745.

322. Subtract JDNs in figure 18 (e.g., Nehemiah JDN 1,558,612 minus Cyrus JDN 1,525,487 is 33,125 days). This harmony is a completely unexpected pleasant surprise, providing far deeper confirmation than anyone should ever need.

323. Genesis 6:15; Exodus 25:10; Ezekiel 40:7–11; also Revelation 21:17, which deems (Fibonacci) "144 cubits" a measurement both *human* and *angelic*.

324. Ulmer, et al. "Clooney"; Astronomer [Johannes] "Kepler truly believed that the Golden Ratio served as a fundamental tool for God in creating the universe." Livio, *Golden Ratio*, 154, see also 115; Speculatively, Fibonacci numbers, seen throughout the universe *and* in our solution, could link our deduced "supernatural Entity," who is "God of the Bible" and "Creator of the universe," with that same Fibonacci-bearing universe's "cause for existence" as deduced by the Cosmological Argument (specifically, the *Kalam*).

325. Because *proof* (per *Webster's*) requires a judgment of sufficiency, "proof of God" can be claimed only by the reader, not the writer (nor anyone else). And don't conflate proof with truth, which is objective. Objective truth exists, no matter if we *accept it or not*, even no matter if we *existed or not*.

326. Deuteronomy 4:29; 2 Chronicles 15:12; Jeremiah 29:13; Matthew 7:7; Luke 11:9; James 4:8, and others.

327. Please note that most people will not actually read a book like this without first hearing a strong endorsement from someone they trust that the book indeed delivers on its claims to provide new, direct evidence of God.

328. A position sometimes called "fideism" or "presuppositionalism."

329. And "with gentleness and respect." See also Proverbs 25:2; John 8:32; Ephesians 6:14; Philippians 4:8. Scripture calls us to seek Truth, to respect Truth, and to love Truth. Jesus is Truth (John 14:6).

330. *Josephus*, 355 (*AJ* 10.11.4) notes Darius as a kinsman of Cyrus, but not his son.

331. *Josephus*, 355 (*AJ* 10.11.4). Note the different father's name.

332. Xenophon, *Cyropaedia*, 7.5.24–26; Burn, *Persia and the Greeks*, 55.

333. Shea, "Vassal King," 113. Of the Babylonian Chronicle's twenty-three death notices [Shea's table X], only one, Bel-etir, may have been non-royal. Ugbaru's death notice is evidence he was a vassal king (not *King of Babylon*) before Cyrus took the title *King of Babylon*, two months later. This is a reasonable time interval for news of Ugbaru's death to reach Cyrus and his response to travel back to Babylon; Daniel 5:31–6:1; Burn, *Persia and the Greeks*, 56.

334. Shea opined that Ugbaru's original name "probably was Gubaru, but since the Babylonian Chronicle refers to him twice as Ugbaru and only once as Gubaru, the name Ugbaru is used for him throughout this study." Shea, "Nabonidus Chronicle," 14; A later section of the Chronicle introduces a different Gubaru, whom Shea (along with most scholars) "maintains that the Gubaru mentioned in later texts is another individual." Miller, *Daniel*, 173.
335. Shea concluded, "When the details are compared they make a good case for identifying Darius the Mede as Ugbaru." Shea, "Nabonidus Chronicle," 14.
336. The key is when Daniel started Cyrus' first year as King of Babylon (chapter 8).
337. The parallel passage Mark 13:14 also directly refers to "Daniel the Prophet" in the original Greek, though this is oddly omitted in some translations.
338. Tanner, "Daniel's Seventy Weeks," 185. The earliest Christian writing on the Seventy Weeks (Irenaeus, c. AD 180) directly links Matthew 24:15 to Daniel 9.
339. The abomination "to which Christ referred was yet future." Miller, *Daniel*, 35.
340. Daniel 11 certainly fits the era of Antiochus IV *Epiphanes* (c. 370 BC), but we can't exclude it also finding future fulfillment during Daniel's seventieth week.
341. Note, there is uncertainty whether Jesus actually spoke these exact words. Although this parenthetical remark seems forced, it is certainly possible Jesus spoke it. People often make aside remarks—I'm making one now—so we can't exclude the possibility. But in our context, the question is moot. The words "let the reader understand" were certainly *intended* by Jesus, even if the Gospels paraphrase them. These words are in Scripture and are authoritative. The key question is, *what meanings do they convey*?
342. For example, Matthew 11:15; 15:10; Mark 4:9, 23; 7:14, 16; 13:14; Luke 8:8; 14:35.
343. Regarding Daniel's "know and understand," Lange asserted, "It directs the notice of both the hearer and the reader to the importance of the disclosures now to be made, and to the duty of subjecting them to serious and thoughtful consideration." Lange, *Commentary*, Daniel, 196.
344. Jesus referred to other prophecies and sometimes explained their meaning (e.g., sign of Jonah), but only here did he urge us to read and *understand* one.
345. Gentry wrote that Daniel 9:25 "requires that both terms [*mashiach* and *nagid*] refer to one and the same person." Gentry, "Daniel's Seventy Weeks," 32; Rabbi Halahawi notes that "*mashiach* is used nowhere in the Hebrew Scriptures as a proper name." Halahawi, *The Way*, 224.
346. Daniel doesn't use a definite article "the" ahead of Messiah, which in Hebrew would be *"hamashiach,"* a word used four times in Scripture (Leviticus 4:3, 5, 16; 6:22), each referring to "the anointed priest" (*hakohen hamashiach*). Daniel refers not to an anointed priest but rather to an anointed prince. Thus, Daniel's omission of "the" before "messiah" does not exclude the promised Messiah.
347. Directly: 1 Samuel 13:14; 25:30; 2 Samuel 5:2; 6:21; 7:8; 1 Kings 1:35; 2 Kings 20:5; 1 Chronicles 11:2; 17:7; 29:22; 2 Chronicles 6:5; 11:22; Isaiah 55:4, or generally: 1 Chronicles 28:4.
348. "In Chron, the theological use of [*nagid*] is restricted to David" and is "a key word linking David's speech when he gives Solomon the plans for the temple, and Solomon's speech after it has been built." VanGemeren, *Dictionary of OT Theology*, 3:21.
349. Tanner, "Daniel's Seventy Weeks," 323.
350. The closest is in Leviticus 4:3, 5, 16; 6:22, *"hakohen hamashiach"* the "anointed

priest," which is a religious, not secular, title.

351. Young asserted that "there is only One in history who fully satisfies the two essential requisites of the theocratic king, Jesus who is the Messiah (Psalm 110:4; Zechariah 6:13; John 4:25)." Young E., *Daniel*, 204. See also John 1:41; "the eschatological Anointed One, the Messiah. Within the canon of the OT there are only two unambiguous references to this figure, both in Dan 9 (25,26)." VanGemeren, *Dictionary of OT Theology*, 2:1126.

352. Tanner noted a "consensus among the early church fathers (a near unanimous position, in fact) that Daniel's seventy weeks prophecy was fulfilled in Christ." Tanner, "Daniel's Seventy Weeks," 200. See also Jerome on Daniel 9:24–27.

353. Per the Talmud, "In [Writings] is contained a reference to the end of days when the Messiah will come." *Talmud*, vol. 20, "Megillah," 3a.1; Rashi added, "The book of *Daniel* contains this information." "Megillah," 3a.1n12.

354. Five thirty-day lunar months in a row is too improbable to assert.

355. Daniel 2:4–7:28 is written in the Aramaic language.

356. Daniel 12:7 time (Hebrew) is also *Kairos*. The original Greek Septuagint (LXX) contained only the five books of Moses (Torah). Later Greek translations of the entire Old Testament are often (also here) inexactly called "the Septuagint."

357. Young speculated, "what led Dan. to employ the m. [masculine] instead of the f. [feminine] however is not clear unless it was for the deliberate purpose of calling attention to the fact that the word sevens [*shabuim*] is employed in an unusual sense." Young, E., *Daniel*, 195.

358. Anderson, *Coming Prince*, 127–128.

359. Anderson, *Coming Prince*, 123. Note, the Astronomer Royal erroneously applied the algorithmic modern [Hillel II] Hebrew calendar to the biblical era (appendix B) long before it was used. This remains a common error.

360. See figure 21.

361. Parker and Dubberstein, *PDBC*, 32. *PDBC* is authoritative for Persia in this era.

362. Anderson, *Coming Prince*, 103. Note Anderson's epact proposition; Hoehner tactfully identified Anderson's error, "Anderson realizes the dilemma and he has to do mathematical gymnastics." Hoehner, *Chronological Aspects*, 137.

363. Anderson, *Coming Prince*, 128n1.

364. Hoehner, *Chronological Aspects*, 138.

365. Parker and Dubberstein, *PDBC*, 32. *PDBC* is authoritative for Persia in this era.

366. Hoehner, *Chronological Aspects*, 138.

367. F. R. Ames wrote, "the interpretation of Daniel 9:25 turns, in part, on the meaning of *dabar* which may refer to the word of a prophet (either Jeremiah [Jer 25:1–14 or 29:1–23], or Daniel [Dan 9:20–27]) or to the decree of a king (Cyrus [Ezra 1:2–4], Darius [6:3–12], or Artaxerxes [7:11–26].)" VanGemeren, *Dictionary of OT Theology*, 1:913. Some expositors tendentiously claim *dabar* to have a specialized meaning. Yet a brief scan of its 1,400 uses in Scripture shows it to be general, not specific.

368. *Taim* from Ezra 6:12; 7:13 is Aramaic, not Hebrew. Note, Daniel 2 and 6 also refer to decrees of kings using words other than *dabar*, and this is sometimes used to exclude Daniel's *dabar* from indicating the decree of an earthly king. However, those references too are in Aramaic, not Hebrew.

369. Daniel 9:22–23. Daniel indeed fully understood the meaning of this prophecy.

370. Ezra 4:8–6:18; 7:12–26; Daniel 2:4–7:28.

371. This Hebrew-Aramaic split referencing may be one of many reasons this prophecy's meaning has remained "secret and sealed" for centuries.
372. The assumption wasn't always dominant. Current consensus is strongly influenced by Thiele's 1983 book *The Mysterious Numbers of the Hebrew Kings*.
373. Horn and Wood, *Ezra 7*, 135–139.
374. David N. Freedman, "The Babylonian Chronicle," *The Biblical Archaeologist* 19, no. 3 (1956), 50, 54.
375. Jehoiachin reigned three months, so "eighth year" refers to Nebuchadnezzar.
376. Here is the raw data: "**accession** year" (no instances); "**first** year" (12 instances), 2 Chronicles 29:3; 36:22; Ezra 1:1; 5:13; 6:3; Jeremiah 25:1; 52:31; Daniel 1:21; 7:1; 9:1, 2; 11:1; "**second** year" (11 instances), 1 Kings 15:25; 2 Kings 1:17; 14:1; 15:32; Ezra 4:24; Daniel 2:1; Haggai 1:1, 15; 2:10; Zechariah 1:1, 7; "**third** year" (7 instances), 1 Kings 15:28, 33; 2 Kings 18:1; 2 Chronicles 17:7; Esther 1:3; Daniel 1:1; 10:1; "**fourth** year" (10 instances), 1 Kings 6:1; 22:41; 2 Kings 18:9; 2 Chronicles 3:2; Jeremiah 25:1; 36:1; 45:1; 46:2; 51:59; Zechariah 7:1; "**fifth** year" (5 instances), 1 Kings 14:25; 2 Kings 8:16; 2 Chronicles 12:2; Jeremiah 36:9; Ezekiel 1:2; "**sixth** year" (2 instances), 2 Kings 18:10; Ezra 6:15; "**seventh** year" (5 instances), 2 Kings 12:1; 18:9; Ezra 7:7, 8; Esther 2:16; "**eighth** year" (2 instances), 2 Kings 24:12; 2 Chronicles 34:3; "**ninth** year" (5 instances), 2 Kings 17:6; 18:10; 25:1; Jeremiah 39:1; 52:4; "**tenth** year" (1 instance), Jeremiah 32:1. *University of Michigan Library*, 1997. Precision may vary across versions and flagging duplicates is in part discretionary. But the point remains, that if Jews had commonly used the accession year, Scripture should mention it directly, but it doesn't.
377. Bible Gateway, https://www.biblegateway.com.
378. Babylonian for "accession year" is *rish sharruti*. Charles Boutflower, "The Historical Value of Daniel V and VI," *The Journal of Theological Studies* 17, no. 65 (1915), 43–60.
379. Some scholars note that Jeremiah 52:29 must be from Babylonian records because only captors count captives. The point is valid re: count of captives, but at issue here is rather the count of *years*, which was well known to Jews. Babylonians didn't edit the Bible; Hebrews did, and for Hebrew readers. Thus, "eighteenth year of Nebuchadnezzar" is with certainty a *Hebrew* date.
380. The Talmud records Jews' changing dating methods: "From the days of Ezra the prophet and onward we never found Elul to be full." *Talmud*, vol. 17, "Beitzah," 6a.1. Jews no longer added a thirtieth day to Elul, as Babylonians often did. See also *PDBC*. Significantly, this calendrical change occurred in the "days of Ezra." Moreover, Horn and Wood remark that, during this time, the Elephantine Papyri indicate "The Jewish Calendar showed some variations from that of the Babylonians" and that "Jews after the exile did not adopt the Babylonian calendar part and parcel." Horn and Wood, *Ezra 7*, 83, 83n25.
381. Seidelmann, *Explanatory Supplement*, 55. Note that the JDN is not associated with the earth's age, nor the Hebrew count of years (*anno mundi*).
382. E. M. Reingold, Dershowitz, N., *Calendrical Calculations: The Ultimate Edition* (Cambridge, United Kingdom: Cambridge University Press, 2018), 16, section "1.5 Julian Day Numbers."
383. NASA, "Julian Day"; Espenak "Converter." Double-check BC/AD years, Gregorian/Julian calendars, and astronomical notation (e.g., 5 BC is −0004).
384. Seidelmann, *Explanatory Supplement*, 588.

385. The Talmud's "seasons" is from *tekufot* (i.e., equinoxes, "cycles"). They define spring and autumn: [If] "autumn is to begin after Succos [Tabernacles] this is a reason for them to proclaim a leap year (Rashi)." *Talmud*, vol. 47, "Sanhedrin," 11b.1–2n10. This kept years from starting too early (but not too late). Thus, Nisan AD 31 began in April not March. Note, the Mishna was recorded c. AD 200, when the natural, biblical Hebrew calendar was still observed.

386. Per the Talmud, "If the summer is to extend fourteen days into Tishrei (so that the equinox is to occur on the fifteenth), autumn would begin on the sixteenth, the second day of the Festival [Tabernacles]. According to the Tanna of 'Others,' this requires intercalation." *Talmud*, vol. 47, "Sanhedrin," 13b.2. Other Talmudic opinions set the cutoff three days later yet would still not alter the conclusion.

387. Napier Shaw, *Manual of Meteorology*, vol. 1 (London: Cambridge University Press, 1926), 51. At its inception in 46 BC, the Julian calendar placed the autumn equinox on September 24.

388. According to the Talmud, "the court did not proclaim leap years during famine years." *Talmud*, vol. 47, "Sanhedrin," 12a.1n1. Also, "we do not extend the year so as not to prolong the grain shortage." "Sanhedrin," 12a.3.

389. The Ezekiel 26 prediction of Tyre's destruction is a clear example of prophecy with time gaps. See also 2 Samuel 7:12–13; Psalm 110:1–3; Hosea 3:4–5; 5:15–6:1.

390. Hoehner, *Chronological Aspects*, 130.

391. The Babylonian *nikkud* punctuation mark *sihpa* "is identical to the Tiberian 'atnach, but the Babylonian accent appears above the word and the Tiberian below the word." Shmuel Bolozky, *Encyclopedia of Hebrew Language and Linguistics*, ed. Geoffrey Khan, vol. 1 (Leiden: Brill, 2013), 270, table I; According to Wickes, in the superlinear ("Babylonian") punctuation system, the "Athnach is the same, but is placed *above* the word." William Wickes, *A Treatise on the Accentuation of the Twenty-One So-Called Prose Books of the Old Testament* (Oxford: Clarendon Press, 1887), 142.

392. Baruch Davidson, "Who Made Up the Way We Sing the Torah?" *Chabad.org*, https://www.chabad.org/library/article_cdo/aid/817346/jewish/Who-made-up-the-way-we-sing-the-Torah.htm; Per the Talmud, "scriptural cantillation is of Biblical origin, and is therefore an intrinsic feature of the 'laws and statutes' taught by Moses." *Talmud*, vol. 29, "Nedarim," 37b.2.

393. Solomon "taught [the Torah] with the symbols of cantillation." *Talmud*, vol. 7, "Eruvin," 21b.3. This predates Daniel. There is ample evidence of cantillation preceding the Masoretes. "In the name of R' Yochanan: whoever reads from the Torah without a pleasant tone, or recites Mishnah without song." *Talmud*, vol. 20, "Megillah," 32a.2. Rabbi Yochanan ben Zakai, was a contemporary of Jesus; The Talmud continues, "he reads without the traditional cantillation (trop) indicated in the punctuated Torah text" and "in some of the ancient Mishnah texts that are punctuated, we find cantillation symbols." "Megillah," 32a.2nn22, 23; "this refers to the [Onkelos] Targum [. . .] to the notes of cantillation." "Megillah," 3a.1. Onkelos was born shortly after Jesus' crucifixion.

394. This book considers punctuation, chapter and verse divisions, titles, headings, and subheadings as outside the scope of inspired text.

395. Tanner, "Daniel's Seventy Weeks," 327n17. Early texts with no *atnach* division (e.g., Septuagint, Symmachus, Syriac Peshitta, Targums, Theodotion, Vulgate, etc.) are all translations and cannot override the Hebrew text. McComiskey

asserted that early Christian writers had the Greek Theodotion, yet still saw "a distinct juncture between the seven and sixty-two weeks," and this was "the dominant view in the early church." McComiskey, "Seventy 'Weeks' of Daniel," 20–21. Here, "direct evidence" would require a fully punctuated *Hebrew* text (i.e., *not* a translation) predating the Masoretes, that either omits the *atnach* in Daniel 9:25, or places it elsewhere. No such text has yet surfaced.

396. Could this *atnach* have been added after Daniel, but before the Masoretes? No known evidence supports that. But in the end, *it doesn't matter*. We deduce a break between the seven and sixty-two weeks based not on punctuation, but on Daniel's wording, which does indeed hold scriptural authority.

397. "With respect to the text of Daniel, all eight scrolls reveal no major disagreements against the Masoretic Text." VanderKam, *Dead Sea Scrolls*, 138; McComiskey, "Seventy 'Weeks' of Daniel," 25.

398. Tanner, "Daniel's Seventy Weeks," 325; Hoehner, *Chronological Aspects*, 129–131. Note that the original 1611 King James Bible displayed a semicolon in this spot. (Refer to a photocopied original, not to often-edited internet sources.)

399. Gentry summarizes modern consensus. "Problems of interpretation arising from following the accents in the Masoretic Text are insurmountable." Gentry, "Daniel's Seventy Weeks," 30. This book will present a viable approach.

400. The *atnach* doesn't force early solution to Daniel 9:25 (e.g., Cyrus, Onias III). Note, many first century AD Jews considered Daniel 9:25 not yet fulfilled. Josephus wrote an "oracle that was also found in their sacred writings, how, '*about that time*, [AD 66–70] one from their country should become governor of the habitable earth.'" *Josephus*, 899 (*Wars* 6.5.4); Beckwith noted, "that prophecy was surely Daniel 9." Beckwith, "Daniel 9," 532; According to the Talmud, penned after Jerusalem's AD 70 destruction, "Since the date of the End that we calculated has arrived and [the Messiah] did not come.'" *Talmud*, vol. 49, "Sanhedrin," 97b.2. Thus, many first century AD Jews saw Daniel 9:25 as yet future.

401. Keil, *Commentary*, 9:729.

402. Shea, "Vassal King," 100, table VI.1; 112–113, table VIII. Tablet examples leading with *Cyrus* in italics are from the collection published by Strassmaier in 1890.

403. Shea, "Vassal King," 112, table VIII.

404. The title "King of Lands" was used for Assyrian emperors (e.g., Ashurbanipal).

405. Shea, "Vassal King," 113, table VIII (e.g., *Cyrus* 22, 23).

406. Shea, "Vassal King," 113, table VIII. An alternate view puts his death in Nov. 539 BC, but still wouldn't alter Daniel's count of Cyrus' years.

407. Some scholars place his death in November 539 BC.

408. Parker and Dubberstein, *PDBC*. Dates for Nisan 1 tallied and graphed.

409. Irenaeus, *Against Heresies*, ed. Alexander Roberts and James Donaldson, trans. Alexander Roberts and William Rambaut (South Bend, IN: Ex Fontibus Co., 2020), 341 (3.21.3).

410. Some (e.g., Finegan) harmonize different sources with reduced regard for the sources' primacy or authority. We have excellent basis for Irenaeus' authority, and his nativity date reference is the earliest we know of. Other later references often appear on non-Judean calendars (e.g., Syriac, Egyptian—each with its own set of caveats and issues) and may simply have been originally sourced from Irenaeus. Note, Finegan (1998 edition) table 137 is correct.

411. Augustus was originally known as Octavius. Suetonius, *Twelve Caesars*, 32 (*Caesar* 83). When Julius Caesar was murdered, and upon "returning to Rome, he took possession of his inheritance. [. . .] He first held the government in conjunction with Mark Antony and Marcus Lepidus, then with Antony only, for nearly twelve years, and at last in his own hands during a period of four and forty." Suetonius, *Twelve Caesars*, 49–50 (*Augustus* 8).
412. Parker and Dubberstein, *PDBC*, 44.
413. Leviticus 23:15-16.
414. In 6 BC, Passover fell on Sunday, April 4. The next weekly Sabbath was Saturday, April 10. Pentecost was fifty days later, on Sunday, May 30.
415. Luke 1:23-24. The date isn't proven from the text but verified in chapter 10.
416. The desolation is different from the captivity (2 Chronicles 36:21; Jeremiah 29:10; Zechariah 1:12). The captivity ended with Cyrus' edict (537 BC), but the seventy years' desolation had not yet ended in the time of Zechariah (520 BC).
417. 2 Chronicles 36:20-22; Ezra 1:1-4.
418. Ezra 4:24.
419. Haggai 1:15; 2:1.
420. Ezra 5:1. Dating methods were uniform concurrently (appendix D.1).
421. Haggai 1:1; 2:10.
422. Fred Espenak, "Six Millennium Catalog of Phases of the Moon," *Astropixels. com*, astropixels.com/ephemeris/phasescat/phasescat.html.
423. "A famine also coming upon us, reduced us to the last degree of despair." *Josephus*, 585 (*AJ* 18.1.1). This rebellion is briefly referenced in Acts 5:37.
424. "The court did not proclaim leap years during famine years," and "we do not extend the year so as not to prolong the grain shortage." *Talmud*, vol. 47, "Sanhedrin," 12a.1n1, 12a.3; John K. Fotheringham, "The Evidence of Astronomy and Technical Chronology for the Date of the Crucifixion," *The Journal of Theological Studies* 35, no. 138 (1934), 157. Although we lack direct records of Judean intercalations, we do know there was famine prior to AD 8.
425. Anderson distinguished "servitude" from "desolations," each lasting seventy prophetic years, and partly overlapping. Anderson, *Coming Prince*, x-xi. Zechariah 1:12 confirms the seventy-year desolation had not expired in 520 BC, yet the captivity ("servitude") had ended with Cyrus' 537 BC edict.
426. Zechariah 1:16-21.
427. Horn and Wood, *Ezra 7*, 135-139.
428. Siegfried H. Horn, "The Seventh Year of Artaxerxes I," *Ministry Magazine (Ministry for World Evangelism)* 26, no. 6 (1953), 25.
429. Horn and Wood, *Ezra 7*, 157.
430. John K. Fotheringham, "Note on the Regnal Years in the Elephantine Papyri," *Monthly Notices of the Royal Astronomical Society* 69, no. 5 (1909), 447.
431. Horn and Wood, *Ezra 7*, 145-146.
432. Horn and Wood, *Ezra 7*, 135-139.
433. Hunger, *Astronomical Diaries*, 21; Stephenson, *Historical Eclipses*, 153, item 1.
434. Neuffer asserts, "a change in Artaxerxes' year numbering afterward [. . .] is unattested by any evidence." Neuffer, "Accession of Artaxerxes," 79.
435. Horn, "Seventh Year of Artaxerxes," 25; Parker and Dubberstein, *PDBC*, 32.
436. Hoehner, *Chronological Aspects*, 31-32.
437. *Josephus*, 602 (*AJ* 18.6.10).

438. Ramsay, W., *Christ Born at Bethlehem*, 202.
439. *Jewish Encyclopedia*, "Temple of Herod." 12:85. October is proxy for the Hebrew month *Tishri*. Note that advancing Herod's years at Nisan and not Tishri would not alter the conclusion.
440. John 2:13. There is no year between 1 BC and AD 1, so subtract a year.
441. Early Christian theologian Tertullian, in c. AD 208, wrote that Jesus was "revealed since the twelfth year of Tiberius." (*Against Marcion*, 1.15). This is strong evidence that Tertullian counted Tiberius' reign from Augustus' AD 14 death and Luke from Tiberius' AD 12 accession as co-regent.
442. Ramsay, W., *Christ Born at Bethlehem*, 201.
443. Luke 4:1–2.
444. Leviticus 23:15–16.
445. Hoehner argued persuasively for a literal indication of time (January/February). Hoehner, *Chronological Aspects*, 57.
446. Hoehner, *Chronological Aspects*, 55–60. Note that the *heorte* doesn't need to be identified (as Passover, Pentecost, or Tabernacles) to draw this conclusion.
447. *Talmud*, vol. 13, "Yoma," 39b.1.
448. Some have won lotteries more than once over a span of years and on many tickets, but nobody has ever won back-to-back Powerball jackpots, and certainly not on single tickets (as of 2024). *Powerball is a registered trademark of the Multi State Lottery Association.*
449. Joseph Spector, "Odds Are, You Won't Like This Powerball Story," *USA Today*, July 7, 2015, http://www.cnbc.com/2015/07/07/odds-are-you-wont-like-this-powerball-story.html. The odds were 1 in 292,201,338 starting in 2015 (and are the same in 2024 yet may change, of course).
450. "The population of Palestine [Judea] in antiquity did not exceed a million persons." Magen Broshi, "The Population of Western Palestine in the Roman-Byzantine Period," *Bulletin of the American Schools of Oriental Research*, no. 236 (Autumn 1979), 5, 7. Note that only King David's descendants were eligible to be Messiah. This was only a subset of the total Jewish population.
451. Bruce Frier, "Roman Life Expectancy: Ulpian's Evidence." *Harvard Studies in Classical Philology* 86 (1982), 245, table 5. Exactly 7.54 percent (col. Cx). We solve this from the perspective of Jesus' age at the crucifixion. Obviously, no one who didn't live to that age can have an identical chronological fingerprint.
452. Frier, *Roman Life*, 245, table 5. Exactly 56.4 percent (col. Cx). Note that relaxing the age constraint only further reduces the odds.
453. Frier, *Roman Life*, 245, table 5. Exactly 0.1056 (col. qx) or 10.56 percent.
454. Exactly 0.0000578, or 0.00578 percent.
455. Some other solutions to this prophecy might not pass this test quite as well. Relaxing gender, ethnicity, or age constraints would only further reduce the calculated odds. Also, don't read too much into the precision. First, we carry at most two significant digits, and second, this exercise can be done differently.
456. The closest is Leviticus 4:3–16; 6:22, *hakohen hamashiach*, "anointed priest."
457. Richard Dawkins, *The God Delusion* (New York: Mariner Books, 2008), 77.
458. Dawkins asserted, [Bertrand] "Russell's point is that the burden of proof rests with the believers, not the non-believers." Dawkins, *The God Delusion*, 76.
459. For example, [Christopher] Hitchen's Razor: "what can be asserted without evidence can be dismissed without evidence," cuts in all directions—meaning

objections must also be evidence-based (i.e., for skeptics and theists alike).

460. Søren Kierkegaard, *Eighteen Upbuilding Discourses: Kierkegaard's Writings*, vol. 5. trans. Howard and Edna Hong (Princeton University Press, 1992), 137.

461. Milton Friedman, "The Methodology of Positive Economics," *Essays In Positive Economics* (University of Chicago Press, 1966), 9.

462. This isn't the only evidence of God. There are other lines of evidence beyond our scope. Note also, this book does not claim finality.

463. There are many lines of evidence informing this topic. This book's solution is certainly one of them but is absolutely not the only one.

464. Daniel 9:27 has split good-faith Bible scholars' opinions for centuries. The two most prominent views couldn't be more starkly divergent and consequential.

465. Matthew 24:44; Mark 13:37; Luke 12:40.

466. *Jewish Encyclopedia*, "Calendar," 3:498.

467. The modern Hebrew calendar was adopted c. AD 359 when the Sanhedrin disbanded and exiled Jews needed a way to maintain a uniform calendar without any central authority. This is long after the last biblical writings.

468. The Hebrew calendar in Jesus' time (observation and reckoning) was first adopted during the exile when Hebrews learned Babylonian astronomical techniques, including how to calculate the equinoxes (*tekufot*). Prior to the exile, the equinox played no direct role in regulating the Hebrew calendar. This transition in the calendar occurred during Daniel's lifetime, and we can't exclude the possibility that Daniel himself, having been set over "the wise men of Babylon" (Daniel 2:48) played a role in this transition. The Hebrew calendar at the time of Cyrus, Ezra, and Nehemiah was observed virtually the same as during Jesus' earthly ministry and is thus the period of our focus.

469. Bradley E. Schaefer, "The Length of the Lunar Month," *Journal for the History of Astronomy* 23, no. 17 (1992), 32.

470. Genesis 1:14; Numbers 28:11; Psalm 81:3–4; 104:19.

471. The Talmud states, "it is a mitzvah [commandment] to sanctify the month based on the sighting of the new moon." Rashi confirmed, "as soon as the new moon is sighted, the month must be sanctified." *Talmud*, vol. 18, "Rosh Hashanah," 20a.1, a.3n26; Schaefer, "Lunar Month," 32; Seidelmann, *Explanatory Supplement*, 588. Evening, immediately after sunset, is the only time of day that a new crescent is first visible by an observer on earth.

472. "Witnesses must desecrate the Sabbath because it is a mitzvah [commandment] to sanctify the month based on the sighting of the new moon." *Talmud*, vol. 18, "Rosh Hashanah," 20a.1.

473. The average cycle "of the moon is 29.53 days, so that a [lunar] month composed of a whole number of days will be either 29 or 30 days long." Schaefer, "Lunar Month," 32. A new crescent was only visible right after sunset, and sunsets happen only once per day in any given location.

474. Seidelmann, *Explanatory Supplement*, 588; Jewish Encyclopedia, "Calendar," 3:499; By Talmudic rule, "a month is never longer than thirty days." *Talmud*, vol. 18, "Rosh Hashanah," 20a.1n6.

475. Exodus 12:2. Traditionally, the month when "barley was in the ear" (Heb. *aviv*) (Exodus 9:31). *Aviv* is "spring" in Hebrew, and *Tel Aviv* means "Spring Hill."

476. Horn and Wood affirmed that Old Testament months "were always numbered from Abib, or Nisan, regardless of whether the reckoning of the year was from

the spring or from the fall." Horn and Wood, *Ezra 7*, 58. The Talmud confirms, "On the first of Tishri is the new year for reckoning the years." *Talmud*, vol. 18, "Rosh Hashanah," 8a.2. So, the civil Hebrew year did not begin with the first Hebrew month. The Hebrew year had four different starting points, see *Talmud*, vol. 18, "Rosh Hashanah," 2a.1. Note, we moderns also have different starting points for the year in different contexts. Not only January 1, but also the school year, fiscal year, sports seasons, etc., start at different times.

477. By Talmudic rule, "we intercalate only an additional month of Adar into the year." *Talmud*, vol. 47, "Sanhedrin," 12a.1.

478. *Talmud*, vol. 47, "Sanhedrin," 11b.1–2.

479. By rule, "the court did not proclaim leap years during famine years." *Talmud*, vol. 47, "Sanhedrin," 12a.1n1. Also, "we do not extend the year so as not to prolong the grain shortage." "Sanhedrin," 12a.3.

480. By rule, "If the summer is to extend fourteen days into Tishrei (so that the equinox is to occur on the fifteenth), autumn would begin on the sixteenth, the second day of the Festival [Tabernacles]. According to the Tanna of 'Others,' this requires intercalation." *Talmud*, vol. 47, "Sanhedrin," 13b.2.

481. *Talmud*, vol. 18, 22b.3, "Mishnah Rosh Hashanah," 2:2.

482. Melamed, "Peninei Halakhah (Festivals)," 9.4, https://www.sefaria.org/ Peninei_Halakhah%2C_Festivals.9.4.2.

483. Fotheringham, "Date of the Crucifixion," 156.

484. William M. Folkner et al., "The Planetary and Lunar Ephemerides DE430 and DE431," *Interplanetary Network Progress Report* 196 (2014), 1. Ephemerides are numerically integrated equations describing the motions and gravitational interactions between the sun, earth, moon, planets, and 120 of the largest asteroids. *Wheaties* is a registered trademark of General Mills IP Holdings II.

485. For lunar position, DE431 is preferred "for times more than a few centuries in the past" (c. AD 1500). Folkner, et al., "Ephemerides," 1. This book applies DE431 to Bernard D. Yallop, "A Method for Predicting the First Sighting of the New Crescent Moon," *RGO NAO Technical Note* 69 (1997).

486. According to the DE431 ephemeris, the ancient (150 BC) value for the moon's mean orbital inclination versus the ecliptic equals its modern value of 5.15 degrees. Yet, Hipparchus and Ptolemy measured this at 5.0 degrees in 150 BC and AD 150, respectively. See R. R. Newton, "The Authenticity of Ptolemy's Parallax Data: Part 1," *Quarterly Journal of the Royal Astronomical Society* 14 (1973), 378–79. These differences are too great to ignore (and are not due to rounding). This wouldn't impact the procession of eclipses, when the moon is by necessity near zero degrees to the ecliptic, but could influence crescent visibility, when the moon cycles away from the ecliptic, closer to maximum inclination—and that precise maximum remains unconfirmed. Note that this does not show the DE431 to be wrong and the ancients right, only that this aspect is not confirmed by history as are other aspects.

487. Ilyas wrote that the earliest "criterion for ascertaining the lunar crescent's first visibility was established in the Babylonian era." Crescent observation requires "more than 24h, i.e., from the time of conjunction (Moon, Sun) to the time of evening observation." M. Ilyas, "Lunar Crescent Visibility and Islamic Calendar," *Quarterly Journal of the Royal Astronomical Society* 35 (1994), 429.

488. M. Ilyas, "Age as a Criterion of Moon's Earliest Visibility," *The Observatory* 103

(1983), 27. Figure 1 shows latitude influences visibility. Average cutoff time is twenty-five hours; See also Bradley E. Schaefer, "Visibility of the Lunar Crescent," *Quarterly Journal of the Royal Astronomical Society* 29 (1988), 520. Since Jerusalem sits at 31.4°N, the average cutoff time is slightly later.

489. ...such as lunar mean orbital inclination to the ecliptic. See also endnote 486.

490. Parker and Dubberstein, *PDBC*, 1. See also appendix B.

491. NASA "Delta T (ΔT)" NASA Eclipse Web Site, last modified January 29, 2009, https://eclipse.gsfc.nasa.gov/LEcat5/deltat.html; Fred Espenak, "Delta T," *EclipseWise.com*, last modified September 28, 2014, http://eclipsewise.com/help/deltat.html. This is why we now add a leap second every few years.

492. Espenak, "Delta T." This can also be written as $\Delta T = TT - UT$, which is mathematically the same. Some sources refer to TD (terrestrial dynamic) time, which in our context is a functional equivalent of TT (terrestrial time).

493. Espenak, "Delta T."

494. Espenak, "Six Millennium Catalog."

495. Espenak, "Delta T."

496. Espenak, "Six Millennium Catalog."

497. Espenak, "Delta T."

498. Espenak, "Six Millennium Catalog."

499. Espenak, "Delta T."

500. *Talmud*, vol. 17, "Beitzah," 6a.1. This applies to Jesus' lifetime. The Rabbi (ultimately) quoted, Abba Arikha ("Rav"), wrote in the early third century AD. Thus, this observation applies from c. 457 BC onward (and continues in the modern Hebrew calendar). Rashi confirmed: "Elul was virtually always a month of twenty-nine days." *Talmud*, vol. 18, "Rosh Hashanah," 18a.5n31.

501. Zuckermann, *A Treatise*, 61; Per the Talmud: Jews did not intercalate a month in a sabbatical year "so as not to prolong the prohibition against cultivation and not into the year following *sheviis* [sabbatical] so as not to delay the omer offering." *Talmud*, vol. 47, "Sanhedrin," 12a.3; "The court did not proclaim leap years during famine years" 12a.1n1; "A famine also coming upon us, reduced us to the last degree of despair." Josephus, 585 (AJ 18.1.1); Note, if intercalated as a normal year, the AD 8 Nisan moon would have conjoined on March 25, well within the normal window. Espenak, "Six Millennium Catalog."

502. Parker and Dubberstein, *PDBC*, 32 (authoritative for Babylon).

503. Espenak, "Delta T."

504. Espenak, "Six Millennium Catalog."

505. Espenak, "Delta T."

506. Espenak, "Six Millennium Catalog."

507. Stephenson, *Historical Eclipses*, 164, eclipse number 27.

508. English astronomer F. Richard Stephenson judged that "when compared with the computed Julian dates, these [ancient observations] are invariably accurate." Stephenson, *Historical Eclipses*, 99. Stephenson's focus was purely technical. He had no religious or historical purpose. His goal was to calibrate delta-T from ancient observations as precisely as possible. Thus, these records are selected for reliability by a disinterested party for a nonrelated purpose. This provides an excellent basis for this, or any study of biblical dates.

509. *Ptolemy's Almagest*, trans. G. J. Toomer (Princeton: Princeton University Press, 1998), 11; Horn and Wood, *Ezra 7*, 128. Horn presents a summary version.

510. For example, the Uruk King List and Assyrian Eponym Canon.
511. According to Thiele, Ptolemy's Almagest records "over eighty solar, lunar, and planetary positions, with their dates" enabling "checks as to its accuracy at almost every step from beginning to end," which "have been verified by modern astronomers" so "the canon of Ptolemy may be used as a historical guide with the fullest confidence." Thiele, *Numbers*, 70–71.
512. Neuffer quotes German astronomer Otto Neugebauer, re: VAT4956: "A text which contains many positions of sun, moon and stars is within many thousands of years uniquely fixed." Julia Neuffer, "Ptolemy's Canon Debunked?," *Andrews University Seminary Studies* 17, no. 2 (1979), 43.
513. Shea, "Nabonidus, Belshazzar," 146. Referencing *PDBC*. See also chapter 2.
514. Neuffer asserted there is a "complete agreement of the Canon with the extant ancient records." Neuffer, "Ptolemy's Canon," 46.
515. Thiele, *Numbers*, 71n8 (i.e., Babylonian accession year with Nisan advance). See also appendix A.4.2.
516. Thiele, *Numbers*, 184; Horn, "Babylonian Chronicle," 20. Carchemish fell in 605 BC, between April 12 (Nisan 1) and Nabopolassar's August 16 death.
517. Parker and Dubberstein, *PDBC*, 12. A tablet dated to Evil-merodach AY in Sippar and one dated to Nebuchadnezzar year 43 in Uruk both date to October 8, 562 BC, meaning news of Nebuchadnezzar's death had reached nearby Sippar but had not yet reached the more distant Uruk on that date.
518. Note the word "first" is absent in the original Hebrew of Jeremiah 52:31.
519. 2 Kings 25:27. Adar 27 in Evil-merodach's accession year was April 2, 561 BC. See also Parker and Dubberstein, *PDBC*, 28.
520. When events provoked a change in dating method, *all* Jews changed.
521. Jews advanced King Xerxes at Nisan and then advanced his son Artaxerxes (Longimanus) at Tishri. See also appendix A.14.1.
522. That is, foreign to *Judah* (e.g., Israel, aka Northern Kingdom, was also foreign to Judah). *Talmud,* vol. 18, "Rosh Hashanah" 3a–3b, records a lively dispute between rabbis over chronology and presents many statements, some true, some false, and some partially true. Unlike the Bible, the Talmud doesn't claim to provide inerrant fact but rather to teach the reader how to evaluate difficult questions. In short, *the Talmud is not gospel* and shouldn't be read as such. Biblical dating methods must be deduced firstly from canonical Scripture.
523. Thiele, *Numbers*, 180, 183, chart 30. Thiele presumed different biblical sources applied different dating systems concurrently. This book asserts the Bible writers applied uniform dating methods at any given time, and those methods would change (for everyone) with changing conditions. We see evidence of such a change at the exile, and then again upon Ezra's return from exile.
524. Keil, *Commentary,* 9:526; Horn, "Seventh Year of Artaxerxes," 25. Elephantine papyri and the scribe Ezra both date Artaxerxes' years identically.
525. Rodger C. Young, "When Did Jerusalem Fall?" *Journal of the Evangelical Theological Society* 47, no. 1 (2004).
526. Young, R., "When Did Jerusalem Fall?," 38n5.
527. D. Freedman, "Babylonian Chronicle," 50, 54; Young, R., "When Did Jerusalem Fall?" 31–32.
528. *Talmud*, vol. 18, "Rosh Hashanah," 3b.1. Note Israel was also foreign to Judah.
529. Thiele, *Numbers*, 182, diagram 20.

530. D. Freedman, "Babylonian Chronicle," 53.
531. A minority of scholars place Daniel 1:1 in 606 BC. Keil, *Commentary*, 9:526; Anderson, *Coming Prince*, 233. Most scholars date this to 605 BC. As will be shown, both scriptural and historical evidence favor the minority view.
532. Thiele, *Numbers*, 184; Horn, "Babylonian Chronicle," 20.
533. Keil, *Commentary,* 9:526; Thiele noted Nebuchadnezzar returned "to the Hatti-land and until [January] marched unopposed." Thiele, *Numbers*, 207. The chronicle doesn't say *when* he rejoined his army after he became king. It only indicates when he again returned to Babylon, in January, 604 BC. Note also, the occasional claim that "Nebuchadnezzar was nowhere near Jerusalem in 606 BC" is without basis. The chronicle is silent on his location in that year.
534. Young asserted the title here "is used proleptically." Young, E., *Daniel*, 35. On pages 115–116, Young gave a detailed account of Belshazzar's title in Daniel.
535. Daniel 1 and 2 Chronicles 36:7 noted that temple implements were carried to Babylon. Neither mention Carchemish, nor fleeing Egyptians. The Jeremiah passages mention Carchemish, but not temple implements (likely because they were already taken). Also, Jeremiah 36:9 notes these prophecies were read in the "fifth year of Jehoiakim" which cannot predate Carchemish in the "fourth year of Jehoiakim" per Jeremiah 46:2, nor predict Daniel's "third year" of Jehoiakim. Jeremiah did not foretell Daniel 1:1.
536. *Josephus*, 945 (*Against Apion* 1.19), quoting Babylonian historian Berosus.
537. *Josephus*, 341 (*AJ* 10.6.1). Note also *AJ* 10.11.1 makes no mention of any quick return to Judah after his accession on September 7 of 605 BC.
538. The 605 BC interpretation traces back to Ussher (maybe earlier) and is often cited without critical examination. It's one example of a persistent conflation.
539. Daniel 1:3–5. Ashpenaz was responsible for educating the captured Hebrew youths. Ashpenaz was in Jerusalem to help select them, so we can't exclude that they may have begun their education in Jerusalem.
540. Daniel 1:18 notes *days* not years, suggesting the three years were precise.
541. Daniel 1:19.
542. Daniel 2:1.
543. Daniel 2:48. Nebuchadnezzar appointed Daniel to be chief over the magi.
544. 2 Kings 25:2; Jeremiah 1:3; 39:2.
545. Parker and Dubberstein, *PDBC*, 12.
546. *Talmud*, vol. 19, "Taanit," 29a2. Hebrew *erev* is very common for "evening." See also note 24. The text may be understood in many different ways, but it seems most likely that the temple's destruction began as evening was falling on Av 9, and the conflagration consumed the temple during that night (as foretold in Jeremiah 6:4–5), which was Av 10 after the Sabbath. Only 587 BC can be understood to fit this passage. Neither 588 nor 586 BC can fit.
547. Parker and Dubberstein, *PDBC*, 28. Adjusted for Hebrew intercalations.
548. Zuckermann, *A Treatise*, 60. Zuckermann's table starts at 535–534 BC (AM 3227, evenly divisible by seven); Wacholder's sabbatical years fall one year after Zuckermann's. Ben Zion Wacholder, "The Calendar of Sabbatical Cycles During the Second Temple and the Early Rabbinic Period," *Hebrew Union College Annual* 44 (1973), 156.

WORKS CITED

Albright, William F. 1943. "The Gezer Calendar." *Bulletin of the American Schools of Oriental Research* 92 (1): 16–26.

———. 1956. "The Nebuchadnezzar and Neriglissar Chronicles." *Bulletin of the American Schools of Oriental Research* 143: 28–33.

———. 1963. *The Biblical Period from Abraham to Ezra.* New York: Harper Torchbooks.

Anderson, Robert. 1957. *The Coming Prince.* Grand Rapids: Kregel Classics.

Baldwin, Joyce G. 2009. *Daniel: An Introduction and Commentary.* Downers Grove, IL: InterVarsity Press.

Beckwith, Roger T. 1981. "Daniel 9 and the Date of Messiah's Coming in Essene, Hellenistic, Pharisaic, Zealot and Early Christian Computation." *Revue de Qumran* 10 (4): 521–542.

Bible Gateway. n.d. Accessed March, 2024. https://www.biblegateway.com.

Bickerman, E. J. 1980. *Chronology of the Ancient World.* Ithaca, NY: Cornell University Press.

Boice, James Montgomery. 2006. *Daniel: An Expositional Commentary.* Grand Rapids: Baker Books.

Bolozky, Shmuel. 2013. *Encyclopedia of Hebrew Language and Linguistics.* Edited by Geoffrey Khan. Vol. 1 of 4. Leiden, Netherlands: Brill.

Boutflower, Charles. "The Historical Value of Daniel V and VI." *The Journal of Theological Studies* 17, no. 65 (1915): 43-60.

Briant, Pierre. 2002. *From Cyrus to Alexander: A History of the Persian Empire.* Translated by Peter T. Daniels. Winona Lake, IN: Eisenbrauns.

Broshi, M. 1979. "The Population of Western Palestine in the Roman-Byzantine Period." *Bulletin of the American Schools of Oriental Research* 236 (1): 1–10.

Burn, A. R. 1968. *Persia and the Greeks: The Defense of the West.* London: Minerva.

Chabad.org. n.d. "The Complete Jewish Bible With Rashi Commentary." Translated by The Judaica Press. Accessed March, 2024. https://www.chabad.org/library/bible_cdo/aid/8165/showrashi/true.

———. n.d. "The Legalities of Destruction." Accessed March, 2024. http://www.chabad.org/parshah/article_cdo/aid/52753/jewish/The-Legalities-of-Destruction.htm.

Clinton, Henry Fynes. 1827. *Fasti Hellenici: The Civil and Literary Chronology of Greece.* Cambridge: Cambridge University Press. 2013 Reprint Edition.

Collins, Francis S. 2006. *The Language of God: A Scientist Presents Evidence for Belief.* New York: Simon and Schuster.

Davidson, Baruch. n.d. "Who Made Up the Way We Sing the Torah?" *Chabad.org.* Accessed March, 2024. https://www.chabad.org/library/article_cdo/aid/817346/jewish/Who-made-up-the-way-we-sing-the-Torah.htm.

Dawkins, Richard. 2008. *The God Delusion.* New York: Mariner Books.

Dio, Cassius. 1925. *Roman History: Books 61–70.* Edited by Herbert B. Foster. Translated by Earnest Cary. Vol. 8. Loeb Classical Library. Cambridge, MA: Harvard University Press.

Espenak, Fred. 2014. "Delta T." *EclipseWise.com*. Accessed March, 2024. http://eclipsewise.com/help/deltat.html.

———. 2014. "Six Millennium Catalog of Phases of the Moon." *Astropixels.com*. Accessed March, 2024. astropixels.com/ephemeris/phasescat/phasescat.html.

———. 2011. "Astropixels Calendar Date Converter." *Astropixels.com*. Accessed March, 2024. astropixels.com/ephemeris/calendarconverter.html.

Evans, James. 1998. *The History and Practice of Ancient Astronomy*. New York: Oxford University Press.

Feinberg, John S. and Paul D. 1981. *Tradition and Testament: Essays in Honor of Charles Lee Feinberg*. Chicago: Moody Press.

First, Mitchell. 1997. *Jewish History in Conflict: A Study of the Major Discrepancy between Rabbinic and Conventional Chronology*. Jerusalem: Jason Aronson Inc.

Foley, Ian. 2014. *The Time Is Near: Volume 1—A Reference Commentary on the Visions of Daniel*. Bloomington, IN: Balboa Press.

Folkner, William M., James G. Williams, Dale H. Boggs, Ryan S. Park, and Petr Kuchynka. 2014. "The Planetary and Lunar Ephemerides DE430 and DE431." *Interplanetary Network Progress Report* (196): 1–81.

Forbes, Bruce D. 2007. "Christmas Was Not Always Like This: A Brief History." *Word & World* 27 (4): 399–406.

Ford, Desmond. 2007. *In the Heart of Daniel: An Exposition of Daniel 9:24–27*. Lincoln, NE: iUniverse.

Fotheringham, John K. 1909. "Note on the Regnal Years in the Elephantine Papyri." *Monthly Notices of the Royal Astronomical Society* 69 (5): 446–449.

———. 1934. "The Evidence of Astronomy and Technical Chronology for the Date of the Crucifixion." *The Journal of Theological Studies* 35 (138): 146–162.

Freedman, David N. 1956. "The Babylonian Chronicle." *The Biblical Archaeologist* 19 (3): 50–60.

Freedman, H., and Maurice Simon, translators. 1939. *Midrash Rabbah: Deuteronomy, Lamentations*. London: Soncino Press.

Friedman, Milton. 1966. "The Methodology of Positive Economics." In *Essays In Positive Economics*, 3–16, 30–43. Chicago: University of Chicago Press.

Frier, Bruce. 1982. "Roman Life Expectancy: Ulpian's Evidence." *Harvard Studies in Classical Philology* 86: 213–251.

Gedalyahu, Tzvi Ben. 2008. "Today Marks Ninth of Av Fast Day – Birthday of the Messiah." *Arutz Sheva*. August 10, 2008. http://www.israelnationalnews.com/News/News.aspx/127128#.Vv17J3rOear.

Gentry, Peter J. 2010. "Daniel's Seventy Weeks and the New Exodus." *Southern Baptist Journal of Theology* 14 (1): 26–44.

Greene, Oliver B. 2011. *Daniel: Verse by Verse Study*. Sixteenth printing. Greenville, SC: The Gospel Hour, Inc.

Halahawi, Rabbi Shalomim Y. 2007. *The Way: The Prophetic Messianic Voice to the path of the Edenic Kingdom Redemption*. Morrisville, North Carolina: Lulu.

Hall, Marion H. 1990. "Definitions Used in Relation to Gestational Age." *Paediatric and Perinatal Epidemiology* 4 (2): 123–128.

Hammel, Eric. 2010. *Six Days in June: How Israel Won the 1967 Arab-Israeli War*. New York: Maxwell Macmillan International.

Henry, Matthew. 1991. *Matthew Henry's Commentary on the Whole Bible*. 6 vols. Peabody, Mass: Hendrickson Publishers.

Herodotus. 1964. *The Histories of Herodotus*. Edited by E. H. Blakeney. Translated by George Rawlinson. 2 vols. London: J. M. Dent & Sons.

Hoehner, Harold W. 1977. *Chronological Aspects of the Life of Christ*. Grand Rapids: Zondervan.

Horn, Siegfried H. 1953. "The Seventh Year of Artaxerxes I." *Ministry Magazine (Ministry for World Evangelism)* 26 (6): 23–25, 45–46.

———. 1967. "The Babylonian Chronicle and the Ancient Calendar of the Kingdom of Judah." *Andrews University Seminary Studies* 5 (1): 20.

Horn, Siegfried H., and Lynn H. Wood. 2006. *The Chronology of Ezra 7*. Calhoun, GA: TEACH Services, Inc.

Hunger, Hermann. 2001. *Astronomical Diaries and Related Texts from Babylonia*. Vienna: Publishing House of the Austrian Academy of Sciences.

Ilyas, M. 1983. "Age as a Criterion of Moon's Earliest Visibility." *The Observatory* (103): 26–28.

———. 1994. "Lunar Crescent Visibility and Islamic Calendar." *Quarterly Journal of the Royal Astronomical Society* (35): 425–461.

Irenaeus. 2020. *Against Heresies*. Edited by Alexander Roberts and James Donaldson. Translated by Alexander Roberts and William Rambaut. South Bend, IN: Ex Fontibus Co.

Ironside, H. A. 2005. *Daniel*. Grand Rapids: Kregel Publications.

Israel Ministry of Foreign Affairs. n.d. "Declaration of Establishment of State of Israel." Accessed March, 2024. https://www.gov.il/en/Departments/General/declaration-of-establishment-state-of-israel.

Jewish Encyclopedia. 1916. ed. Singer, Isidore, 12 vols. New York: Funk And Wagnalls Company.

Josephus, Flavius. 1999. *The New Complete Works of Josephus*. Revised and Expended Edition. Translated by William Whiston. Grand Rapids: Kregel Publications. (*Wars*, c. AD 75; *AJ*, AD 94; *AA*, post AD 94)

Keil, C. F., and F. Delitzsch, 2001. *Commentary on the Old Testament*, 10 vols. Trans. J. Martin and M. G. Easton. Peabody, Mass.: Hendrickson Publishers.

Kierkegaard, Søren. 1992. *Eighteen Upbuilding Discourses: Kierkegaard's Writings*. Vol. 5. Translated by Howard and Edna Hong. Princeton University Press.

King, Leonard W., Reginald C. Thompson, and Ernest A. W. Budge. 1907. *The Sculptures and Inscription of Darius the Great on the Rock of Behistûn in Persia*. London: British Museum.

Lange, Johann P. 1978. *A Commentary on the Holy Scriptures: Critical, Doctrinal, and Homiletical*. 12 vols. Trans. P. Schaff. Grand Rapids: Zondervan.

Lewin, Thomas. 1865. *Fasti Sacri or a Key to the Chronology of the New Testament*. London: Longmans, Green, and Co.

Livio, Mario. 2003. *The Golden Ratio: The Story of Phi, the World's Most Astonishing Number*. Paperback. New York: Broadway Books.

Llewellyn-Jones, Lloyd, and James Robson. 2012. *Ctesias' History of Persia: Tales of the Orient*. New York: Routledge.

Marshall, Benjamin. 1728. *Three Letters in Farther Vindication of the Late Bishop*

Lloyd's Hypothesis of Daniel's Prophecy of the Seventy Weeks. London: James and John Knapton.

McComiskey, Thomas E. 1985. "The Seventy 'Weeks' of Daniel Against the Background of Ancient Near Eastern Literature." *Westminster Theological Journal* 47 (1): 18–45.

Meyer, H. A. W. 1884. *Critical and Exegetical Hand-Book to the Gospels of Mark and Luke*. Translated by R. E. Wallis and W. P. Dickson. New York: Funk & Wagnalls.

Melamed, Rabbi Eliezer. n.d. "Peninei Halakhah (Festivals)." Accessed March, 2024. https://www.sefaria.org/Peninei_Halakhah%2C_Festivals.9.4.2.

Miller, Stephen B. 1994. *The New American Commentary: Daniel, An Exegetical and Theological Exposition of Holy Scripture*. Vol. 18. Nashville: B&H.

Montagu, George. 1845. *The Times of Daniel: Chronological and Prophetical*. London: James Darling.

Montgomery, James A. 1927. *A Critical and Exegetical Commentary on the Book of Daniel*. Edinburgh: T. & T. Clark.

Moore, Keith. 2015. "How accurate are 'due dates'?" *BBC News*. February 3, 2015. http://www.bbc.com/news/magazine-31046144.

NASA. 1998. "Julian Day and Civil Date Calculator." Goddard Space Flight Center. Accessed March, 2024. https://core2.gsfc.nasa.gov/time/julian.html.

———. 2009. "Delta T (ΔT)." NASA Eclipse Web Site. Accessed March, 2024. https://eclipse.gsfc.nasa.gov/LEcat5/deltat.html.

Neuffer, Julia. 1968. "The Accession of Artaxerxes I." *Andrews University Seminary Studies* 6 (1): 60–87.

———. 1979. "Ptolemy's Canon Debunked?" *Andrews University Seminary Studies* 17 (2): 39–46.

Newton, Isaac. 1733. *Observations upon the Prophecies of Daniel and the Apocalypse of St. John*. London: J. Darby and T. Browne.

Newton, Robert R. 1973. "The Authenticity of Ptolemy's Parallax Data-Part 1." *Quarterly Journal of the Royal Astronomical Society* 14: 367–388.

Parker, Richard A., and Waldo H. Dubberstein. 2007. *Babylonian Chronology: 626 BC - AD 75*. (PDBC) Paperback. Eugene, OR: Wipf and Stock Publishers.

Pascal, Blaise. 1910. *Thoughts*. The Harvard Classics. Edited by Charles W. Eliot. Translated by W. F. Trotter. Vol. 48. New York: PF Collier & Son.

Pink, Arthur W. 1922. *Gleanings in Genesis*. Chicago: Moody Press.

Pirkei Avos. 2020. ed. Rabbi Menachem Davis. *The Schottenstein Edition*. Rahway, NJ: Mesorah Publications (ArtScroll).

Poole, Matthew. 1990. *A Commentary on the Holy Bible*. 3 vols. McLean, VA: MacDonald Publishing Company.

Ptolemaeus, Claudius. 1998. *Ptolemy's Almagest*. First Princeton Paperback Printing. Translated by G. J. Toomer. Princeton: Princeton University Press.

Ramsay, G. G. 1904. *The Annals of Tacitus: Books I–VI: An English Translation*. New York: E. P. Dutton & Company.

Ramsay, William M. 1898. *Was Christ Born at Bethlehem? A Study on the Credibility of St. Luke*. London: Hodder and Stoughton.

Reingold, Edward M., and Nachum Dershowitz. 2018. *Calendrical Calculations:*

The Ultimate Edition. Cambridge: Cambridge University Press.

Robertson, Archibald T. 1922. *A Harmony of the Gospels for Students of the Life of Christ.* New York: HarperCollins Publishers.

Schaefer, Bradley E. 1992. "The Length of the Lunar Month." *Journal for the History of Astronomy* 23 (17): 32–42.

———. 1988. "Visibility of the Lunar Crescent." *Quarterly Journal of the Royal Astronomical Society* (29): 511–523.

Schwartz, Howard. 2007. *Tree of Souls: The Mythology of Judaism.* Paperback. New York: Oxford University Press.

Segev, Tom. 2007. *1967: Israel, the War, and the Year that Transformed the Middle East.* First US Edition. Translated by Jessica Cohen. New York: Metropolitan Books.

Seidelmann, P. Kenneth. Ed. 2006. *Explanatory Supplement to the Astronomical Almanac.* United States Naval Observatory. First Paperback Impression. Sausalito, CA: University Science Books.

Shaw, Napier. 1926. *Manual of Meteorology.* Vol. 1. London: Cambridge University Press.

Shea, William H. 1972. "An Unrecognized Vassal King of Babylon in the Early Achaemenid Period: Part 3." *Andrews University Seminary Studies* 10 (1): 88–117.

———. 1982. "Nabonidus, Belshazzar, and the Book of Daniel: An Update." *Andrews University Seminary Studies* 20 (2): 133–149.

———. 1991. "Darius the Mede in His Persian-Babylonian Setting." *Andrews University Seminary Studies* 29 (3): 235–257.

———. 1996. "Nabonidus Chronicle: New Readings and the Identity of Darius the Mede." *Journal of the Adventist Theological Society* 7 (1): 1–20.

———. 2001. "The Search for Darius the Mede (Concluded)." *Journal of the Adventist Theological Society* 12 (1): 97–105.

Sigal, G. 2013. *The 70 Weeks of Daniel: (9:24–27).* Bloomington, IN: Xlibris LLC.

Spector, J. 2015. "Odds Are, You Won't Like This Powerball Story." *USA Today.* July 7, 2015. http://www.cnbc.com/2015/07/07/odds-are-you-wont-like-this-power-ball-story.html.

Stenger, Victor J. 2008. *God: The Failed Hypothesis - How Science Shows That God Does Not Exist.* Amherst, NY: Prometheus Books.

Stephenson, F. Richard. 1997. *Historical Eclipses and Earth's Rotation.* Hardback. New York: Cambridge University Press.

Steudel, Annette. 1993. "'The End of the Days' in the Texts from Qumran." *Revue de Qumran* 16 (2): 225–246.

Suetonius. 2014. *The Twelve Caesars.* Edited by T. Forrester. Translated by Alexander Thomson. Oxford: Benediction Classics.

Tacitus, Cornelius. 1982. *Tacitus: The Histories.* Translated by Kenneth Wellesley. New York: Penguin Books.

Talmud. 2021. *Talmud Bavli* (Babylonian Talmud), *Schottenstein Edition.* 73 vols. Rahway, NJ: Mesorah Publications (ArtScroll).

Tanner, J. Paul. 2009. "Is Daniel's Seventy Weeks Prophecy Messianic? Parts 1 & 2." *Bibliotheca Sacra* 166 (662): 181–200, and 166 (663): 319–335.

Thiele, Edwin R. 1994. *The Mysterious Numbers of the Hebrew Kings.* Paperback.

Grand Rapids: Kregel Academic.

Tomasino, Anthony J. 2008. "Oracles of Insurrection: The Prophetic Catalyst of the Great Revolt." *Journal of Jewish Studies* 59 (1): 86–111.

Ulmer, Hanno, Cecily C. Kelleher, and Martin W. Dunser. 2009. "George Clooney, the Cauliflower, the Cardiologist, and Phi, the Golden Ratio." *BMJ: British Medical Journal* 339. Accessed March, 2024. https://www.bmj.com/content/339/bmj.b4745.

United States Naval Observatory. n.d. "Julian Date Converter." Accessed March, 2024. https://aa.usno.navy.mil/data/JulianDate.

University of Michigan Library. n.d. "Bible: King James Version Simple Searches." Accessed August 4, 2022. http://quod.lib.umich.edu/k/kjv/simple.html.

VanderKam, James, and Peter Flint. 2002. *The Meaning of the Dead Sea Scrolls: Their Significance for Understanding the Bible, Judaism, Jesus, and Christianity.* New York: HarperSanFransisco.

VanGemeren, Willem. Gen. Ed. 1997. *The New International Dictionary of Old Testament Theology and Exegesis.* 5 vols. Grand Rapids: Zondervan.

Vermes, Geza. Trans. 2011. *The Complete Dead Sea Scrolls in English.* London: Penguin Books.

Wacholder, Ben Zion. 1973. "The Calendar of Sabbatical Cycles During the Second Temple and the Early Rabbinic Period." *Hebrew Union College Annual* 44: 153–196.

Walvoord, John F. 1989. *Daniel: The Key to Prophetic Revelation.* Moody Paperback Edition. Chicago: Moody Press.

Webster, Noah. 1913. *Webster's Revised Unabridged Dictionary of the English Language.* Springfield, MA: Merriam.

Wickes, William. 1887. *A Treatise on the Accentuation of the Twenty-One So-Called Prose Books of the Old Testament.* Oxford: Clarendon Press.

Xenophon. 1910. *The Education of Cyrus (Cyropaedia).* Edited by F. M. Stawell. Translated by H. G. Dakyns. London: J. M. Dent & Sons.

Yallop, Bernard D. 1997. "A Method for Predicting the First Sighting of the New Crescent Moon." *Royal Greenwich Observatory NAO Technical Note 69.*

Young, Edward J. 1972. *The Prophecy of Daniel: A Commentary.* Eighth printing. Grand Rapids: Wm. B. Eerdmans Publishing Co.

Young, Rodger C. 2004. "When Did Jerusalem Fall?" *Journal of the Evangelical Theological Society* 47 (1): 21–38.

Zuckermann, Benedict. 1974. *A Treatise on the Sabbatical Cycle and the Jubilee.* Translated by A. Löwy. New York: Hermon Press.

SELECT SUBJECT INDEX

Abijah, 52, n158, n413

abomination, 14, 122, n339

accession year, 22, 46, 47, 67, 83, 127–130, 135–138, 140–143, 173–176, 180–182, n376, n378, n515, n519

Adar II, 20, 132, 133, 157, 158

Africanus, Julius, n95

age of responsibility, 69, 70, 73, 75, 76

Alexander the Great, 2

Almagest (Ptolemy), 171, n486, n509, n511. *See also* Ptolemy's Canon

Anderson, Robert, 16–21, 30, 125, 126, n19, n58, n70, n74, n85, n362, n425

Anointed One, 123, n8, n296, n351. See also *mashiach nagid*; Messiah

Antiochus IV (Epiphanes), n340

Aquinas, Thomas, 113

Archelaus, 33

Arnon River, 99

Artabanus, 21, 22, 100, 142, n73, n278, n279

Artaxerxes I (Longimanus), Persian Emperor, 16–19, 47, 125–130, 174, n521
  decree to Nehemiah, 21–25, 28, 30, 37–39, 43, 105, n45, n70
  decree to Ezra, 39, 80–82, 101, 105, 168, n45, n126, n367
  accession date of, 47, 81, 100, 101, 126–130, 141–144, 174, n434, n524

Ashpenaz, n539

atnach, 34, 134, n114, n391, n395, n396, n400
  sihpa (proto-*atnach*), 134, n391

Augustus Caesar, 11, 83, 137, 138, 144, 145, n227, n228, n411, n441

Babylon, 6–3, 22, 24, 25, 45–47, 65–67, 79–82, 85, 97, 127, 158, 164, 168, 169, 171, n36, n333, n336, n535
  fall of, 8–12, 121, 122, 135–137, n26, n32, n134

Babylonian captivity, 7, 8, 13, 32, 45, 58, 64, 65, 74, 78, 79, 93, 96, 129, 130, 139–141, 174, 177–179, n19, n158, n179, n208, n255, n416, n425, n533

Babylonian Chronicle, 10, 11, 122, 127, 134, 173, 177, 178, 181, 182, n28, n333, n334, n533

Bardiya (aka Smerdis, Gaumata) Persian

Emperor, 65, 67, 129, n192, n200

barley, 157, 158, n152, n475

bar mitzvah, 70, n205

Bede (Venerable), 49

Belshazzar, 9, 10, 135, 177, 178, n32, n33

Belteshazzar, n21. *See also* Daniel

Ben-Gurion, David, 61

Bethlehem, 36, 37, 47, 51, 53, 54, n146, n151, n167

Caesarea (*Maritima*), 90, 91

Caleb, 99–101

Cambyses II, Persian Emperor, 67, 121, 129, 135–137, n134, n200

Cana in Galilee, 145

cantillation marks, 134, n392, n393, 396, n400, n401

Carchemish, battle of, 8, 173, 175–180, n516, n535

Cassius Dio, 89, 90

census enrollment, 51, n148, n151

Chaldee Year. *See* prophetic year

Christos Kyrios, 149

Clement of Alexandria, n110

conjunction (lunar). *See* new moon

Coponius, 33

cosmological argument (*Kalam*), n324

Ctesias, n72, n73

Creator, God as, 117, 118, n324

crucifixion, 2, 17, 27, 29, 54, 87, 99, 137, 138, 146, 147, n451

Cyaxares, 121. *See also* Darius the Mede

Cyrus II (the Great), Persian Emperor, 8–12, 38–40, 44–47, 65, 78, 121–123, 134–137, 175, n33, n134, n208, n281, n330, n333

Cyrus Cylinder, n195

Darius the Mede (vassal king in Babylon), 11, 12, 46, 47, 121, 122, 135, 136, n36, n134, n330, nn333–335

Darius I (the Great), Persian Emperor, 37–40, 65–69, 73–77, 107, 126, 140, 141, 166, n197, n200

David, King, 98, n159, n211, n348

Dead Sea Scrolls, 2, 58, 110, 134, n48

decree, 16, 24, 33, 37–43, 95–97, 101, 102, 104, 105, 112, 117, 126, 134, n45, n120, n126, n179, n254, n283, n301, n368

of Artaxerxes to Ezra, 17, 79–82, 84, 100, 143, 168, n218
of Artaxerxes to Nehemiah, 16, 21, 24, 25, 28, 29, 93, 130, 143
(Edict) of Cyrus, 38, 39, 45–49, 57–67, 74, 75, 79, 126, 134, 135, 139, 140, n129, n195, n281, n416, n425
of Darius the Great, 40, 65–69, 73–77, 140, 141, 166
Descartes, René, 113
desolation of Jerusalem, 74, 77, 93, 96, 139–141, n208, n416, n425
Dionysius Exiguus (monk), 49

Ecbatana, 65, 66
Edict of Cyrus. See decree(s)
Egypt, 7, 8, 88, 98, 99, 127, 141, 142, 177, 178, 180
Elephantine Papyri, 81, 141, 142, 175, n224, n380, n524
Elizabeth (mother of John the Baptist), 53, 62, 139, n164
ephemerides (ephemeris), 161–163, 167–169, nn484–486
equinox, 132, 158, 159, nn385–387, n468, n480
Essenes (sect), 58, n179, n296
Etemenanki Tower, 11
Euphrates, 8, 10, 11, 66, 80, 81, 177, 178
Evil-merodach, king of Babylon, 129, 172, 173, 180, 181, n517, n519
Ezekiel (prophet), 18, 58, 59, 63, 88, 110, 175, 181, n178, n318
Ezra (scribe), 17, 37, 39, 45, 46, 67, 80–82, 85, 97, 101, 107, 129, 135, 137, 140–144, 167, 168, 175, n45, n198, n221, n224, n255, n380, n468, n524

Fibonacci numbers, 117, 118, n323, n324
forty years before the Roman destruction of Jerusalem, 87–89
Fotheringham, John, 142, 159, n87
Friedman, Milton, 151

Gabriel (angel), 18, 53, n187, n188
Gessius Florus, 90, n244
Gobryas, 121
Golan Heights, 76
Goren, Rabbi Shlomo, 78
Gregorian calendar, 24, 60, 75, 125, 126, 130, n183, n383
Gubaru, 121, 122, n334

Haggai (prophet), 38, 67, 70, 140
Hatikvah (The Hope), 60, 64
Hebrew calendar, 132, 155–159, 161, n87, n96, n359, n385, n467, n468, n500
Hebrew holidays, and advents of Jesus, 106–108
Herod the Great, 50, 145, n106, n144
Hillel II calendar. See modern Hebrew calendar
Hoehner, Harold, 16–21, 27, 30, 125, 126, n85, n362, n445

Irenaeus, 111, 137, 138, n300, n338, n410
Isaiah (prophet), 38, 133, n124
Ishbosheth, 98, 100, n262
Israel, land of. 45–47, 60–64, 66, 80–82, 95, 97, 99, 100, 102, 130, 138, 140, 159, n184. See also Judah; Judea
Israel, Northern Kingdom, 32, 87, n522
Israel, modern state of
1947 UN Partition Plan 63, 64, 75
British Mandate Palestine, 61, 62
Jerusalem returned to, 75, 107
rebirth, 61–64, 74, 75, 87, 104, 106
Syrian attack on, 76, 77

Jacob (patriarch), 32, 97, n104, n108
Jehoiachin (Jeconiah), King, 127, 129, 173, 175, 180, 181, n375
Jehoiakim, King, 171, 173, 175–178, n19
Jeremiah (prophet), 96, 110, 116, 129, 139, 140, 174–176, n318, n367
Jerusalem, 24, 26, 44, 51, 58, 69, 72, 118, 146, 153, 159, 162, 164–169, n146, n151, n488, n533
Babylonian sieges and destruction of, 7, 8, 127, 129, 130, 139–141, 171, 176–182, n208, n267, n539
decrees to restore and rebuild. See decree
exile from, and return to, 60, 62, 65, 66, 72, 75, 79–82, 96, 97, 100, 127, 130, 143, 168, n255
Jesus' triumphal entry into, 27–30, 87, 106, 107, 165
Old City of, 1967 return to Israel, 72–77, 106, 107, n211,
Roman siege and AD 70 destruction of, 2, 86–93, 108, 148, n400
and Seventy Weeks Prophecy, 2, 3, 13–16, 19, 33, n45, n109, n122
Jesus Christ, x, 2, 4, 63, 118–120, 137, 139, 148, n293, n329, n341, n441 See also

mashiach nagid; Messiah,
ages at key events, 71
all messianic Scripture fulfilled in, 31–33, 133, 150–151, n62, n97, n293
baptism of, 17, 83–85, 87, 92, 145, 146, 169, n226
biblical decrees linked to key advents of, 41, 104–108
birth of, 48–57, 63, 133, 137, 138, 149, 166, n174, n188, n410
conception of, 53, 139
crucifixion of, 2, 17, 27, 29, 99, 146, 147, n95
earthly ministry of, 50, 84, 85, 99, 111, 145, 146,155–159
first temple entry of, 65, 69–71, 73–77, 97, 98, 167, 168
as fulfilling Daniel's Seventy Weeks, 2, 31, 39–43, 57–64, 104–108, 109–112, 115, 123, 148, 149, 151, n352
knowing God and, 116, 117
as Messiah, 2, 4, 109–112, 117, 133, 149, n13, n351
return of, 5, 120, 122, 152
Seventy Weeks Prophecy as predating, 2, 110
triumphal entry of, 16, 19, 27–30, 87, 92, 165
Jewish-Roman War (AD 66), 89–92
John (apostle), 116, 137, 138
John the Baptist, 52, 53, 56, 62–64, 75, 83–85, 138, 139, 144–148, n188, n226
Jonah (prophet), 88
sign of, n62, n344
Joseph (patriarch), n21
Joseph (husband of Mary), 50–54, 73, 88, 149, n167
Josephus (Flavius), 32, 50, 89–92, 121, 144, 168, 178, 180, n6, n144, n159, n239, n244, n299, n330, n400
Joshua's conquest, 97, 99, 100
Josiah, King, 175, 177
jubilee cycle, 15, 40, 41, 43, 57, 64, 77, 97, 99, 101, n48
Judah (kingdom of, land of), 7, 45, 78, 80, 87, 128–130, 140, 141, 169, 174, 175, 177, 178, n194, n208, n299, n522, n528
Judah (patriarch), 32, n104
Judah (tribe of), 32, 36, 47, 55, 58, 66, 82, 87, 88, 98, 127, 130, 140, 148, 174, 176, 177, 182, n104, n105, n108, n522, n528

Judea (Roman province), 33, 51, 83, 90, 132, 140, 144, 161, n299
population of, n450
Judean dating method (ABC), 21–23, 30, 47, 67, 73, 81, 83, 127–130, 137, 138, 174–177
Julian calendar, 24, 28, 58, 60, 74, 75, 85, 89, 92, 125, 126, 131, 132, 158, 161, 171, n387
Julian Day Number (JDN), 28, 30, 57, 62, 73–76, 84, 87, 89, 92, 104, 130–132, 140, 141, 145, 146, 165–169, n91, n92, n322, n381
Julius Caesar, 137, n411
Justin Martyr, n300

Kadesh Barnea, 99, 100
Keil, C. F., 134, n19
Kepler, Johannes, n324
Kibbutz Gadot, 76
Kierkegaard, Søren, 151, n460
Kotel. See Western Wall

laws of nature. *See* natural law
Law of Moses. *See* Torah
LBAT 1419 (artifact), 20, 22, 143, n74
lehashib (to restore), 96, 97
Lepidus, Marcus Aemilius, n411
Lloyd, William (bishop), 16, n58
lunar calendar, 15, 16, 20, 24, 53, 124, 132, 154–169, n86, nn467–489
lunar conjunction. *See* new moon
lunations calculated, 164–169

Ma'ariv (newspaper), 76
Maimonides (Rambam), 159
Malachi (prophet), 32, 70
Manetho (priest, historian), n278
Mary (mother of Jesus), 51, 53, 54, 88, 137, 138, 149, n167, n188
mashiach nagid, 15, 123, 149
Masoretic Text, 34, 134, n397, n399
mathematical audit, 183
Melchizedek Scroll, 110, n296
Messiah. *See also* Jesus Christ; expectations for, 111, n299
rejection of, 88, 89
and Seventy Weeks Prophecy, 13–19, n299, n351, n352
Micah (prophet), 37, 38, n318
modern (Hillel II) Hebrew calendar, 24, 29, 30, 155, 158, 161, n87, n96, n359, n467

Mosaic law. *See* Torah
NASA, 28, 130, 131, n92
Nasser, Gamal Abdel, 76
nativity, 48–57, 62, 64, 87, 104, 106, 137–139, 166, n174, n188, n410
natural law, 1, 2, 112, 113, 116, n1, n315
Nebuchadnezzar, king of Babylon, 8, 9, 12, 181, n517, n533, n543
  chronology of reign, 127, 129, 130, 171–182, n375, n379, n517
Nehemiah, 16, 21–25, 81, 107, 126–130, 136, 137, 143, 144, n70, n76, n468
new moon, 125, 154–159, 162–169, n471, n472, nn486–488
Newton, Sir Isaac, 3, 17, 34, n13
nonaccession year, 22, 25, 127–130, 143, 174–176
null hypothesis, 109

Octavian. *See also* Augustus Caesar

Palm Sunday, 19, 27–32, 35
Parker and Dubberstein's Babylonian Chronology (*PDBC*), 24, 47, 81, 125, 126, 168, 169, n86, n408, n517
Pascal, Blaise, x, 115, n314
Passover, 27, 29, 49–54, 60, 70, 81, 84, 85, 99, 138, 139, 145, 146, 175, n146, n169, n414, n446
pause(s) in prophecy, 133, 134, n110, n389
  separating the seven weeks and sixty-two weeks, 33–35, 40–43, 57, 64, 77, 84, 93, 95, 97, 99, 101, 102, 105, 117, 118, nn113–118, n280, n283
Pentecost, 51–54, 139, 146, n287, n414
Persian taking of Babylon. *See* Babylon
Pesach. See Passover
physical laws of nature. *See* natural law
Polycarp, 137, 138
Pontius Pilate 144, n107
prediction, x, 2–5, 14, 28, 35, 112, 115–117, 149, n317, n318, n389,
  key tests for, 1, 2, n3, n315
proof, 5, 113–118, 134, 151, n311, n325, n458
prophetic year, 16, 19, 40–43, 57, 59, 74, 77, 87–93, 101, 102, 123–125, 140, 141, n53, n55, n58, n208, n425
Ptolemy's Canon, 171, n511, n512, n514
  See also *Almagest* (Ptolemy)

Rambam (Rabbi Moshe ben Maimon). *See* Maimonides
Ramsay, William, 51, 145, n227
Rashi (Rabbi Shlomo Yitzhaki), 123, n101, n353, n385, n471, n500
rish sharruti, n378
Rome (Roman Empire), 2, 10, 11, 33, 87, 90, 92, 140, 144, 145, n227, n228, n411
rosh chodesh, 156–159
Rosh Hashanah, 25, 52, 89, 90

Sabbath, 27, 52, 54, 56, 61, 73, 79, 81, 85, 89–92, 106, 133, 139, 145, 146, 156, 169, 182, n159, n167, n182, n221, n238, n287, n414, n472, n546
sabbatical cycle, 15, 40, 41, 43, 57, 64, 84, 85, 99, 101, n48, n548
sabbatical year, 168, 182, n153, n501, n548
Sagan, Carl, n17
Sanhedrin, 158, 159, 161, n87, n108, n467
Saturnalia, n139
Saul, King, 98, n262, n267
scepter, 32, n103
Second Coming of Jesus, 152
shabua/shabuim, 15, 125, n46, n52, n357
Shavuot. See Pentecost
Shea, William H., n33, n36, n334, n335
shepherds, 51, 54, 149, n146
Shiloh, 32, n101, n102
Six-Day War (1967), 72, 75–78, 87, 107, 117, n211
Sol Invictus, n139
solar years, pauses between weeks measured in, 40–43, 57, 95, 97–102, n283
Solomon, King, 97, 98, 134, n348, n393
State of Israel. *See* Israel
Stephenson, F. Richard, 173, n508
Suetonius, 89, n299
Sukkot. See Tabernacles
supernatural, 1, 2, 5, 116, 117, 151, nn1–4, nn316–318, n324
Syria, 76, 178

Tabernacles, feast of, 51, 52, 73, 106, 132, 139, 146, 148, 158, 159, n385, n386, n446, n480
Tacitus, 32, 89, n82, n228, n299
Tattenai, 65, 66, n194
tax, taxation, 25, 51, 66, 81, 175, n148
Temple, 55, 117, 118, 156, 158
  First Temple (Solomon's Temple),

8, 97, 98, 101, 141, 182, n208, n261,
    n348, n546
  Second Temple, 32, 38–40, 44, 45,
    47, 50, 52, 65–70, 73, 75–77, 79,
    81, 86–89, 91, 95–99, 101, 102, 107,
    108, 132, 140, 145, 146–148, 158,
    n122, n192,
Temple Mount, 1967 return to Israel, 62,
    72, 75–78, 87, 107, 158
Thiele, Edwin, 174, n75, n78, n80, n372,
    n511, n523, n533
360-day year. *See* prophetic year
Tiberius Caesar, 83, 84, 144, 145,
    nn226–228, n441
timeline of decrees, 39, 42, 104
Tisha b'Av, 54–56, 67, 68, 106, 139, 166,
    167, 182
Titus Caesar, 145
triumphal entry. *See* Jesus Christ
Tyre, destruction of, 35 n389

Ugbaru, 10–12, 46, 121, 122, 135, 136, n36,
    n134, nn333–335. *See also* Darius the
    Mede
United States Naval Observatory, 184,
    n92

VAT 4956, 171, 172, n512
Venerable Bede (monk). *See* Bede

Wacholder, Ben Zion, 182, n153, n548
welibnot (to rebuild), 96, 97
Western Wall (*Kotel*), 72, 78

Xenophon, 121, n26, n32
Xerxes (Ahasuerus), 67, 129, n193
    father of Darius the Mede, 121, 136,
    Xerxes the Great, Persian Emperor,
        20–22, 126, 142, 143, n521

yamim (days), 15, n49
Yom Kippur, 52
Young, Rodger C., 175

Zechariah (prophet), 27, 29, 38, 67, 140,
    n416
Zechariah (father of John the Baptist),
    52, 139, 145, n187
Zedekiah, King, 181, 182
Zered (brook), 99
Zerubbabel, n194, n255
Zuckermann, Benedict, 182, n48, n50,
    n153, n548

SCRIPTURE INDEX

Numerals indicate page numbers, and "n" indicates endnotes. For example: "123" references page 123. "n346" references endnote 346. Page numbers and endnote numbers are displayed in order of their appearance in the book.

Genesis
1:14	155, 159, 160, n470
6:15	n323
7:11	124
8:3–4	124
31:13	123
37–50	n21
49:10	32, n101

Exodus
9:31	157, n475
12:2	n475
12:3	n88, n169, n285
12:6	n170
12:41	n56, n180
23:12	n90
23:14–17	n150, n161
25:10	n323
30:10	146

Leviticus
4:3, 5, 16	n346, n350, n456
6:22	n346, n350, n456
8:10	123
12:2–4	n233
ch. 16	146
ch. 23	106
23:8	169, n230
23:11	n171
23:15–16	n287, n413, n444
25:8, 10	n48
ch. 26	59, 64, 77, n182
26:18	59, n39, n209
26:19	n182
26:34–35	n182

Numbers
9:13	81
14:34	n178
21:12–13	n273
28:11	n470
29:1	n238

Deuteronomy
2:14	n272
2:18	n273
3:12, 16	n274
4:29	n326
5:14	n90
16:16	n150, n161
17:10	n108
18:22	n124, n318
19:15	n319
30:1–5	n184

Joshua
11:18	n275
11:23	n276
14:7	n271
14:10, 15	n277

1 Samuel
9:16	123
10:1	123
13:14	n347
24:6	123
25:30	n347
26:23	149

2 Samuel
2:4	n263
2:10	n264
2:11	n267
4:7–8	n265
5:1–3	n266
5:2	n262, n347
5:5	n267
6:21	n347
7:2	n257
7:8	n347
7:12–13	35, n389

1 Kings
1:35	n347
2:11	n267
6:1	n376
6:38	n256, n268
8:16	98
14:25	n376
15:25, 28	n376

15:33	n376
22:41	n376

2 Kings
1:17	n376
8:16	n376
12:1	n376
14:1	n376
15:32	n376
17:6	n376
18:1, 9–10	n376
20:5	n347
22:3	175
23:23	175
24:10–12	127, 173, 175
24:12	n376
ch. 25	130
25:1	n376
25:2	182, n544
25:8	130, 182
25:21	130
25:27	129, 130, 173, 181, n519

1 Chronicles
11:2	n347
17:7	n347
21:18	n260
22:1–6	n261
22:7–8	n258
22:14–19	n260
24:10	n160
28:4	n347
28:11–19	n259
28:13	n158
29:19	97, n261
29:22	123, n347
29:27	n267

2 Chronicles
3:2	n376
6:5–6	98, n347
11:22	n347
12:2	n376
15:12	n326
17:7	n376

23:8   n159
29:3   n376
34:3   n376
36:19–21   n131, n208
36:20–22   n417
36:21   140, n182, n416
36:22   134 n376
36:22–23   n123, n132

Ezra
1:1   126, 134, n376
1:1–4   n128, n132, n417
1:2–4   45, n123, n367
1:8   n105
4:11–24   n192
4:1–6   n191, n216
4:6–7   129, 67
4:21   n122, n192
4:24   n122, n192,
            n376, n418
5:1   n420
5:3–5   n194
5:13   134, n133, n376
6:1–3   n195
6:1–12   n128
6:3   126, 135, n126,
            n376
6:6–12   66
6:12   126, n126, n368
6:13   n196
6:14   38, 39, 43, n120,
            n126
6:15   67, n376
7:5–6   n218
7:7   n376
7:9   n198, n219
7:12–25   81, n218
7:13   126, n126, n368
7:28   n222
9:1–2   n217

Nehemiah
1:1   23
ch. 2   21
2:1–8   n67, n69, n83
2:4–8   n128
2:3–5   n125
2:7–9   n84
2:9   126

Esther
1:3   n376
2:16   n376
4:11; 5:2   n103

Job
31:37   123

Psalms
19:1   118
81:3–4   n470
95:9–11   n237
104:19   n470
110:1–3   35, n389
110:4   n351
137:5   72

Proverbs
25:2   94, n254, n329
28:16   123
30:4   103

Isaiah
1:18   121
9:6   133
11:1   56
39:7   n18
40:3   n190
41:21   121
44:28   38, 44
45:1   123
45:13   38
46:9–10   170
48:5–6   170
ch. 53   n293
53:2–6   n124
55:4   n347
61:1–2   133
66:8   62

Jeremiah
1:3   182, n544
6:4–5   n546
16:15   n184
ch. 25   139, 177, 178
25:1   176, n376
25:1–11   n38, n367
25:3   175
25:8   n318
25:11   139, 140 n208
25:11–12   74
26:18   n318
ch. 29   139
29:1–23   n367
29:10   96, 139, n131,
            n181, n318, n416
29:13   n326
32:1   n376
36:1   n376
36:9   n376

39:1   n376
39:2   182, n544
45:1   n376
46:2   173–177, n376,
            n535
51:59   n376
52:4   n376
52:12   129, 182
52:27   130
52:29   130, 151, 182,
            n379
52:31   173, n376, n518

Ezekiel
1:2   n376
3:27   n318
ch. 4   58, 74, 87, 93,
            104, 151
4:3   n182
4:4–7   58
4:5   n179
4:6   n237
4:13   n317
11:17   60
14:14, 20   n318
ch. 26   35, n389
33:21   181
39:28   n184
40:1   181
40:7–11   n323

Daniel
1:1   151, 171, 177–179,
            n19, n376, n531,
            n535
1:1–6   n18
1:3–5   n539
1:7   n21
1:18   180 n540
1:19   n541
1:19–21   n24, n376
ch.2   18, n368
2:1   n21, n376, n542
2:4–7:28   n355, n370
2:12–13   n22
2:48   n23, n468, n543
5:1–6   n27
5:25–28   9
5:31–6:1   11, n333
6:2   n37
6:28   121
7:1   135, 177, n376
7:25   124, n54
8:1   135

8:7–8	n4
8:14	n51
8:20–21	n4
ch. 9	104, 108, 120, 122, 123, n14, n50, n62, n296, n300, n338, n400
9:1	121, 135, n135, n376
9:2	96, n38, n318, n376
9:3–19	n40
9:11	59
9:13	59
9:20–23	n41
9:20–27	n367
9:22–23	18, n369
9:23	126, n318
9:24	15, 33, 107, 108, 120, n109
9:24–27	3, 13–15, 122, n52, n179, n296, n352
9:25	2, 4, 5, 13–19, 24, 25, 27, 29–35, 37–39, 43, 45, 49, 57, 64, 65, 69, 71, 77, 79, 83, 92–96, 102, 104–112, 115–117, 120–126, 134, 147–152, n15, n65, n120, n126, n254, n300, n302, n317, n345, n367, n395, n400
9:25, 26	n8, n351
9:25–27	n50
9:26	34, 86, 89, 107, 108, n7, n293
9:27	3, 14, 123, n464
10:1	47, n281, n376
10:2–3	n49
ch. 11	122, n340
11:1	135, n135, n376
11:2–4	n4
ch. 12	111, 120, 122, 149
12:4	111
12:4, 9	17, 18, 37, 43, 47, 149, n14, n15, n301

12:7	124, n54, n356
12:9	4, 111, 149

Hosea
3:4–5	35, n389
5:15–6:1	35, n389

Micah
2:12	n184
3:5	n318
5:2	36, 37, 149

Haggai
1:1	n376, n421
1:13–15	n194
1:15	n193, n197, n376, n419
2:1	n419
2:7	n202, n207
2:7–9	n100, n130
2:10	n376, n421
2:16–17	n217
2:21	n194

Zechariah
1:1	n376
1:7	n376
1:12	141, n208, n255, n416, n425
1:16–21	n426
6:13	n351
7:1	n376
7:1–3	67
8:19	55
9:9	26

Malachi
3:1	32, n130, n202, n207, n269

======================

Matthew
3:13–17	145
3:16–17	n229
4:1–2	n235
7:7	n326
11:15	n342
12:39–40	n62
15:10	n342
ch. 24	n62
24:15	118, 121, 122, n9, n43, n62, n338
24:35	114
24:36	152
24:44	n465
28:19–20	120

Mark
1:9	n229
1:9–11	n225
1:9–13	145
1:10	n288
1:15	n98
4:9, 23	n342
7:14, 16	n342
11:9	149
11:7–11	n68
13:14	n43, n62, n337, n342
13:37	n465
15:38	146

Luke
1:5	n156, n160
1:10	52
1:20	n187
1:23–24	n157, n415
1:24–38	n155
1:36	139, n188
1:57	62
1:76	n190
2:1	n148
2:4–5	n147
2:7	53
2:8	51
2:9–11	149
2:11	54
2:19	149
2:22–23	n234
2:22–38	69
2:41–50	n203
2:41–51	70
2:42	n207
2:46	n99, n205
2:51	149
3:1–3	84, 145, n226
3:21	n229
3:21–22	145
3:22	n288
3:23	50, n231
4:1–2	n443
4:16–21	133
8:8	n342
10:23–24	n298
11:9	n326
12:40	n465
12:56	31, 111
13:35	146
14:35	n342
19:35–39	n90
19:44	88, 111, 149, n89,

	n98
24:44	31, 118, 150
John	
1:12	119
1:19–52	145
1:23	n190
1:41	149, n351
2:13	146, n440
2:20	50, 99, 145
4:25	n351
4:35	146
5:1	146
6:4	146
8:32	n329
13:1	146
14:6	n329
14:6–7	117
18:31	n107
19:27	137, 138
19:31	106
Acts	
1:3	n236
2:1–4	n172
5:37	n423
17:11	121, n146, n291
Romans	
1:20	118
10:17	119
1 Corinthians	
5:7	n88

2 Corinthians	
13:1	n319
Ephesians	
6:14	n329
Philippians	
4:8	n329
Colossians	
2:16–17	n287
1 Thessalonians	
5:2	152
5:21	121
Hebrews	
9:7	146
11:1	115
James	
4:8	121
1 Peter	
3:15	n326
1 John	
4:1	121
4:1–3	n291
Revelation	
11:2	124, n54
11:3	124, n54, n55
12:6	124, n54
12:14	124, n54
13:5	124, n54
21:17	n323

ACKNOWLEDGMENTS

Eternal gratitude to all who provided the encouragement, editing, proofing, and advice that helped put this book into shape:

Adam S, Andrew B, Ania K, Ann N, Anthony W, Ariel C, Arnon S, Benjamin K, Bill V, Bill W, Brian S, Brian W, Brigid M, Damon D, Dan L, Dan O, Dan S, Daniel O, David B, David L, Don F, Don S, Douglas J, Greg M, Hermann H, Jack M, Jan L, Jeff A, Jeff B, Jennifer E, Jim B, JJ J, John A, John O, Jonathan P, Jonathan H, Jonathan R, Josie S, Karen E, Katie T, Kelli S, Kelly B, Linda C, Madison C, Mark H, Matt L, Mel H, Michele W, Olga S, Patrick F, Rachel B, Rachel K, Rachel L, Rebecca M, Rich J, Sabrina G, Sanjay M, Sarah A, Sarah H, Sue F, Susie S, Teresa C, Thom P, Tim S, Tom D, Tom S, Tomas B, Virginia E, Wade B, and William G.

This is certainly an incomplete list. If you have helped on this project and your name doesn't appear, then please accept my apologies and inform me. I will correct the next revision.

Extra special thanks to Jenne Acevedo at Acevedo Word Solutions, and to Gail Cross at Desert Isle Design. You won't find a better project manager or a better graphic designer to work with.

A labor of love

ABOUT THE AUTHOR

In 2013, James Brown heard a presentation on how the book of Daniel predicted the exact day that Jesus triumphantly entered Jerusalem. He wondered: *"If this is true, then why doesn't everyone know about it?"*

Months later that topic came up in conversation with a relative, and James sent him the link to that same presentation. After pressing "send," James quickly felt the need to re-check the presentation's timeline calculations, to see if they were true.

What followed was years of deep diving into the solution to that Daniel passage. Not only did James find the correct date of Jesus' Triumphal Entry, but he also discovered that this text foretold much more than just one event. In fact, Daniel foretold the precise dates of Jesus' key advents to an extent that leaves no doubt that Jesus is the Messiah that Daniel wrote about.

Even more intriguing, those findings reconcile other Old Testament time prophecies and are objectively verifiable. Such a discovery just couldn't be kept private. Everyone should know about it.

James is a chemist who lives in Arizona with his daughter and two beagles. He is a member of the *American Scientific Affiliation*, and volunteers with the Arizona State University chapter of *Ratio Christi*, an organization that provides "reasons for Christ" to university students.

For more information, please visit
www.threeproofsofgod.com